PUT YOUR HANDS ON YOUR HIPS AND ACT LIKE A WOMAN

# PUT YOUR HANDS ON YOUR HIPS AND ACT LIKE A WOMAN

Black History and Poetics in Performance

GALE P. JACKSON

UNIVERSITY OF NEBRASKA PRESS | LINCOLN

© 2020 by the Board of Regents of the University of Nebraska
Acknowledgments for previously published material appear on page xvii, which constitutes an extension of the copyright page.

All rights reserved
The University of Nebraska Press is part of a land-grant institution with campuses and programs on the past, present, and future homelands of the Pawnee, Ponca, Otoe-Missouria, Omaha, Dakota, Lakota, Kaw, Cheyenne, and Arapaho Peoples, as well as those of the relocated Ho-Chunk, Sac and Fox, and Iowa Peoples. ∞

First Nebraska paperback printing: 2024
Publication of this volume was assisted by the Virginia Faulkner Fund, established in memory of Virginia Faulkner, editor in chief of the University of Nebraska Press.

Library of Congress
Cataloging-in-Publication Data
Names: Jackson, Gale, 1958– author.
Title: Put your hands on your hips and act like a woman: Black history and poetics in performance / Gale P. Jackson.
Description: Lincoln: University of Nebraska Press, [2020] | Includes bibliographical references and index.
Identifiers: LCCN 2019030006
ISBN 9781496217684 (hardback)
ISBN 9781496238894 (paperback)
ISBN 9781496220905 (epub)
ISBN 9781496220912 (mobi)
ISBN 9781496220929 (pdf)
Subjects: LCSH: African American women—Music—History and criticism. | Slaves—Southern States—Music—History and criticism. | African Americans—Music—History and criticism. | African American dance—History. | African American women dancers. | African Americans—History.
Classification: LCC ML3556 .J405 2020 | DDC 305.48/896073—dc23
LC record available at
https://lccn.loc.gov/2019030006

Set in Garamond Premier Pro by Laura Ebbeka.
Designed by L. Auten.

For Eddie

Edwene "Song" Bey-Jones

the one who sings

always and forever

with love

Aa yea yea aa oo
Aa yea yea aa oo
Aa yea yea aa oo
   Khoisan healing circle incantation


Lilo ntwe Mama
Milo ntwe
Lilo ntwe Mama
Milo ntwe
   "Corn Pounding Song," Zambia, twenty-first century


Deep river
My home is over Jordan
Deep river
I want to cross over into camp ground
   African American spiritual, traditional, eighteenth century

In a little time after, amongst the poor chained men, I found some of my own nation, which in a small degree gave ease to my mind. I inquired of these what was to be done with us. They gave me to understand we were to be carried to these white people's country to work for them. I was then a little revived, and I thought if it were no worse than working, my situation was not so desperate.

OLADUAH EQUIANO

Yemaya hace su
Hace su Yemaya
Yemaya hace su
Hace su Yemaya

Orisha song, African diaspora, twentieth century

Ships at a distance have every man's wish on board. For some they come in with the tide. For others they sail forever on the horizon, never out of sight, never landing until the Watcher turns his eyes away in resignation, his dreams mocked to death by Time. That is the life of men.

   Now, women forget all those things they don't want to remember, and remember everything they don't want to forget. The dream is the truth. Then they act and do things accordingly.

   ZORA NEALE HURSTON, *Their Eyes Were Watching God* (1937)

Hamida had a baby
She named him Abdu el-Samad,
she left him in a canal bed,
The kite swooped down and snatched off his head!
Shoo! Shoo! Away with you! Oh kite! Oh monkey snout!

The children would repeat the song, so rapidly that the first line sounded before the echo of the last had died down and the last line seemed to follow on the tail of the first. Because they were circling and singing uninterruptedly, it was impossible to pick out the song's beginning or end by ear, just as it was impossible to tell by looking where the circle began and where it ended. For they were children, and when children play they grasp each other by the hand and form a closed circle.

NAWAL EL SAADAWI, *The Circling Song* (1989)

But you now, dear girl, who I loved like a flower whose name
I didn't know, you who were so early taken away
I will once more call up your image and show it to them,
beautiful companion of the unsubduable cry.

    RAINER MARIA RILKE, "The Sonnets to Orpheus" (1922)


Kawolin Akawo mdanse kongo jouk kom fe mwen malo
Kawolin Akawo mdanse kongo jouk kom fe mwen malo
Mdanse kongo, mlaye kongo
Mdanse kongo, mlaye kongo
Kawolin Akawo, negnwe tizo reyan raje
Kawolin Akawo, negnwe tizo reyan raje.

    KAWOLIN AKAWO, Kongo song, Haiti, traditional

# Contents

List of Illustrations ..................................... xiii

Acknowledgments ........................................ xv

Past and Prologue as Prelude:
Eurydice's Black Flight ..................................... 1

1. The Way We Do: An Introductory Mapping .......... 11

2. Juba Danced: Following a Story in Motion .......... 47

3. The Ancestors and the Lullaby: Passing It On ....... 75

4. Put Your Hands on Your Hips:
   Rites of Passage in Performance ..................... 103

5. Rosy, Possum, Morning Star:
   Work Songs and the Blues ........................... 133

Coda: Circling Back Around ............................ 173

Notes .................................................... 185

Bibliography ............................................. 199

Index .................................................... 217

# Illustrations

1. *Female Figure* .................................................... xx
2. Sheila (Chela) Anozier, *Danto* ............................ 46
3. Sheila (Chela) Anozier, *Bousou* .......................... 73
4. Carole Byard, *If I Could* .................................... 102
5. George "Geo" Smith, *Dance Sister* .................... 172

## Acknowledgments

Many skilled and generous weavers contributed to the fabric of this work. The wisdom and grace of ancestors and elders, the supportive embrace of family and community, every teacher, student, collaborator, and fellow traveler I have ever had the privilege of learning with—a village vast and wide beyond enumeration has informed, illuminated, opened the way, and guided my coming into imagination, voice, and storytelling. For this I give abundant thanks and the promise to continue to work on the dropped stitches of my own, apprentice, learning.

In this limited space, I wish to acknowledge my esteemed and beloved mentors: Frank Randall, who pushed me from the nest with a smile and a challenge; W. Ofautey Kodjoe, Colin Palmer, and James Hatch, who nurtured the seed of this work and supported it to flower; as well as Lucia Jack, June Jordan, Grace Paley, Valerie Maynard, and Carole Byard, whose examples are embracing, enriching, inspiring, encouraging, and abiding.

In addition to the world of artistic and intellectual influence I hope to have begun to acknowledge in my citations, I wish to express my gratitude to Charles Frederick, Kathy Engel, Dr. Alexis DeVeaux, Nana Mushenheim, Dr. Zala Chandler, and Dr. Danielle Boutet, each of whom has graciously and generously offered thoughtful, and thought-provoking, reading, comment, and conversation on versions of this manuscript. Preliminary investigations toward this book were presented, over twenty years ago, at the American Historical Association, and I thank those scholars for their attention and incisive critique in the earliest stages of this work.

I also wish to acknowledge and appreciate the Faculty of Humanities and Education of the University of the West Indies, Mona, Jamaica, including

Professor Carolyn Cooper and Dean Aggrey Brown, who welcomed and encouraged me to bring this project back to my mother's country (where they say the healing ingredient can always be found); Professors David Williams, Mawena Logan, Gregory Stephens, Norval Edwards, and Anthea Morrison, of the Department of Literatures in English, who supported this work through to its culmination; and Ms. Mary Gray, who facilitated keeping me in touch with this distinguished network over a fruitful period as a fellow and has, no doubt, been a key support person in the successful completion of many a dissertation. My heartfelt thanks as well to Dean Stanley Moore, a true brother and scholar, and to Wayne Modeste, formerly of the Institute of Jamaica, whose kind and consistent counsel made the work in Jamaica possible. *Obligado*.

Here too I wish to give thanks in abundance to Pat Hall and Pamela Patrick, whose Afro-Caribbean Dance and Movement community was an essential ingredient, for body and mind, in the completion of this writing; Shelia Anozier, whose collaborative presence in sisterhood, song, and dance continues to teach me so much; Scott Barton, who has fed my soul and helped with everything; and Susan Buroker, who lovingly worked with me and Scott to make the image files happen. With profound humility, I also wish to offer infinite gratitude and blessings to the formidable and honorable Professor Rex Nettleford, who, master dancer that he is, stepped into my life "right on time" and, with divine grace and extraordinary generosity, lifted me into the "inward reach and outward stretch," my own rite of passage, in this work closing as an opening.

Finally I give thanks to my family "committee": Norma Patricia, my very first reader, and our dad, Vernon B.; my aunts and uncles, Barbara and Roy Alexander; my roots advisers, Yvonne Hope, Denise Jean, and Trevor Thompson, who introduced me to language and the truth of song, dance, and story; and my "grand women and men," Edith Brooks, Muriel Thompson, and Cyril Adolphus Hayes, who hold the flame. This work is dedicated to them, to the men and women of Chapelton and Darliston at the roots of our Jamaican branching, and to my father, James Jackson, and my paternal grandparents, Irene and Jerimiah, of Calhoun Falls, South Carolina, our ancestral line on this Great Turtle Island.

Portions of this book have previously appeared, in different form, in the *Journal of Black Studies* 46, no. 8 (2015); Ellen Goldner and Safiya Henderson Holmes, eds., *Racing and (E)rasing Literature* (New York: Syracuse University Press, 2001); Hazel Arnett Ervin, ed., *African American Literary Criticism, 1773–2000* (New York: Twayne, 2000); Janice D. Hamlet, ed., *Afrocentric Visions* (Thousand Oaks CA: Sage, 1998); *The Medicine Show* (New York: Coast, 1994); and the *Black American Literature Forum* 25, no. 1 (Spring 1991).

PUT YOUR HANDS ON YOUR HIPS AND ACT LIKE A WOMAN

1. *Female Figure*, ca. 3500–3400 BCE. Terracotta, pigment, 11½ x 5½ x 2¼ in. (29.2 x 14 x 5.7 cm). Brooklyn Museum, Charles Edwin Wilbour Fund, 07.447.505. Creative Commons-BY. Photo: Brooklyn Museum, 07.447.505_SL1.jpg.

## PAST AND PROLOGUE AS PRELUDE
Eurydice's Black Flight

**"Death brought me to this place."**
This is a story with many beginnings, a story about herstory and history, and how it is held and told, in song and dance, in invocation and inscription, in African American culture and performance traditions. The seeds for my storytelling were planted and cultivated by the travelers and storytellers of my maternal line, immigrants who talked story across current events, world politics, geography, and time, and who spoke always, with blue light longing and cutting imagination, of Jamaica as "home." Novelist Paula Marshall wrote of the blessing of "kitchen table wisdom" in her upbringing. In our sprawling household, the kitchen extended into the living room where, in my memory, "big people" music, blues, soul, gospel, calypso, ska, mento, "old time" Caribbean rhythms, ballads, and love songs, played in the background. On Sundays extended family and friends would gather in circles of food and conversation and, particularly the younger ones, dancing. I learned to dance, to sing, and to love story in the middle of those circles and have come to understand that the seeds that they planted in me fell from a tree rooted in deep ancestral time.

The performance inscriptions and (art)iculation traditions of African diaspora women, the quick tongue lineage this work engages with and within, have very old roots in human practice and in the visual record of the female figure as symbol and sign. Those roots can be traced back to our shared African beginnings. Among our early human artifacts, for instance, are a profusion of clay figures, excavated from predynastic Egyptian and Nubian grave sites dated to the fourth millennium BCE, sculpted in the image of women with wide hips, generous buttocks, slender waist, long torso, pendulant breasts, birdlike heads, and upwardly extended arms that, at the fingertips, appear to become wings.[1] In the "pure word" of embodied text, the sculptures speak. They are syntax in which woman is subject and the verb is transitive—invoking song, cry, motion, and flight, in their visual statement, even as their interment with the dead marks recognition of ancestral presence and the animating role of the female figure in liminal migration. The image is a symbol and a sign of fertility and fecundity traversing time, reminding us that we are dancers in the swirling star swarm of the cosmos.

Avian icons of singing and dancing women, bridging the lands of the dead and the lands of the living, resound throughout Africa's art histories, ancient and modern, abounding in the vignette texts that embody the sacred performances of Sudanic and Egyptian antiquity—their rites of effective utterance, storytelling, and reincarnation.[2] Among these images are those of the winged goddess Ast (Isis), and of Hathor before her, wearing the emblem of the vulture seated within a crown of bovine horns. These renderings are, in turn, reminiscent of even older images painted on the rock face of southern Africa, where in circles on the vast stretches of parietal canvas of rock and "cave art" ancestral women can be found clapping their hands in trance dance conjuring of flight and celestial vision. Among these paintings there are images of women masked in vulture headdress and of women whose vaginas open into landscapes.[3]

These ancient renderings of the female body as icon, sign, and symbolic writing offer a point of entry into an exploration of the richly layered texts of African diaspora performance and, within it, the self-told stories of African American women, the subject of this writing, and its own performed invocation. African diaspora performance draws on what Robert Farris Thompson has called "ancient organizing principles" to remember and record ancestral journey and contemporary testimony in story, song, and dance and to pass it on in transforming circles of communal creation. Like the poet's invocation of the liminal woman, this storytelling is a conjuring that attempts to weave findings from far-flung locations toward engagement with and within vibrant webs of tradition.

The "texts" of cultural performance beautifully complement and illuminate conventional historical sources, including the potent though slender body of writing by pre-twentieth-century African and African American women; disrupt the "master narrative" that excludes the founding, informing, and persistently enriching presence of Africans and their descendants in this region; and provide windows into expansive discourses and paradigms for locating and identifying the history, philosophy, and theory embedded in African diaspora traditions. The songs and dances of the first generations of African diaspora women record a lineage of thought and reflection on identity, journey, imagination, and agency, in polyphonic "collective autobiography" and in fluid improvisation on the "deep rivers" of African traditions.

Extensive scholarship maps the continuum between the music, dance, visual art, language, and cultural practice of the African diaspora and that of the old worlds of West and Central Africa, identifying the sources of those cultural streams while offering wider implications for the study of human history and my telling attempts to draw on that generative body of study.[4] There are worlds of story, history, and poetics in performance act and artifact—stories within each story within the telling. While this study looks primarily at the lives of women during the sixteenth through the early twentieth century, with some focus on nineteenth-century life and experience, herstories sit within an epic that very much frames this writing.

All that we know at this juncture of human history bears witness to the wisdom of reimagining one "mother tongue" as that of an African woman. Archeological evidence, evolutionary linguistic study, and theory from human genetic history all point to an African homeland long before "Africa" was so named. At generative intersections, studies following the branches of the human genetic family tree identify members of the Khoisan language–speaking family as bearing the genetic marks of an "ancestral" human population and support the extensive, though "controversial," work in language universals that has also identified Khoisan-speaking peoples as the children of our shared—some thirty thousand years ago—great-great-grandmothers. The work of these researchers abounds in the popular literature, yet the significance of these root and route connections has not been fully brought into our historical and literary imagination, much less our social thinking, academic constructs, or curriculums.[5]

What the ancients knew has been lost in the sands of history and time and on the battlegrounds of hegemonic paradigms. We in Western discourses speak, for instance, of historically specific constructs to propose concepts, like "Victorian manners," as metonym and draw on Greek and Roman mythology, like the story of Oedipus, to make universal statements. Our very concept of time, "classic," "modern," "postmodern," is framed by Euro-centric, racialized, and patriarchal paradigms. As in the now-popular use of specifically gendered terms like "seminal" to praise the work of women, these hegemonic paradigms have led us to uncritically reproduce structural hierarchies that, in turn, narrow our vision. Despite the fact that, in Thompson's words, "listening to rock, jazz, blues, reggae, salsa, samba, bossa nova, juju, highlife, and mambo, one might conclude that much of the popular music of the world is informed by the flash of the spirit" of Africa and the African diaspora, despite the high five, zombies, spirituals, rock and roll, and soul, we do not yet have the vocabulary to locate our intellectual history and our shared humanity in our San, Mbuti, BaBenzile, ancient Nubian, Sudanese, Egyptian, Ashanti, Kongo, Yoruba, Ijaw, Malian, Watusi, or Oromo heritage, philosophy, and epistemology. Though the call for decolonization resounds, the fragmentation wrought by colonial constructions of social and racial hegemonies, inextricably bound with practices of empire, imperialism, and the rise of capitalism, have bequeathed to us a legacy of dismembered knowledge and a shattered human terrain that must be recognized, recovered, remembered, and reclaimed. Such a midwifery of critical imagination continues to call for the generative sweep of storytelling, griot works, to assist us in reimagining ourselves. The performance lineages of Africa and the African diaspora provide example, illumination, and an essential telling.

Evolutionary biologists offer the image of human lineage as a chain of women holding hands in a line that stretches over hundreds of miles and over three million years of time, and naturalist Elizabeth Marshall Warren evokes it in her writing about the first people of the Kalahari, the Khoisan language–speaking people now called San.[6] To begin this exploration of a recent cohort of this female line, I would like to add to that image the motion of the circle dance, the sound of singing, and the percussive punctuation of hand clapping, feet keeping time. We might then envision our ancestral line as a spiraling cosmos of movement and song. As in the rock art–recorded trance dances of the earliest people, the dancing figures among ancient Egyptian tomb inscriptions, and the sculptural representations interred with ancestral Nubians, each girl and woman in our ancestral spiraling could be seen as both altar and icon, named in her time as well as within the continuum human. Each could be seen as Eurydice, and before her Ast and the stars themselves, in motion and flight. Each could be seen as a speaking subject, in a tapestry of performance, beckoning us to listen to her storytelling.

"A story is like the wind. It comes from a far quarter and we feel it." (//Kabbo, circa 1871)
My exploration of African diaspora history and poetics told in performance is animated by an engagement with storytelling traditions, the voices of women in history, and the practice and performance of writing. It arises out of an ongoing inquiry into African American cultural history and identity within the context of the larger motion of the human journey. Long enchanted by how our storytelling maps human migrations, and in fact, the cycles of both human and universal seasons, I have become increasingly intrigued by the cyclical forms, the conversations across time, the acts of witness and liminality, embedded in cultural performance. While natural history and the work of the human genome tell the story of our human lineage through the narrative of mitochondrial DNA, this small study proposes a consonant telling in a circling lineage of song and dance. That's, of course, more than I can do, and my study is, in many ways, a preliminary investigation toward a vast work in progress, a poet's parsing of a grand synthesis, and in homage to that lineage.

My approach is Africanist, a humanist proposal conscious of the necessity of recognizing Africa as a place of human cultural beginnings, and interdisciplinary, in an attempt to address a wide breath of knowledge. I speak of cultural performance in a broadly inclusive sense, encompassing dynamic ritual and day-to-day expression. The work gathers documentation and description of a selection of African diaspora performance, of songs, dances, and musical practice, and situates those performances in a narrative of journey, story, cultural history, ancestry, and cosmology. I draw on a range of sources from the African diaspora and African American vernacular and early literary traditions, including spirituals and sacred song, blues, secular rhymes, ballads, work and play songs, folklore, poetry, novels, the "slave narratives," and the oral histories recorded by the U.S. Works Progress Administration (WPA). I draw also from sixteenth-, seventeenth-, and eighteenth-century travelogues and from the collections of nineteenth- and twentieth-century artists, folklorists, documentary historians, anthropologists, ethnologists, musicologists, practitioners, and students of performance. Though I focus on the voices of African American women, my telling is guided and illuminated by the larger voice of the Afro-Atlantic.

The "blues suite" of *Put Your Hands on Your Hips and Act Like a Woman*, my song, dance, and ritual exploration, arises from the intersection of three distinct paths of inquiry into African American culture. The first path comprises an engagement with African diaspora women's entries into Western discourses, the spectrum of their narrative, oral and literary, articulations, and the study of the "voices" of women within broader, and constantly changing, performance tradition. My project is directly animated by three decades of black feminist scholarship, which includes the work of North American writers Toni Cade Bambara and Ann Allen Shockley, who brought their skill with fiction into expanding understanding of the geography of African diaspora women's identities; Barbara Christian, who in her "Toward a Black Feminist Criticism" called for new theoretical paradigms in critical writing; Alice Walker and Jean Fagan Yellin, who brought a literary anthropology to bear in their studies of Zora Neale Hurston and Harriet Jacobs; Toni Morrison, Mary Helen Washington, Hortense Spillers, and Hazel Carby, who wrote, alternately, of song, flight, invention, kin, conjuring, and reconstruction as central to the discursive strategies of African and African diaspora women authors. These writers, among others, including Angela Davis and June Jordan, engaged with the voices and authorial strategies of over three hundred years of women's writings.

Their work is the legacy of an even older black feminist—or as Alice Walker reminds us, "womanist"—humanism. Anna Julia Cooper, the nineteenth-century scholar, wrote of the "darkened eye" of a vision that does not fully see the presence of women and of the possibility, "the darkened eye restored," of "seeing a circle where before it saw a segment."[7] "Tis the woman's strongest vindication for speaking that the world needs to hear her voice," Cooper wrote.[8] The call to restorative work persists, and Cooper's image of the circle is particularly resonant when we see the circle as the dynamic heart of ritual performance.

Much of the ovarian work of a black feminist and womanist scholarship proposed alternative critical paradigms, improvisation rather than binary opposition, and a concurrent expansion of the literary landscape toward an embracing humanism. This work, and this charge, is essential to re-presenting, locating, and identifying how, as Henry Louis Gates wrote in his *Signifying Monkey*, the black tradition "has theorized about itself." Yet so much of the critical work that has been done, identifying the "black" wordplay, figurative tropes, metaphor, metonymy and synecdoche, of "signifying" and "reading," focuses on men's articulations, on Orpheus's daring song. Clearly there is more to be found, as the aforementioned and other writers have continued to point out, in the specific articulations of women.

The second path of inquiry that flows into this study arose naturally from the first and is animated by a protracted query into the African roots of African American culture. This layer of the work is as much informed by W. E. B. Du Bois's inspired and oft-told tale of his great-grandmother's African lullaby as by the image of the strings of DNA that connect us. Here I attempt to situate the multivocal text of women's voices within a wide range of critical cultural study, art and social history, as well as literary theory, moving out from a number of sites of bedrock, including Henry Louis Gates's theory of signifying, the vernacular and African American literature, Sterling Stuckey's study of the circle as a signal form in the cultural performance of enslaved Africans, and Robert Farris Thompson's work on African philosophy and artistic continuities in African diaspora art.

Here too contemporary scholarship has late nineteenth- and early twentieth-century roots, among them the work of Katherine Dunham, Zora Neale Hurston, Darwin Turner, and W. E. B. Du Bois. Work focused on the North American continent has similarly been informed by Caribbean-focused African diaspora scholarship, including the discourse expanding work of Aimee Cesaire, C. L. R. James, Fernando Ortiz, Linda Cabrera, Eric Williams, Louise Bennett, Rex Nettleford, Errol Hill, Orlando Patterson, John Nunley, and Stuart Hall, among others.

Following these paths, of course, leads into a forest of knowledge, in art, language and linguistics, archeology, studies of the mind, physics and metaphysics, wherein myriad trails chart our human footprints, and brings me back to storytelling as a place of deep knowledge, pedagogy, and inclusive truth. In homage to Eduardo Galeano, that "poor student" who effervescently retold the history of the Americas through its indigenous voices; Paul Robeson, who found and sang a shared story in the voice of world music and song; the honorable Drs. Louise Bennett ("Miss Lou") and Rex Nettleford, who brought the fierce wisdom of Jamaican folk culture, in story, poetry, dance, and choreography, back into our national and international conversation; and Federico Garcia Lorca, that passionate poet of ritual and vision, this work is dedicated to telling the story within the story of all of us.

**"To be naked is to be silent." (Dogon Proverb)**

"In the spirit," the form, and the tradition, *Put Your Hands on Your Hips and Act Like a Woman* is a composition akin to a multi-strip weaving. The threads are story, song, choreographic notes, and situating texts. A selection of songs and movement or "play" texts form the foundation for the weaving and are presented in blocks in the narrative, periodized or dated when appropriate, and noted to source throughout, following the mighty lead of W. E. B. DuBois in *The Souls of Black Folk*. Some of the lyrical texts I use have been anthologized widely, and I refer the interested reader to compendiums in my more extensive resource listing. While texts of songs are abundant, documentation of the visual statement of dance and movement are more challenging to represent, and for this I turn to a range of practitioners and informants.

The second layer of my narrative explores these texts in performance. The place of pride in this framing goes to the critical authority of practitioners. Often, in an attempt to give frame to the stories of "anonymous" early women, I have drawn on the writings of their literate contemporaries and the observations of outside informants. The eighteenth-century biography *The Interesting Narrative of Olaudah Equiano* provides narrative support in this regard, and subsequently I bring in narrative support from the life and work of the eighteenth-century poet Phillis Wheatley and the fictions and narratives of Harriet Jacobs, Harriet Wilson, Hannah Craft, Sojourner Truth, and others.

Each chapter begins with a creation story and, in most cases, riff and commentary on the tale as a cultural performance. Primarily these tales re-member the epic sweep of ordinary lives and are intended to suggest ever-widening webs of connection. If the voices of communal creation, this long line of women holding hands, is the warp thread, then these archetypal tales are the weft. All are my own adaptations and sites for discovery and recovery in the telling. I refer the reader to primary sources in my notes. In conversation with these mythic or folkloric archetypes, each chapter takes an increasingly expansive look at the presence of ancestry, journey and history, witness and pedagogy, circles of communal art making and the creation of liminal space in the performance practice of African and African diaspora women. Consideration is given to the ways in which improvisations on those forms mark shifts in African diaspora visions over time in a complex dialectic of articulation and becoming.

The first chapter begins with a personal snapshot, a remembering of urban girls' street play. I go on to invoke, in survey form and some panoramic riffing on storytelling, some of the expansive terrain of Pan-African philosophy and practice that inform African American culture, with special attention to the role of San, Yoruba, and Kongo influence and inspiration. Chapter 1 also introduces some of the stories and voices that guide my narrative.

Subsequent sections of the narrative focus on specific performed texts and propose a constellation of routes for engaging with them. Chapter 2 situates an early nineteenth-century performance of the "Juba" within an exploration of African and early African American women's performance to illuminate its telling reconstruction of black identity in act and artifact. Chapter 3 begins with a discussion of W. E. B. Du Bois's recollection of an African lullaby in his magisterial homage to the African American spirituals, "the sorrow songs." The song sets the stage for examining the African American lullaby, and its relationship to the spiritual, as a historical document and a formative rite of passage for women and children. Chapter 4 expands on the rites-of-passage theme, drawing concentric circles of remembering from WPA informants and other narrative sources and exploring sacred and secular performance in the context of both art and social history. The closing chapter traces the documentation of African American women's identity in work songs and in the compositions of early blues-singing women. From the voice of the blues, the narrative circles back, in coda, toward a wide-angled contemporary perspective on the collective autobiography told in black song and motion.

# THE WAY WE DO                                       1
An Introductory Mapping

**Spider and the Calabash of Knowledge: An Asante Story**
*They say that once, Spider came to possess all the world's knowledge, stuffed it into a calabash, and tried to hide it, in a treetop. Well, according to the story, the calabash fell, or was flung, from Spider's hands to the ground, where it shattered, and the bounty of story was fragmented and scattered on the four winds. Now the task of the storyteller, like that of the Spider, is to weave the broken pieces back together.*

An African diaspora storytelling demands movement over a vast, complex, terrifying, and broken terrain, of old and new worlds in violent transformation, and looking at a crossroads of being, metamorphosis, and becoming. Appropriately Spider, the divine trickster and storyteller, an ancient with many names who has traveled far and wide and is always returning, weaves a web that spans these multiple locations. Among this region's indigenous first nations, Cherokee, Keres, Dine, and Pueblo traditions speak of Grandmother Spider, and of Thought Woman, the weaver, as an avatar of existential creation, complexity, and illumination. Though the ancestral peoples of this region were ravaged by the genocidal land grabbing of European occupation and settler colonialism, their story, lore, knowledge, and traditions live on in those who survived them, in the earth itself, and in any true telling of the history of this land. So it begins.

The African peoples, who came to this region in the course of close to four hundred years of forced migrations, brought their own rich cosmological and philosophical traditions to the Caribbean archipelago and the American mainlands. Many of these people were from West and Central

Africa, and among them were Akan- or Twi language–speaking people, from the area that is now the country of Ghana, and among the many traditions they brought with them to this region were their anansesem, their stories of Ananse the spider, a trickster, a troublemaker, and a creative progenitor. In the cross-cultural fusions and re-articulations of the African diaspora imagination, Spider, whom the Akan sometimes call "Kwaku Ananse," is hero and clown, creator and fool, intercessor between the small and the powerful, the Gods and mortals, and a metaphoric uncle of storytelling. In Jamaican tradition, as in that of the Akan, all folklore is often called "Ananse story," and Spider remains an honorific kin who storytellers address with a familial name, sometimes flipping the gender frame, by calling it Brother Anansi, or Brer 'Nancy, Nancy, Sis, or Auntie Nancy. Metaphysical and morphing on the Great Turtle Island, Spider (as well as the hare and the jackal tricksters of East Africa) reappears as the fabled Brer Rabbit of African American lore. Though not a deity, like the Yoruba orisha Esu Elegba and the Fon loa Papa Legba, Spider is a divine trickster who also embodies symbolic crossroads and liminal portals in its webbing. According to the preeminent folklorist Louise Bennett, "is Anansi meck it."

Spider's extensive web of presence in the African diaspora deftly represents the complexity, multiplicity, fragmentation, and convergence, the "something torn and new" as Kamau Braithwaite poets, embedded in an ever-emerging concept of "black" identity. Among those Akan peoples who carried their anansesem across the Atlantic crossing were citizens of the Asante kingdom. Asante was a state with a deeply cosmopolitan genesis, like the Akan language itself, as well as a lavish poetic and visual art tradition, a state arising at the crossroads of centuries of intercontinental migrations, wars of empire and commerce dating back to the twelfth century, rising militarism, and the catastrophic explosion over the tragic centuries to come, of a transatlantic trade in human beings. Basil Davidson, in his *The African Past*, points out how the Asante state became, with Dahomey and the delta city states, "one of the strongest slaving nations in Africa" playing, among them, "the same leading part that Brittan, France and Holland represented on the European side." So "it go" and so we begin.[1]

### Yimbala y sona: Singing and Drawing a Point

> Head and shoulders baby
> One, two, three
> Head and shoulders baby
> One, two, three
> Head and shoulders head and shoulders head and shoulders baby
> One, two, three
>
> "Head and Shoulders," African American street game, twentieth century[2]

When I was a child, performing the rituals of urban childhood on New York City sidewalks and streets, we played through a repertoire of ring games that, it seemed, we learned from each other or just made up and passed on. Each of these games, and there were many, inextricably paired dance and song, was ritually circular, polyphonic and responsive, syncopated and percussive, multi-metered, subtly competitive, formally improvisational, and held moments, in collective performance, for transforming individual flights. Most of these games were sung and danced to the music of hand clapping. Most of these games contained both sculpted moments and pure wildness. Many of these games had components of articulation that were bantering or derisive. Much of the language of this play was "black," or what we, as African American children, understood as being "black" then. They were dances or plays, songs or games, full of signs, signifying, and ciphering. When we wagged the finger of one hand, put the other on our hip, and set our upper torso to swaying, we certainly knew, but probably "felt" more than understood, what we were saying. These street performances were caldrons of continuous articulation and improvisation. In each of the games we played, we rehearsed the social performance of childhood and learned something of the dance of acting like a woman. Of course, the best illustration would be to see and hear us.

I realize now the figure we were cutting, how the characteristics of our play were those of African music, dance, and visual arts, sacred and secular performances, as they had been brought together and transformed in the African diaspora. Arms raised, hands moving quickly from the head to the shoulders, breaking with a hand clap and, on the "one two three," beating out three alternating hand pats with our partners before bending to the concrete, which might have once been earth, touching our knees and then our ankles and then our knees again in rapid fire succession, we danced a distillation of performances of greeting and naming, of ritual identifying. We danced a fusion of traditions of historical recitation in performance. And we, the children of Birmingham, Selma, and Jamaica, the civil rights movement, Black Power and the rise of the Black Panthers, African independence, urban protest and anticolonial struggles, sang and danced in the wake and the midst of a world wrestling with and within its own historical motions.

Numerous folkloric and ethnographic studies collect the games of African American girls and examine their historic and social meaning. Pairing this energetic body of sociological and ethnographic explorations with the literature on African art, aesthetics, philosophy, and performance traditions, and dancing in the intersecting circles of our African diaspora street games and a wide spectrum of the performance practices of West and Central African girls and women, presents a powerful, and illuminating, web of connections.[3]

> Knees and ankles baby
> One, two, three
> Knees and ankles baby
> One, two, three
> Knees and ankles knees and ankles knees and ankles baby
> One, two, three
>   "Head and Shoulders"

In our rings of play, dance, and song, we were actually recalling a number of the formal structural requisites specific to performed African and African American articulations. Our "Head and Shoulders" was sung and danced, for instance, in traditional African antiphony or "call-and-response." And our motion of play, using call-and-response, the three-line stanza, and the circle as a setting, is common to the expressive heritage of the African diaspora, spanning a panorama of place and time, from Rio de la Plata to the Housatonic and Hudson, from early African American burials, community and religious celebrations, to the performance practices of Caribbean Carnival and our own street games.

The web of stories connecting these circles of generative action is both abiding and guiding. African diaspora carnival, festivals, parades, and processions, for instance, all draw from a mixture of public art, assembly, and masking traditions, the oldest of which reach back to community ritual performance and sacred practice. These performances are sites for social organization, healing, and transformation. "The organization of social life in traditional societies gives a special place to the festival," Rex Nettleford writes in Nunley and Bettelheim's *Caribbean Festival Arts*, "for there is a general consciousness of its potentials as a vehicle for communicating or affirming the values of a society and for strengthening the bonds that bring its members."[4] In his introduction to the same volume, Robert Farris Thompson fruitfully examines the relationship between African diaspora carnival and Yoruba and Kongo aesthetics.[5] Masquerades and carnival gatherings, combining dance, music, and visual art statement in performance, are a strong thread in the lineage of African diaspora art and articulation. Our girls' street play moves in this continuum. And when we did the number, arms akimbo, or with one hand on our hip and one hand in the air, we were formally restating the Kongo, Yaangalala, position.[6]

In terms of musical architecture, our recitations play with and within an African-derived metric structure, using the three-line stanza, the "blues form," that underlies popular regional music and has been traced by practitioners and ethno-musicologists to West African storytelling and the historical narrative performance practices of griot traditions.[7] Of course, the blue notes of our play are also telling. The blues is a poetic form. A lyrical lament that contains "duple rhythms," "syncopated patterns," an A B A arrangement, and four-measure phrasing and that moves from the repetition, the call-and-response, of its initial two lines to resolution, revelation, and "philosophical commentary" in its closing. The form both invites and represents dialog, across space and time. Musicologist Eileen Southern reminds us that the "distinctive three-line stanza" is "an apparent throwback to African origins, for the three-line stanza is uncommon in American and European folksong repertories," and that the formal "condensation" of measures in the song line creates a "break at end of each vocal line, during which the accompanying instruments (guitar, piano, or instrumental ensemble) improvises, and the singer interjects spoken asides such as "Oh, Lordy."[8]

> Round the world baby
> One, two, three
> Round the world baby
> One, two, three
> Round the world, round the world, round the world, baby
> One, two, three
>   "Head and Shoulders"

Dance phrase and text in complement, our "Head and Shoulders" embodied the geography of historical and social identity; mapping and continuing the physical and metaphysical journey of the African American story. In words and movement we danced "apart" though together in the African tradition, not holding hands, as in a waltz, but deeply connecting as we constructed our recitation in inscription. We were poetry in motion. And yes, there was language, symbol, signifying, and storytelling in our hands. Cultural historian and educator J. D. Elder's studies of similar plays among girls in the Caribbean point to paired hand clapping and to the articulation of the "open palms" as widely used phrases associated with mutuality and cooperation. We were learning and teaching community and communion, as well as personal responsibility and artistry, in our play in "the tradition."

The statements of the hands, head, and shoulders are potent African echoes in our dancing, saluting, and indicating. Africanist scholars, including Robert Farris Thompson and Maureen Warner-Lewis, remind us of the Central African custom of clapping hands as an act of greeting and write that the head and shoulders are symbolic sites of power in Central African ritual performance traditions. Contemporary practitioner and performance artist Marilyn Worrell, in line with the work of Katherine Dunham, identified the West African danced tropes of self-presentation in our "sassy" dancing and recognized our restatement of female orisha in the fan-like fluttering of our hands as derivative of Yoruba sacred performance. And as our quick hand movements embody the "inward stretch outward reach" of diasporic motion as we leap and return from a "grounded" position, our sculptural attentiveness also makes strong reference to the iconography and aesthetic values of African dance, the statements of vitality, readiness, and "flash of the spirit" that Thompson has documented extensively. Dance is a language, sound is its root, and our dance remembered African languages that, despite the diasporic dismemberment, were never quite lost. The concrete we stamped percussively had truly once been earth.[9]

The language of the body, and its conscious articulation in dance as visual culture, is an old one, and dance study draws on "vocabulary" very similarly to literary disciplines. Within this choreographic chronicling, the critical vocabulary of African dance is highly developed, and its antiquity is in alignment with those evident in sculptural traditions. Some of the breath of this critical oeuvre is highlighted in Thompson's documentation of a range of commentary on the dance as a visual art in his *African Art in Motion*. Thompson's practitioner informants address Pan-African compositional and aesthetic values, including the positional "attentiveness" and "readiness" with which a dancer enters into the dance.[10] This concept of self-presentation is a critical one in movement aesthetics and criticism. It is also a familiar in terms of vernacular understanding. We speak, for example, of "keeping your head up," holding "head in hand," and of extending "welcoming arms." Thompson finds myriad instances of tropes of self-presentation in the movement language of Yoruba dance traditions, in which the dancer makers of the body a sculptural iconography. These aesthetic dictates are deeply philosophically based. "Many traditional people in Africa believe that when they dance or strike an honorific pose they are standing in the image of the ancient divine fathers," Thompson writes.[11] Here too Thompson writes about clapping as a form of salutation among the Kom of Cameroon.[12]

The use of these movement metaphors reverberates in African diaspora dance in concert performances that draw on African and African diaspora folk roots. Luminous examples of contemporary choreographic mapping for professional staging include Katherine Dunham's extensive body of work in Haitian traditions and Rex Nettleford's fulsome re-presentation of Jamaican folk tradition, as well as the shining oeuvre of Alvin Ailey. Nettleford uses the danced phrase of open palms with powerful effect throughout and strikingly in his danced history of the African diaspora *The Crossing* (1978) and the eloquent phrasing of open palms similarly frames the penultimate movements of Alvin Ailey's tour de force danced exploration of "Negro religious music" in *Revelations* (1960), a work in which the flutter of fans restates the ritual appearance of the orisha in Yoruba religious performance.

> Ham bone ham bone where you been?
> All round the world and back again
> Ham bone ham bone what you do?
> I got a chance and I fairly flew
> Ham bone ham bone where you stay?
> I met a pretty girl and I couldn't get away.
>
> "Ham Bone," African American play song, nineteenth century[13]

In our confluence of West and Central African performance articulations, we were clapping, dancing, and singing, ancient canons of speaking, "drawing a point" of power in an amalgam of traditions. At the time, as we would have said then, we weren't "studying" that. We knew "we were saying something," but we weren't deconstructing. We were challenging each other in a dexterity of performance from which, hands on hips with a dizzying precision, would arise a communal "winning." We took flight within and against tradition, in the jazz idiom, taking the word from each other's mouths and making it our own.

Black and proud jazz—the jazz idiom in our play demands another underlining. Ralph Ellison, every bit the "jazz man," wrote of "the subtle rhythmical shaping and blending of ideas, tone and imagination demanded of group improvisation." "This tradition," wrote Ellison, "insisted that each artist achieve his creativity within its frame. He must learn the best of the past and add to it his personal vision." Jazz, what my father's generation called "the new music," arises, according to musicologist Eileen Southern, "from the fusion of blues and ragtime with brass band music and syncopated dance music." And "the most salient features of jazz," Southern writes, "derive directly from the blues. Like the blues jazz emphasizes individualism. The performer is at the same time the composer, shaping the music into style and form. A traditional melody or harmonic framework may serve as the takeoff point for improvisation, but it is the personality of the player and the way that he improvises that produces the music." Southern also notes that jazz uses the call-and-response form of the blues by "employing an antiphonal relationship" between two voices as well as bringing attention to the etymological relationship between the word "jazz" and the Ki-Kongo term *jizz*.[14]

Hidden in the complex hermeneutics of our play, even (or perhaps especially) from us, were the traces to a canon of played performance that had brought us to our particular place in an old grammar of expression. Our performance had come from somewhere, had meaning there, and continued to gather meaning in our complex re-presentation. But when a new family from "down south" moved on to our block, and Cookie taught us to "pat the Juba" to the words of "Ham Bone" in 1968, we simply took it up, not for a moment caring from whence this new play had come, who this Ham Bone was, and what it was saying. Now taking up the literary and historical anthropology of that expression in performance, re-membering the fragments of the broken calabash of Asante story, is central to my own adult work.

Ham Bone, this traveler, is a metaphor for the experience of diaspora, an experience inherently in motion. Here we honor the path by beginning with a selection from the divination text of the Yoruba and an excerpt from the oral history of Kossola, Cudjoe Lewis, one of the founders of Africatown, a settlement of freed Africans in the U.S. state of Alabama, in 1866, who was reportedly among the last Africans to be brought enslaved to the U.S. mainland—both injunctions to speaking and recognition. We go on, in protracted introduction, to look at a selection of documents of African diaspora and African American performance in conversation with the practices of West and Central Africa and the hunter-gatherer legacy of the San. We then turn to the stories of other travelers and storytellers whose voices open several paths to re-cognition.

### Journey Geography and Circles of Ancestry

Speak to me so that I may speak to you.
By our voices we recognize each other in the darkness.

*Ifa* divination verse, traditional/classical[15]

It bout daybreak when the folks dat sleep get wake wid de noise when de people of Dahomey breakee the Great Gate. I not woke yet. I still in bed. I hear the gate when dey break it. I hear the yell from the soldiers.... I jump out de bed and lookee. I see the great many soldiers wid French gun in de hand and de big knife.... Oh lord, lord! I see de people gittee killed so fast!

The old ones dey try run way from de house, but dey dead by de door.... Oh lord, lord! One gate lookee lak nobody dere so I make hate and runnee towards de bush, but de man of Dahomey dey dere too. Soon as I out de gate dey grabee me, and tie de wrist. I beg dem, please lemme go backo to my mama, but dey don't pay whut I sat no 'tenshun.

Oluale Kassola (Cudjoe Lewis), founder of Africatown, Alabama, 1866[16]

House a' fire.

In the violent, and exponentially gapping, rent in time between the late 1400s and late 1800s, millions of people from diverse communities on the African continent, people from remote rural villages, small towns, and family holdings, people from ancient urban centers and global ports, cosmopolitan metropolises, and powerful city-states, were caught in the vortex of the tragedy of massive proportions, the social and political upheaval, horrific displacement, forced and enforced migrations, the *Maafa*, set into motion by a burgeoning transatlantic economy based on the buying and selling of human beings. The devastation wrought on individuals and communities, as well as on the collective consciousness, over the course of four hundred years of apocalypse, echoes still, and the physical and metaphysical journey of crossing over "the waters" of what came to be called the "Middle Passage" remains central to telling African diaspora story and American history.[17]

According to one telling, and much classic and contemporary testimony and scholarship, those peoples, many from West and Central Africa but hailing from the breadth and depth of a vast continent, those people who found themselves caught in the sprawling nets of trade and traffic in "slaves," were kidnapped and stolen from their homes, taken prisoner in wars and raids, roped, chained, and incarcerated in dungeons, cells, and barracoons, traversed a continent and an ocean, plunged off the edge of the universe, and were brought face to face with chaos, terror, and death; those people began to forge a new Pan-African identity in the crossing.[18] And from the Portuguese colonies in the islands of Cape Verde, Madeira, and São Tomé to Peru, Brazil, Colombia, Santa Domingo, Cuba, Barbados, Jamaica, Suriname, and Mexico, from the Caribbean islands through the continental mainlands, the story of the peoples' journey was inscribed in nascent, and ever transforming, Pan-African identities and is remembered in the poetics of African diaspora performance and its universal embodiment of "the enduring human spirit."

> Orunmilla carry me in your bag; carry me in your purse
> So that we may go together slowly;
> So that wherever we may go we may go together.
> *Ifa* divination verse, traditional/classical period[19]

The diverse peoples of the African continent carried radiant ancestral sources to those waters of mortal struggle, and the sacred and secular performances of the African diaspora arise from a dynamic amalgam of multiple streams of knowledge and ways of knowing, traditions of cosmology, language, history, voice, recognition, and reconnection. Among those ancestral sources were recognizably West and Central African cultural practices, as well as echoes of older practices, like those of the southern San, practices characterized by prodigious engagement with questions of journey, geography ancestry, witness, history, pedagogy, and social transformation.

One ancestral source of African diaspora influence flows out of the art and philosophy of the Yoruba people, of the nation now known as Nigeria, and the voice of Yoruba divination verse, which long predates the terror of the Middle Passage, speaks potently across the physical and metaphysical distance later crossed by kidnapped African people and their descendants. The prophetic text simultaneously points to a rich past. Yorubas trace their descent, and the origin of *Ifa*, to the fabled medieval city of Ile-Ife, where terra-cotta sculpture found in archaeological sites suggest a link between Yoruba and the Nok civilization of the first century BCE. As an ancient urban hub, Ife can be seen as a nexus of cultural traditions and Yoruba practices as gathering the knowledge of the multiplicities of people who have migrated through that region over the millennia. The documentary work of Migene Gonzalez-Wippler and William Bascom has opened fertile terrain for engagement with the widespread presence of *Ifa* divination practice, and the philosophical tenets within it, among "related" peoples of West Africa and records of *Ifa* divination in the diaspora dating to the latter part of the seventeenth century.[20]

Yoruba philosophy, speaking expansively of journey and historical memory, remains vital in the performance practice of West Africa and the diaspora. According to Kolawole Ositola, a seventh-generation *Ifa* priest and diviner practicing in the Ijebu Yoruba town of Imodi, Nigeria, in alignment with numerous traditional ontologies, Yoruba see "the whole life span of a person [as] a journey." The Abenaki concept of life as an "earth walk" comes to mind. Anthropologist Margaret Thompson Drewal, in her *Yoruba Ritual*, expands on how the Yoruba understanding of journey is similarly widely embracing. "Yoruba peoples of southwestern Nigeria conceive of rituals as journeys—sometimes actual sometimes virtual," Drewal writes of funerals and birth celebrations, professional incantation and divination, sacred possession and masking, among contemporary Yoruba. By extension Drewal makes the connection between Yoruba performance and the practices of the African diaspora. "Wherever Yoruba religion thrives—Brazil, Cuba, the United States—this practice persisted. Cast in performance in a myriad of ways—as a parade or a procession, a pilgrimage, a masking display, or possession trance—the journey evokes the reflexive, progressive, transformative experience of ritual participation."[21]

Yoruba history and philosophy, like that of the Asante, offers a generative critical frame for interpreting the performance texts of the African diaspora as well as for the kind of "black reading" of the African American literary canon Gates explores so brilliantly in his *Signifying Monkey*. "The Negro Spirituals," for extraordinary example, elegantly interlace articulations of journey, physical and metaphysical geography, and historical memory in a way that recognizes the injunction of the *Ifa* as well as the flung fragments of the broken calabash of Asante story. This recognition is resplendently restated in the spiritual "You May Bury Me in the East."

> You may bury me in the east
> You may bury me in the west
> But I'll hear the trumpet sound
> In the morning
>
> "You May Bury Me in the East," African American spiritual, eighteenth century[22]

It's an old song with a rich history in its content and its chronicling. The early Africanist thinker, clergyman, and founder, in 1787, of the African Methodist Episcopal Church, Bishop Richard Allen included "You May Bury Me in the East" in his 1801 collection of African American sacred songs. In *The Souls of Black Folks*, the eminent scholar and public intellectual W. E. B. Du Bois called "You May Bury Me in the East" the "voice of exile" and an example of "African" music at the beginning of African American spiritual tradition. In these songs, Du Bois wrote, "the slave spoke to the world." Echoing the trope of cultural translation provided by eighteenth-century African writers of the diaspora James Albert Okawsaw Gronomiosaw and Olaudah Equiano, Du Bois recognized the performance acts of the early spirituals as "speaking texts" or "talking books," which represent genesis and journey even as they gather meaning in historical motion, shifting geographies, living devising, and continuous improvisation.

Presciently, the Yoruba divination text, brought to the Americas in waves of forced migrations, names the epistemological "darkness" that obscures recognition and bids the practitioner to "speak" across the narrative gulf. In response to this larger call, the song "You May Bury Me in the East" takes a speaking journey that restates the proverbial principle in another time and setting drawing on a similar impetus to represent, to speak, the journey of the diaspora in African American ritual performance. The people who were torn from home and found themselves scattered in the cardinal directions, the ancestral "Lost Body" twentieth-century Pan-Africanist poet and statesman Aimee Ceasire grieved for and celebrated in his epic poem is remembered and resurrected by the trumpet's voice in "You May Bury Me in the East," and that remembering, that resurrection, is an act of creative transformation.

African American performance traditions sing insistently of place and of migrations in acts of remembering and spiritual healing. In his study *Ride Out the Wilderness: Geography and Identity in Afro-American Literature*, Melvin Dixon evokes Dr. Martin Luther King Jr.'s prophetic sermon, delivered in Memphis, Tennessee, on April 3, 1968, to underscore the African American performance lineage that illuminates King's vision from the mountaintop. Dixon points out that, within that lineage of remembering, "the wilderness, the underground and the mountaintop are broad geographic metaphors for the search, discovery and achievement of self."[23] These tropes thread throughout African American performance text, and Dixon's contemporary critical investigation sits beautifully in the lineage of Du Bois's praise song. Du Bois wrote of the poetry of the spirituals as wrest from "nature's heart"—of a body of song in which "life was a 'rough and rolling sea' like the brown Atlantic of the Sea Islands; the Wilderness was the home of God, and the 'lonesome valley' led the way to life."[24]

> Wade in the water
> Wade in the water children
> Wade in the water
> God's gonna trouble the water.
>
> "Wade in the Water," African American spiritual, nineteenth century, traditional[25]

Visions of water and its crossing also wind throughout the performed text of Africans in the diaspora, echoing ancient waters, coalescing cosmologies, and deep histories. Du Bois wrote of the spiritual "Wade in the Water" as among the second generation of African songs and representative of the genesis of an "African American" identity.[26] The waters of this baptismal song are, literally and metaphorically, a threshold at which indigenous enactments of creation are restated, marking new tributaries of human narrative.

> Who's that yonder dressed in white
> God's gonna trouble the water
> Must be the children of the Israelite
> God's gonna trouble the water
> "Wade in the Water," St. Simons Island, Georgia, twentieth century

In her study, learning, and ethnographic collecting among communities in the Georgia Sea Islands, folklorist Lynda Parrish was taught to recognize the centrality of "Wade in the Water" to the performance of religious baptism and to see, in the community's sacred performance and ritual observance of motions of the tide, lunar cycles, and physical immersion, a profound connection between this artifact and the "river cults of Africa."[27] Notably within Yoruba, Fon, and related West African cosmologies, water is associated with the feminine and, as within central African geo-cosmologies, with the fecund liminal space between life and death. Another rich ancestral stream flows from the Mende peoples of West Africa, whose cultural connection and continuum with the Gullah people of South Carolina has been extensively and generatively documented in the cultural history and linguistic studies of Darwin Turner and others, and this fecund terrain continues to invite our attention. According to art historian Pamela McClusky, "'Black' and 'wet' are both designated by the Mende word *teli*," and "Blackness and wetness refer to the ultimate origin of Sande knowledge—the nature spirits who dwell in rivers in the bush." These philosophical notions are abundantly reinscribed throughout the sacred performance of the diaspora. In the practice of Haitian Vodun (Vodou), for expansive example, performance of ritual in homage to the Dahomean deities Damballah and Agwe reproduces the wavelike motions of the sea in dance to announce divine presence. In spiritual alignment with these sacred performances, Yoruba-influenced representations of female deities Yemaya and Oshun utilize fans, shells, mirrors, and color symbolism to evoke the movement, bounty, and infinite reflectivity of river, sea, and ocean.[28] Ailey eloquently restates the confluence of these traditions in his choreographic representation, in *Revelations*, of the sacred performance of the African American church. The antiquity, and universality, of these waters is invoked, in turn, by the healing performances of nineteenth-century /Xan San peoples whose "trance"-induced spirit travel reportedly took them underwater; practitioners understand the immersion as an expression of otherworldly journey.²⁹

The African American spirituals, within a dynamic tradition of African diaspora sacred song, are the vessel, vehicle, symbol, sign, and recording of continual historical crossings and are ever expressing a complexity of crossroads in performance. Twentieth-century scholar John Lovell, in his *Black Song: The Forge and the Flame*, writes of "Wade in the Water," first recorded in the nineteenth century, as a song of spiritual possession, as among the body of "signal" songs used by Harriet Tubman to convey secret messages to fugitives, and as a revolutionary text. Those visions continue to resound in contemporary works, in which, in the words of poet Langston Hughes, "The Negro Speaks of Rivers." Examples abound, flowing from the old sacred song and dance into popular movement and sound. Performer, musicologist, and cultural historian Bernice Johnson Reagon writes, in her *If You Don't Go, Don't Hinder Me*, about the role of this spiritual in the American civil rights movement. Over a hundred-year historical span, "Wade in the Water" sings of "God" shaking things up, troubling the stagnant waters of oppression, as well as of the longer memory of the Middle Passage and of ancestral waters of baptism, journey, and vision.

Those visions resound in "modern" and contemporary works and cultural production, in which, in the words of poet Langston Hughes, "The Negro Speaks of Rivers." Examples abound, flowing from the old sacred song and dance into popular movement and sound. Nettleford's "Crossings" and reggae musician and composer Jimmy Cliff's "Many Rivers to Cross," for two potent instances, draw powerfully on this metaphor and web of references, and building, recall Paul Robeson's renditions of the spirituals "Deep River," "Water Boy," and "On My Journey." The continental source waters also continue flowing. Novelist, critic, and theorist Ngũgĩ wa Thiong'o reminds us, in his collected essays *Something Torn and New*, of the postcolonial African writers' continual reference to the continent's ancient rivers and their indigenous source. The list of musical riffs on this theme from the continent is oceanic.[30]

## Witness and History

> Go tell it on the mountain
> Over the hills and everywhere
> Go tell it on the mountain,
> That Jesus Christ is born.
>
> "Go Tell It on the Mountain," African American spiritual, traditional[31]

Some say a new vision of African identity was forged in the holds of the slave ships, in the new political and historical reality of racially based slavery, but that is only a part of the story.[32] Long before the terrible waters of the Middle Passage, there were what Mende Sande society practitioners, of Liberia and Sierra Leone, call "the radiant waters" of indigenous tradition.[33] The cultural wellsprings for a "new" Pan-African identity after the fifteenth century CE may have had everything to do with older ways of knowing, performing knowledge, and "recording" history, in cultural acts of storytelling, personal and communal witness, circles of ancestral reverence, and a worldview that incorporates concepts of metaphor, metamorphosis, duality, and transformation. Traditions of knowing and performing the self in history, and in the cosmos, that were prodigiously present among the diverse people living on the continent of Africa long before the explosion and dismembering of the transatlantic trade in humans. Those griot traditions, as we have come to know them from Malian naming, can generatively be seen as an essential source, guide, and illumination. For, in the words of griot Mamadou Kouyate, "the world is old but the future springs from the past."[34]

The polyphonic histories of Africa continually reveal how all peoples know themselves (and can be known, historicized, and understood) through their cultural articulation. That knowledge is embedded in performance texts, dance, song, story, formal historical recitation, as well as in the inscribed and sculpted motion of visual arts traditions.[35] In kinship with the sacred performances of ancestral memory and "naming" of Yoruba, Fon, and other peoples of what are now the countries of Benin and Nigeria are the griot or bardic traditions among ancient and contemporary Wolof, Mandinga, Limba, and other West and Central African people.[36] The griots of Mali, poets, dancers and singers, musicians, remembering history in performance, have been keepers of political lineages and community stories that predate Timbuktu's great universities.[37] On other sites of ancient sacred performance, Amharic priests and their congregations, in Ethiopia and the diaspora, perform lineage in liturgical recitation, remembering their history in call-and-response in order to create peace and harmony in the universe.[38]

Impetus for communal historicizing in performance is also present in less urbanized or hierarchal societies. The Dogon of southwestern Sudan traditionally engaged in practices of astrological observation, mark making, and ceremonial engagement fundamentally tied to the agricultural cycle and the idea of maintaining the necessary balance between the worlds of the ancestors and the living. Among the Baluba and other peoples of Zaire, small pendants representing ancestral faces are worn so that revered individuals will be remembered, and their character traits will positively influence posterity. Contemporary Rashids, in northeastern Africa, shout their own name—"Rashida"—in the dances of their annual festival gatherings.

These historicizing traditions, and within them the mnemonic, linguistic, poetic, and epistemological devises of oral literatures, all inform the performance of the African diaspora, where historical memory becomes central to black identity.[39] Scholars in the fields of religion, literature, language, and the arts remind us that the Yoruba priests who were enslaved in the African diaspora brought with them a sacred text of over five hundred stories held in their memories and of the continuities of West and Central African in the literary and grammatical structures as well as the sacred traditions of the diaspora. Black history in performance contains old and new ways of calling one's name, statements of tradition, and continual revision, like improvisations on a standard in the jazz tradition.[40]

While discerning the Genesis and Exodus stories of human migration told in ancient footprints is, of course, a matter of speculation over deep time, and beyond the scope of this writing, what wonderful webs of connection and illumination lay within.[41] The text, parable, and history of Yoruba divination, for instance, also record older cosmological visions as well as waves of migrations, from a northeastern homeland, and point to interaction with the indigenous, click language–speaking peoples. In *The African Past*, Basil Davidson writes about the record of the Neolithic giving way to the Iron Age in Africa and what it might reveal to us about human identity rooted in long history: "In this long and complex disintegration of the Neolithic pattern and its reconstruction within an Iron Age framework we can find the origins of modern African societies, showing as these do, in a multitude of ways, the unity in diversity that is none the less rooted in a profound and ancient unity. This large theme of unity in diversity runs throughout subsequent African history. . . . Pan-African unity is a political ambition of modern times, but its roots go far back into the past."

Though the potential cartography of lineage between founding human populations and the sprawl of subsequent West African civilization, as well as of their "meeting and parting" and reuniting over the courses of the millennia, is in fact vast, the juxtaposition of Davidson's synthesis of historical and archeological studies of Yoruba origins pairs convincingly with Joseph Greenberg's work on language universals and his speculations on the antiquity of proto-Yoruba culture.[42] Much that was gathered along the way would, in turn, become a part of an African American articulation as, in new locations, received traditions of performance of memory and history would be continually infused with layers of human journey. If the Yoruba call is "speak to me," the African American response is the impetus to tell the story.

> When I was a seeker
> I sought both night and day
> I asked the Lord to help me,
> And he showed me the way.
> He made me a watchman
> Upon a city wall
> And if I am a Christian
> I am the least of all.
>     "Go Tell It on the Mountain," second stanza

For the African, the overriding collective truth to be told in the early history of these transforming nations was the story of their journey, slavery, and liberation. In thousands of work and play songs, ring shouts and sermons, lullabies and spirituals, testimony and blues songs, in a groundswell of "slave narratives," a body of testimony like no other in history, African Americans voiced a communal desire to tell their story from the elevated moral ground of the highest mountain. African Americans sought, in the words of William L. Andrews, to "tell a free story" and to have that story passed on.[43] And their outpouring of witness often drew on a mytho-poetics that prefigures the formal religious witness of the Afro-Christian churches but is consistent in its passion, urgency, and sense of mission. The griot of another place and time became, as in the song, "a watchman." The bardic performance became a spiritual, a children's play, a lullaby, a work song recalling the sacred and the profane, the epic and the mundane.

> No more drivers lash for me
> No more No more
> No more drivers lash for me
> Many thousands gone
> No more peck of corn for me
> No more No more
> No more peck of corn for me
> Many thousands gone.
>
> "No More Auction Block," spiritual/work song, antebellum period[44]

How many gone? How many millions?[45] Kidnapped Africans included agriculturalists, artisans, poets, musicians, priests, historians, traders, travelers, warriors, political leaders, and children. Many were very young. Many were killed or took their own lives, having been herded like animals and packed like goods, in the crossing. Those who survived worked to lay the foundations for the settler colonial nations that enslaved them. Africans brought essential skills and innovation to cultivation and production in the fields of their enslavement. Enslaved Africans brought with them technologies of metalworking and building, animal husbandry and farming, architecture and medicine. They cut the rows African style for planting, cared for the personal needs of adults and children, and remembered seeds and cooking styles that substantially affected crop diversity and regional culinary history.[46] African women, particularly, cultivated, cared for, and nurtured others in their bondage. The nation they built, housed, and fed in turn brutalized African women and men and children and condemned the offspring of rape to perpetual enslavement. Those who lived to tell the tale, found a container for a mythic telling in cultural performance. Perhaps only a story could contain all that they had seen.

Historian Eric Foner closes his book *A Short History of Reconstruction* with the observation that, despite the twists and turns of mainstream historiography, the African American folk tradition had always contained and maintained a critical clarity on the American Civil War and the question of national identity.[47] His work, along with that of contemporary thinkers in all the humanities, suggests that it is to these folk traditions, in ritual, in story, in narrative, in material culture, in song, that those looking to tell the whole story must return. The African American work song "No More Auction Block" can be understood, in this light, as a historical documentary performance.

The song "No More Auction Block" was recorded across the U.S. South during and after the Civil War and paints a stunning picture of a communal African American recollection of slavery and of how that recollection works.[48] The song recounts the rations of slavery: the peck of corn, the pint of salt. It recounts the abuse of slavery: the hundred lash, the thousands gone. Alternate versions recount some of the particular features of nineteenth-century slavery in North America. Reference to the "driver," in the above version of the song, reflects the hierarchy of that era's plantation society. In another variation one stanza sings "no more mistress call for me" chronicling some of the intersections of racialized and gendered constructions of shifting identity and status in the economies of slavery over this period. In this moment of historical transformation, war, emancipation, economic and political realignments, the song recounts the many thousands left behind before it closes in an open-ended yet weary yawn into the future. A future written from the past.

"No More Auction Block" bears witness, testifies, using a pattern of call-and-response that re-members African concepts of artistic expression, community, and historical documentation and, embedded in its performance of collective autobiography, is both the process and product of formal witness. Asked, in 1862, where the people of Port Royal, South Carolina, had gotten the songs they sang, one community member told abolitionist minister and black song collector James McKim, that the people "had made them." When McKim pressed further, asking "how" the songs were made, the man reportedly told him: "It's this way. My master call me up and order me short one peck of corn and a hundred lash. My friends see it and is sorry for me. When they come to the praise meeting that night they sing about it. Some is very good singers and they know how, and they work it in, work it in, you know, until they get it right; and that's the way."[49]

This Port Royal informant's description of compositional process is strikingly similar to that of the bluesman Son House a hundred years later. Talking about the music he made, Son House gave this comment: "People keep asking me where the blues started and all I can say is that when I was a boy we always was singing in the fields. Not real singing, you know, just hollering; but we made up songs about the things that was happening to us at the time and I think that's where the blues started."[50]

In their autobiographical recollections of antebellum life, song, and story, the first generations of African Americans "wrote" a communal text imbued with a mission urgent and holy. It is a text that documents day-to-day, backbreaking labor expressed in a field holler. It is a story, a historical drama, of individuals and community being moved to moments of revelation that swept them into actual and metaphorical wilderness and flight. It is a story of escaping the physical and spiritual clutches of slavery and surviving. It is a story deeply engaged with moral instruction, with the lessons of folktale, with values and witness moving hand in hand. And the witness, the telling of that story, is a ritual, a performance, that remembers, encodes, and perpetuates the possibility of survival, through the valleys of slavery's inhumanity and despair, across the wilderness of reconstructing a universe, to freedom's metaphorical mountaintop.

By in large African diaspora performances are all about motion. Wading in the water. Going to the mountaintop. A soul tossed east to west but, nonetheless, hearing the trumpet sound. These performances are also sites of conversation. "Ham Bone," the song asks, "where you been?" "Round the world," we respond, "and back again." The rhetorical strategy of these performance practices calls for testimony, for alternating solo and choral bearing witness. These voices respond to the animating call of older text within the persistent contemporary question of journey and location. In the act of bearing witness the journey is transforming. In body and voice bearing witness, practitioners make of themselves a polyphonic sculptural statement, an altar or a staging, for metamorphosis.

## The Altar / The Stage

Night falls and we lay our sleeping mats.
Day breaks and we roll them up.
The one who lays the warp threads must walk back and forth.
*Ifa* divination verse, medieval period[51]

In the oldest sense, performance is a conversation with the universe, an altar to the cosmos, and an engagement with staving off its imminent chaos, in the creation of sites, of theaters, that embody righteous living, accountability, and "effective utterance," like the founding sacred theaters of ancient Egypt. In this spirit, according to Ositola, ritual accompanies the Yoruba initiate in successfully achieving a predestined journey with fate, interceding and negotiating with the ancestors, as they go along on their path, by making use of the proverb, prescription, and divine writing of *Ifa* to navigate the chaos of incomplete knowledge, and as a guide on the road of life.[52] The *Ifa* divination practice creates an altar for communication and transformation, an altar from which the human journey sets off. And as the history of the *Ifa* divination, which is practiced among Fon as *fa* and among Ewe speakers as *Afa*, "sets the stage" of life's journey, the history of

*Ifa* in the diaspora begins with the journey embedded in the many texts Africans brought with them into this region, texts drawn from our oldest meditations on the turning of time, the cycles of human life, the seasons, and the universe.

> Nzung! N'zungi nzila. Man turns on his path.
> N'zungi! N'zungi-nzila. He (merely) turns on his path.
> Bamganga bam'el E ee! The priests the same.
> Lemba Society ritual verse, Kongo, nineteenth century[53]

Central African altars also resplendently shape and inform diaspora tradition. The Kongo cosmogram, or sacred ground drawing, and its constellation of diaspora relations, is one radiant example of these webs of connection. Kongo tradition identifies its own first kingdom as looking down from a mountain and the lands of the living and the dead as flipped mirror images walking the same ground. Consonant with the Kongo view of the cosmos, Kongo altars are deeply embedded in landscape and geography, and Bakongo people identify sites of power and transformation in rock, tree, root, and wood formations, in caves, rivers, and road crossings.[54] According to Thompson, the pervasive presence of Kongo altars is sometimes difficult "to pinpoint."[55] Kongo cosmograms articulate these locations, and the existential and cosmological quest and questions presented in the above ritual song, in elaborate circles with crosses drawn within.

Parsing the Kongo inscription of the cross, art and cultural historian Fukiau Kia Bunseki reminds us, "Contrary to what many students have said, the sign of the cross was not introduced into this country and into the minds of its people by foreigners. The cross was known to the BaKongo before the arrival of the Europeans and corresponds to the understanding in their minds of their relationship to the world." The cross is called *yowa* and is understood as divine inscription given or written by the ancestors. Thompson's exploration of this form, in *Flash of the Spirit*, reminds us that Cuban descendants of the Bakongo call their neo-African cuneiform *la firma*, or "the signature of the spirits." The vertical line of the *yowa* represents a path of entrance, a path that crosses into the next world and on which the practitioner symbolically gains wisdom and age. The horizontal line represents the division between this world and the next. Together these lines mark a point of intersection between the worlds of the living and of the ancestors, a liminal space, an altar of inter-worldly conversation and resultant transformation.[56]

The Bakongo *yowa* sits at the center of a cosmic circle, marks "the four moments of the sun," as a metaphor for the endless cycle of life. It signifies "the compelling vision," in Thompson's words, "of the circular motion of human souls about the circumference of its intersecting lines.... Initiates read the cosmogram correctly respecting its allusiveness. God is imagined at the top, the dead at the bottom, and water in between."[57] In a performance set on a continuum from ancient time to the present, Bakongo and Bakongo-influenced practitioners enact inscription while singing ritual words, singing and drawing a point, *yimbila ye sona*, according to tradition. Their performance of oath on the symbolic crossroads remembers the relationship between the living and the dead, individual and community, communion and continuity in Bakongo belief and brings divine force, creativity, power, and possibility to the point where the practitioners stand.

Discussing the rich elaboration of Bakongo-rendered stages of spiritual inscription in the diaspora's fusions of West and Central African traditions, Thompson notes, "There are analogous ground signs, mediatory cuniforms, found among the Tu-Chokwe of northern Angola, the Ndembu of northwestern Zambia, and the Pende of western Zaire, doubtless fragments from a larger, yet to be 'discovered' western Bantu field of visual expression."[58] Thompson and other scholars recognize a proliferation of related traditions in the diaspora embracing the brilliantly imagined divine inscription in the *veve* of Haitian Vodun, the *firmas* "signatures" of Cuban Abakua religion, the *pontes riscados* "drawn points" of Kongo-influenced sacred practice in Brazil, and the Afro-Christian crosses and calligraphic and liturgical inscriptions of St. Vincent, Trinidad, Tobago, and St. Kitts.[59] This lineage of practice, particularly those of Trinidad's "Shouting" Baptists and the Garifuna rites of St. Vincent, including liturgical drawing, sacred "testifying," and antiphonal plays of rhyme and repetition, also indicate a rich kinship to the sacred ring shout of North America as well as to the vernacular philosophical certainty that what goes around still comes around.

Members,
Plumb the line.
Members,
Plumb the line
O members
Plumb the line
Want to get to Heaven got a plumb the line.
You got to sing right
Plumb the line
You got to sing right
Plumb the line
You got to sing right
Plumb the line
Want to get to Heaven you got a plumb the line
Oh sister
Plumb the line
You got to shout right
Plumb the line

"Plumb the Line," African American shout, traditional, twentieth century[60]

The lyrics and performance of "Plumb the Line" were recorded by Lydia Parrish in the Gullah communities of the U.S. Georgia Sea Islands, communities rich in African cultural retention in language, linguistics, agriculture, and spiritual practice.[61] In incandescent incidence of cultural synthesis, continuity and change, and the fusions of West and Central Africa in the African diaspora, the Gullah, whose name harks to "Ngola" or Angola, continued to sing songs in the related Mende language of West Africa into the 1930s, when Parrish was collecting.[62] Their sacred shout performances, like "Plumb the Line," set the cadence for religious worship in a circular ritual that involves counterclockwise motion; driving repetition; sung, hand-clapped, and stamped antiphonal voice; and lyrical improvisation that addresses each participant by name. Linguist Darwin Turner, whose early work tracing Africanisms in the language among the North and South Carolina Sea Islanders did much to define the discipline of African American and African diaspora studies as well as to redefine the contours of American history, explored the etymological relationship between the shout and an Arabic *saut*, which means "a dance around the Kaaba." Contemporary folklorists Jones and Hawes concur with this historical connection, which, though refuted by later scholars, seems to bear further exploration.

The African American shout and the Bakongo oath involve the communal creation of a moment of potentiality and regenerative possibility, a theater, a stage, an altar, for existential drama. Central to this creative act, and the African experience of ritual participation, is the practice and theory of antiphony, or call-and-response, the alternating voices characteristically at the heart of African and African American performance. These alternating voices are a gathering principle for African articulation of ancestry, journey, and witness in transformational articulation. The Yoruba text we began with offers this imperative: "Speak to me," calls the divination verse, "so that I may speak to you."

African and African-influenced music and lyrics have made the world familiar with the dynamic dialogs of antiphonal composition and the "stage" these dialogs set for transformative communal creation. The lead line sings, "Wade in the water," the chorus sings back, and the vision of the divine arises out of the conversation. The communal creation of call-and-response is generously present in a range of African performance and wonderfully mirrored and redoubled in the rhetorical strategies of African diaspora storytelling. "Ago," we call out in the Twi language of the Akan, calling the people to attention. "Ame," the people respond, "we are here, we are listening." In Haiti and Martinique, a game of call-and-response sets and maintains the "stage" for a story in a way that recalls the *ago/ame* exchange of the Akan as well as a similar Ki-Kongo, *riya/raya*, ritual opening to storytelling. "Krick!" the Haitian storyteller calls out, and the community responds, "Krack!" *E'Krii. E'Kraa. E'misticrii/e'misticraa* is the exchange in the storytelling traditions of Martinique. The *krick/krack, e'misticrii/e'misticraa, riya/raya,* and *ago/ame* exchanges all precipitate dynamic communal creation in call-and-response. Contemporary artists working with and within African diaspora traditions, like filmmaker Eulzan Palcy, in her

The Way We Do

*Sugar Cane Alley*, and novelist Patrick Chamoiseau, in his exploration of the death of the oral tradition, *Solibo Magnificent*, deftly use these devices in composing and representing ever transforming identities in performance "in the tradition."

Since the early years of the diaspora, Africans and their descendants have told the stories, the histories of their nations, through danced and chanted text arising from circles of performance. In the legacy of West and Central African reunification in the African diaspora, a radiant spectrum of sacred practices, including Brazilian Candomblé and Umbanda, Haitian Vodun, Cuban Abakua, and the ring shout of North America, remember the past and represent the cosmos on altars and stages of spiritual performance. Circling, drawing, and re-creating space in motion, embodying the living and the dead, the ancestors and the divine. "Dancing" and, as Charles Frederick writes in his study of the African American spiritual, "singing freedom into being" in vibrant call-and-response over space and time.[63]

> Up on the mountain Jehovah spoke
> Out of his mouth came fire and smoke
> Wade in the water
> Wade in the water children
> Wade in the water
> God's going to trouble the water.
>> "Wade in the Water," alternative version, nineteenth century[64]

> Aa yea yea aa oo
> Aa yea yea aa oo
> Aa yea yea aa oo
>> Khoisan healing circle incantation, twentieth century[65]

These rites of remembering and transformation may have roots in ancient migrations, art, and influence, and a storied inquiry into reimagining our mother tongues might fruitfully begin with the dream song dancing circles of Khoisan-language speakers, particularly since, according to proverbial wisdom, "the San is the teacher of us all." In his *Face of the Gods: Art and Altars of Africa and the African Americas*, Thompson presents the San healing trance dance, along with the altars of indigenous central Africa, as generative cultural locations.[66] While Thompson properly cautions against positing of San practices as rites frozen in time, the evidence of their widespread influence is compelling. Genetic evidence, culled from the ongoing human genome project, indicates that contemporary Khoisan speakers are descendants of humankind's oldest lines, the children of our common human beginnings. Linguistic evidence supports this locating of ancestral legacy. Khoisan (or click)–language speakers, including the groups of peoples called "San," appear to share "genetic markers" from the starting line of human language dispersion and from the deep history of our hunter-gatherer lineage. Pan-African proverb and practice, studies of the archeological records, patterns of inter-African migration, and historical centers of the Atlantic trade—all suggest the influence of San culture in Africa and the African diaspora. Cultural characteristics that we recognize as definitively African are generatively present in their cultural performance.

Central to traditional San culture is the ritual performance of a community healing circle that "sets the stage" for "trance," journey, and transformation. These ceremonial community circles are woven in call-and-response, using body and voice as instruments to form "a moving altar" of polyrhythmic performance, in hand clapping, foot stamping, yodeling, and singing. The practitioner who enters into trance in the vessel and the vehicle of this performance will travel through cosmic water, a liminal "baptism," to garner the insight and power, the *N/um*, for community healing. In the multiple "rings" of the healing circle, those who will "trance," practitioners, healers, both men and women, circle the fire and are brought into their power by the circle of incantation and movement, dance, sound and song surrounding them. The songs, the rhythms, that will carry the healer on this essential journey are drawn, traditionally, from dreams. Ancestral presences, known and unknown, form a numinous "outer" circling.

San practice may in fact present a window into the deep history of ritual performance; the reenactment of the cycles of life, stars, planets, and seasons; and the embodied reconstruction of the torn universe at the root of our theater traditions. Like the mysteries and passion plays of antiquity, from the Isis/Osiris of rituals of ancient Egypt to their restatement in the

Greek Elysian and Orphic rites, the circles of Khoisan speakers dream song dance healing performances represent an older knowing. Surely the songs of the wandering indigenous inhabitants of a wide swath of the African continent, northeast to south and notably the central African region of Angola, also echo in the diaspora in ways that can illuminate our visioning and re-visioning.[67]

**Hush, Hush, Somebody's Calling My Name**
Hush, Hush, somebody's calling my name
Hush, Hush, somebody's calling my name
Oh lord oh lord what shall I do?
"Hush, Hush, Somebody's Calling My Name," African American spiritual, traditional[68]

Among the rare early publications by writers of the African diaspora is *The Interesting Narrative of Olaudah Equiano or Gustavus Vasa the African Written by Himself*, which he first published with Leeds of London in 1789. In his narrative the abolitionist and mariner Olaudah Equiano (or Enkwuno) weaves a tapestry of story, memoir, autobiography, history, and exacting moral argument against the enslavement of the African brethren. His story and the story of his sister, whose name is never called in this writing, resound in our collective memory and call us to some fundamental questions.

Equiano begins his narrative with recollections of an African homeland, in a remote area of the current-day Benin province of Nigeria, and of its "manners and customs," including how he was named "Olaudah," meaning "one favored and having a loud voice."[69] In the course of his epic storytelling, Equiano tells of being kidnapped with his sister, as a child of eleven, and of two children bound, gagged, and marched through the woods by their abductors, then torn from each other's arms and sold to different "masters." "I cried and grieved continually; and for several days did not eat anything but what they forced in my mouth," he writes.[70] Equiano recalls being taken from town to town, sold from hand to hand, occasionally joining caravans of other bound women, men, and mostly children, while being taken ever farther from home, and seeing his sister once again, in the household of a strange town, before they were separated once more and he was embarked on the slave ship that brought him to the North American mainland. He recalls the "pestilential air" of the slave ship, "the shrieks of the women and the groans of the dying," and the spirits of those who escaped by drowning. He writes of persisting thoughts of suicide and of the saving grace of kinship. "In a little time after, amongst the poor chained men, I found some of my own nation, which in a small degree gave ease to my mind. I inquired of these what was to be done with us. They gave me to understand we were to be carried to these white people's country to work for them. I was then a little revived, and I thought if it were no worse than working, my situation was not so desperate."[71]

He writes of arriving in Virginia, "continually grieving and pining for death rather than anything else," and of entering a plantation house and seeing an enslaved black woman cooking with irons around her legs and a muzzle over her head and mouth, a muzzle "locked so fast that she could scarcely speak, and could not eat or drink."[72] He recalls being called "Michael" on the first slave ship, then "Jacob" on the plantation, and later Gustavus Vasa "the African" after fate brought him back to the sea and the slave ships, first as an enslaved hand and subsequently as a nominally free black sailor with a growing reputation for competence at his craft. His recollections of life at sea, in Europe and the West Indies, including taking charge of a slave ship and saving the lives of the people held captive in its hold, its crew, and its incompetent captain, compose the bulk of Equiano's narrative of an interesting life indeed, a narrative in which Equiano claims the authority of his experience and the prophetic power of his name to call for the abolition of slavery.

While contemporary historians have come to question the veracity of Equiano's story of African origins, citing documents that indicate he was born in the U.S. state of South Carolina (not, may I say, an uncommon phenomena among migrants and immigrants in my personal experience) and the historical complexity of his claim to Ibo (Eboe) ethnicity, his travels as well as his literary prowess are well documented; so is the veracity of the collective memory he represents. His narrative, this narrative of a global citizen in an era marked by African identities in transformation and the idea of Western "self-invention," does in fact authentically tell the story of many.[73] *The Interesting Narrative of Olaudah Equiano* remains a "founding" text in the African diaspora literary tradition and a prototype for the "slave narratives" of thousands of women and men bearing witness and testifying to the humanity, and right to freedom, of the African and against the inhumanity of the institution of slavery. Henry Louis Gates points to Equiano's narrative as "the silent second text" within *The Narrative of the Life of Frederick Douglass*. Equiano and those narrators who followed in his wake wrote, and rewrote, in and against discourses on race, hegemonic narratives arising specifically from and in support of what began as European trade, raids, and incursions on the African continent and had become systems of economic, political, and historical domination that continue to bedevil us in our time.[74]

> Sounds like Jesus
> Somebody's calling my name
> Sounds like Jesus
> Somebody's calling my name
> Oh Lord, oh lord what shall I do?
>
> I am a poor pilgrim of sorrow
> I'm in this wide world alone
> No hope in this world for tomorrow
> I'm trying to make heaven my home.
>
> "City Called Heaven," African American spiritual, traditional[75]

Europe and the burgeoning settler colonial nations of the Americas were writing their own narratives in the eighteenth century and creating what North American historian Nathan Huggins would call a "deforming mirror of truth" and "a holy history." And this "conspiracy of myth, history, and chauvinism served to create an ideology as the dominant historical motif against which all history would resonate. In the United States, Huggins reminds us, "this 'master narrative' like the constitution itself, could find no place at its center for racial slavery or the racial caste system which followed emancipation."[76] The canonical practice of "literature" as a sister discipline, and in the most ancient poetic tradition, a twin practice, has certainly wrestled with the same demons. In his narrative Equiano aptly presents himself as a "poor pilgrim," a stranger, attempting to shine a light on the strange land he has come to live in.

> Didn't my Lord deliver Daniel
> Deliver Daniel
> Deliver Daniel
> Didn't my Lord deliver Daniel
> So why not every man?
> "Didn't My Lord Deliver Daniel," African American spiritual, traditional[77]

The performed narratives of Africa and the diaspora propose deliverance in the chronicling.

> Oh where oh where is Ma Teodora? / She's chopping sugar cane.
> With her bongo and bandola? / Yes chopping sugar cane.
> Ah poor Ma Teodora. / She's chopping sugar cane. / She's chopping sugar cane.
> "Ma Teodora," work song, Cuba, sixteenth century[78]

We have, of course, been speaking generally, riffing on Equiano's powerful story, but can fruitfully now listen for the specific experience and articulation of the women of the diaspora. For me, the silent text within Equiano's narrative is the story of his sister's journey, the voice of the woman whose mouth was chained shut, the haunting presence of the girls and women he encountered "in the pestilential air" of the slave ships. The Cuban song "Ma Teodora" lets us know that African women in the earliest centuries of slavery in these regions consciously held on to the instruments and identities of their home though laboring in bondage and knew themselves to be both cane cutters and musicians, both enslaved workers and the mediums of their royal ancestors. The song "Ma Teodora" sings enduring humanity and continuing virtuosity against the pernicious dehumanization of the slave system, in the antiphonal, community building, and historicizing three-line blues structure of griot recitation. In this people's herstory, we are reminded, as was the community of singing workers at the time of the song's recording, that though, like Teodora, Africans took on the names and language of their enslavement, and were embattled and torn by its violence, they held on to, among their own people, the titles of their homelands.[79] In the "bantering" performance of "Ma Teodora" are powerful examples of African women's names for themselves and of what Angela Davis, in *Women Race and Class*, called the "standards for a new womanhood," which African women wrested from their enslavement.[80]

The prodigious performance of her story in the belly of the beast of slavery is also evident in recordings of the songs of African people in eighteenth-century Jamaica, apart from work, in a circle of gathering, movement, and incantation.

> If me want to go in a Ebo. Me can't go there.
> Since them thief me from a Guinea. Me can't go there,
> Since them thief me from my tata. Me can't go there.
> If me want to go in a Kingstown. Me can't go there.
> Since massa go in a England. Me can't go there.
> If me want to go in a Congo. Me can't go there.
> Since them thief me from my tatta. Me can't go there.
> If me want to go to Kingstown. Me can't go there.
> Since massa go in a England. Me can't go there.[81]

The first contains a chronicling, a longing, a knowing, a remembering, and layers of meaning hidden within, recalling both the multitudinous expressive languages of home and the violently renting upheaval of the journey into slavery.[82] The second records a circular performance of a song in a woman's voice.

> Hipsaw! My dear! You no do like a-me!
> You no jig like a-me! You no twist like a-me.
> Hipsaw! My dear! You no shake like a-me!
> You no wind like a-me! Go-yondaa!
> Hipsaw! My dear! You no jig like a-me.
> You no work like a-me! You no sweet him like a-me!

Jamaica. Turning their words over in my mouth, I think of our street recitations, of Olaudah Equiano's missing sister, and of the particular violence against women on the slave ships and on the plantations, the forced "dancing," the woman muzzled, chained, and cooking, the unremitting psychosexual abuse of the deforming narrative he and others do bear witness to, and I find myself leaning in more closely, listening for her telling.

2. Sheila (Chela) Anozier, *Danto*. Courtesy of the artist.

# JUBA DANCED     2
Following a Story in Motion

### The Woman and the Rain Bull: The First San Story

*Once, according to the cosmology of the /Xam San, the rain came, in the form of a bull, to the hut of a young woman. She could smell it coming. She could feel its breath billowing. She lay the babe beside her down in her kaross and, with medicinal herbs in hand, met the bull at her door, climbed on its back, and rode him. After they had gone some long distance, she demanded that the bull stop below a tree so that she could rest. There, she rubbed the bull with her herbs until it slept and she escaped.*[1]

I return to the circles of the stories of the /Xam San to begin again and to offer a frame for reading the performed herstories of the earliest women of the African diaspora and their nineteenth-century descendants. In the late nineteenth century, //Kabbo, an /Xam San cultural practitioner, collaborated with German linguist Wilheim Bleek to transmit, transcribe, and preserve something of his own language and culture, which was then at the verge of extinction in the face of European colonialism. That publication, Bleek's *Specimens of Bushman Folklore*, is the primary source for this story, which //Kabbo reports was told to him by his mother. The /Xam San story of the woman and the rain bull, reminiscent of Zeus's courting of Europa and his rape of Io, as well as of the abductions of Eurydice and Persephone by death itself, suggests a web of connection. Presaging the mythos of Greek antiquity, the storied cosmological inscription of the /Xam San crosses universal symbolic terrain to speak of multiple layers of journey and creation. The woman is abducted from her home, rides the powerful rain bull, the embodiment of water, traveling across worlds and liminal space to the sacred tree where she puts the beast to sleep with her herbs and escapes. Within the metaphor and metamorphosis of the tale is the text of women's performance, journey, agency, and transformation, in which her intimate knowledge of botany, geography, and cosmology are keys to her mythic achievement and a vehicle for her freedom. How she will meet elemental challenges. How she will triumph.

I can imagine elements of this text further illuminated by the fire-lit healing circles of the /Xam San and animated by their "dream song dancing," chanting, and rhythmic hand clapping. On these "moving altars," the song, dance, motion, and sound, /Xam San women articulate a ritual journey and set the stage for the spiritual flight, across worlds and back, deemed necessary for the community's health. Centuries of San visual representation, and the deep history of parietal art that proceeds them, support later ethnographic reports that connect San circles of singing and clapping women with major cultural performances, including healing, fertility, rites of passage, and hunting celebrations. In all these cultural performances, women's articulations have specific functions and meaning. Archeologist David Lewis Williams, among other students of the San and their cosmological enactments of community, recognizes the role their long sessions of repetitive percussion and dance play in creating the psychosocial conditions for ecstatic experience or trance. Williams's study also fruitfully explores the use of mythological and folkloric text as a framework for reading and understanding material culture in parietal art.

San practice is paradigmatic of African and African diaspora performance traditions in its multi-metered embodiment of articulation, in its communal construction of vehicles for social transformation, and in its attention to the human body, in voice and motion, as an altar, a platform, for spiritual flight—grounding the community in the present and evoking the ancestral past. A further note on all that is in a name. The Dutch called these click-language-speaking hunter-gatherers "Bushmen," and their central African forest linguistic kin were dubbed "Pygmy." The names most of these now-scattered groups of people call themselves translate well as "us."[2]

**Legacy Song**

> We mold the pot as our mothers did.
> The pot where is the pot?
> The pot it is here.
> We mold the pot as our mothers did.
>
> "We Mold the Pot," children's game, southern Sudan, twentieth century

Daughters of Africa and the diaspora have drawn from, remembering and reconstructing, widespread traditions of women's performance, art, and articulation, documenting ancestry, identity, and history in generative creative action, teaching and passing these traditions on in the doing. "We Mold the Pot," a children's play from southern Sudan, recorded at the turn of the twentieth century, illustrates theory and praxis in movement and sound. Writer J. H. Driberg's description of this play informs our telling. "Down they sat cross legged in a circle, holding hands, and one sang very slowly," according to this chronicling. "They all answered, thrusting their clasped hands to the center" of the circle, until their fingers were touching, and then leaning all the way back on their hips, arching their backs, hands still clasped, arms outstretched. Rocking their collective bodies back and forth, swaying from left to right, left to right, in between these motions, the circle of children enacted the sculpting of a vessel on the spinning of a potter's wheel. In the way of children, the circling went on and on, "leader" and "chorus" repeating verse and motion again and again, their "backs curving and their arms straining more and more forward to shape the pot down to its mouth."[3]

In a singing and dancing circle, their bodies pantomiming the wheeling motion of the potter's art, which is traditionally women's work in many African societies, including that of the Didinga, the girls act out the molding of pots as a metaphor, evoking woman as sculptor as well as holder of tradition, while "playing" the journey of becoming women. Their play is a communal gesture woven, hands clasped, telling a story in word and motion, recalling received experience, in call-and-response, and completed with a leap and a shout. The performance text "molds the pot" in tradition while, in the dialectical motion of play and song, girls and women also continually mold a new pot, as their mothers did, shaped by specific moments in journey, location, and time.

In the early part of the century, Didinga girls played "pots," evoking the architecture of women's work in their society. In the 1960s African American girls sang and danced street plays integrating African metrics, forms, and movement aesthetic with a "sassy" urban attitude. In kinship with Caribbean plays during that period, all of our plays, "in the tradition," articulated the consonance between the past and the present by incorporating current history and changing values in performance. Perhaps also within our plays are kernel lessons for riding the bull wind from an older crossroads of /Xam San influence.

> Sakere, sakere ho, ho
> Sakere, sakere ho, ho
>> West Africa, modern Liberia, sixteenth century

The slender record of writing by African women in the early years of the diaspora is complemented, illuminated, and enriched by the greater bounty of their voices in performance. Music historian Eileen Southern, in her study *The Music of Black Americas*, underscores the "striking" centrality of music and dance to seventeenth- and eighteenth-century African life, a fact that early European travelers "seldom failed to comment upon this." Scholars since have returned to this aspect of the documentary record. Africans of the period engaged in music, song, and danced performance with and within a range of activities and social locations, from individual and group work practices to ceremonial public occasions and sacred ritual to familial and communal rites of passage. On these multiple sites, where "art" was embedded in daily life, Southern notes the extent to which, as a Pan-African musical phenomenon, "occasions associated with children, adolescent girls, and funerals, in particular, generally called for musical performance by women."[4]

The performance practices of African women "speak" in potent and poetic creative act throughout what Robert Farris Thompson, in his *African Art in Motion*, calls "the danced history of Africa" from the fifteenth century on. In the period paralleling the slow, steady, and subsequently meteoric rise, expansion, desecration, and devastation of what would become known as the Atlantic slave trade, African women's "voices" form a powerful thread of storytelling in the chronicling of Europe's "contact" with the continent. Though these "histories" come to us through the writings, and the gaze, of European men, they offer a useful chronicling that later historians, including and following Southern and Thompson, have drawn on. In around 1455 Senegalese women greeted Venetian trader Ca' da Mosto with danced welcome and introductions.[5] On December 2, 1497, "about two hundred" women, men, and children of South Africa's Mossel Bay welcomed Vasco da Gama with a harmonious statement in flute and dance performance "in the style of Negroes." Of course, Vasco da Gama's journeys, would in turn herald the destruction of the African civilizations he encountered and wrote about.[6] In another ill-fortuned African welcoming, between 1556 and 1557, on the eastern portion of the coast of modern Liberia, West African women greeted British "explorer" William Towerson's company with an assembly performance of music, dance, and song. "He seems to have caught the refrain" of one of their songs, writes Thompson, who suggests that the inscription "sakere, sakere ho ho" may be the first written documentation of the characteristically African form of call-and-response in performance.

The performances of these African women speak of self-presentation, of welcome, and of an invitation to exchange, dialog, and cooperation, in this early period of trade association. The people of these West African communities, states, and nations "met" Europe in full recognition and articulation of their own equality, or superiority, and their performed welcome is a diplomatic expression of credential and politics.[7] As ambassadors for their own ascendant nations, in the act of greeting and welcoming, these women of the regions known to Europeans as Senegambia and the Guinea coast were representing ancestry and lineage, philosophy and aesthetics, in an introduction merging dance, hand clapping and antiphonal singing, formal presentation, and the creation of the milieus for spirit or ancestral possession.[8] Far more than entertainment, the performances of these fifteenth- and sixteenth-century African women made essential statements about history and society, social values and cohesion, virtuosity and communal creation, and performance as both "an ornament to their state" and a site for perpetual transformation.

> The winds roared the rain fell
> The poor white man faint and weary
> Came and sat under our tree
> He has no mother to bring him milk
> No wife to grind his corn.
> Let us pity the white man no mother has he.
>
> Bambara women, extemporaneous work song, eighteenth century

The eighteenth-century chronicle of less formalized historicizing and social commentary in the "bantering" traditions of African women is also revealing. Mungo Park's *Travels in the Interior Districts of Africa, Performed under the Direction and Patronage of the African Association in the Years of 1795, 1796, and 1797* is an oft-cited text in the study of the "encounter" between Africa and Europe. Park, a Scottish surgeon "exploring" the upper regions of the Niger River in the eighteenth century, lost his way and was given shelter by village women of the Bambara states. The women improvised a record of his visit among themselves by scatting against the above refrain, in call-and-response conversation, as they spun their cotton. Park slept and woke to their song and, finding through a translator that it was about him, wrote the words down.

As in the more formal assemblies, Bambara women composed extemporaneous historical documents that wove a narrative of contemporary experience into the larger historical, and critical, record. "Let us pity the white man no mother has he," they sang of this stranger who had no name, no home, and presumably, no one to properly record his history or his ancestry. What they have to say about the white man is evident. What the song tells us about Bambara women and the role they assumed in historical inscription, framing, and interpretation is intriguing. Clearly the white man was literally lost, but their commentary suggests a more layered figurative reading and offers prescient comment on what would come to be known, in Western discourse, as "the white man's burden."[9]

The performed record of West African interaction with Europeans in the seventeenth and eighteenth centuries also chronicles community circles of women dancing and hand clapping, uplifting and keeping time, and these circles' vitality, multi-vocality, multipart movement, percussive and rhythmic precision, and social and historical statement. Thompson makes note of philosophical and aesthetic values these circles articulate, including the value placed on personal and representational balance, multiple meter movement, swing, percussive body movement, danced suppleness, and played suspension of the beat, and elaborates on how these values remain very much evident in the contemporary composition and critique. Within these circles, as the practitioner makes of herself altar, sculpture, stage, and syntax, the performance offers epistemological, philosophical, poetic, and pedagogical text. Central to that text is the circle itself.[10]

Historian Sterling Stuckey, recalling the widespread presence of the "counter clock wise dance ceremony" in Africa and the African Americas, points out that the circle symbolizes a connection with the past and a veneration of ancestry common to and uniting these traditions.[11] The circle is also, naturalist Elizabeth Marshall Thomas reminds us, an architecture of nesting and protection that can be traced back to the circular round house encampments of "the first people" in the upper Paleolithic.[12] In both continuity and influence, the circle makes physical the meta-dialogue of journey, communal creation, witness, and transformation that is characteristic of African and African diaspora performance.

Thompson's "danced history" of Africa also includes a traveler's description of a Fanti dance circle in 1830:

> A noise of singing and clapping of hands attracted us to a party of women who were enjoying themselves in the cool of the evening with a very strange dance. Standing in a circle, one of them advanced, and challenged another in performing two or three different steps and motions of the arms which consisted in bringing the hands from the back of the head to the front, clapping them, jumping up in the air, and striking the ground with the right or

left heel, accompanied by the cry of "Osarah." These motions were performed two or three times; and if the challenged party executed them correctly, the challenger went round to the next, and gave place to one who had made a mistake. This dance is a very favorite one on the Gold Coast.[13]

The danced circle is a literal and metaphorical site of beginning and, as a site of connection, relation, and metamorphosis, inherently a place of pedagogy. In its multiple inscriptions of the composition, tradition, and improvisation, the danced circle is also a place where the grammar of performance is learned in call-and-response dialog, communal creation, and layered storytelling.

The Fanti women's circle of song and dance call-and-response weaves together statements of communal and personal identity in a resonant series of dialogues between dancers, drummers, singers, and audience, as well as between the dancer/practitioner and her own body as an instrument. Philosophically and artistically the performance is an architecture of conversations, "signifying" and significant. The circle draws on and represents a shared vocabulary of sound, motion and meaning, symbol and sign, creating a vessel and a vehicle of story and telling.[14]

In their performances African women styled themselves as vessels of the past and as locations for creative transformation, as representatives of powerful lineages and as critical commentators within them. The story of her abduction and rape resounds in "the unsubduable cry" of Afro-Atlantic performance, among them the Juba, one of the oldest recorded diaspora (art)iculations, a performance of hand clapping, call-and-response, embodied instrumentation, sculptural presentation, fancy footwork, and the voice of resistance.

**Song in a Strange Land**
  Juba this and Juba that
  Juba killed a yellow cat
  And get over double trouble.
    Juba, traditional ring play, nineteenth-century version[15]

This version of Juba was performed by Georgia Sea Island children in the 1930s. Describing the movements of one of the performers, Parrish writes, "By rapidly crossing his hands to first one knee and then the other Snoops pats out an intricate rhythm to the above staccato lines. When he gets to 'now Juba' he does some clever footwork that matches the coordination of his hands." The roots and the routes of the Juba text in performance brings us back to Equiano's sister and the first generation of African diaspora women.

She may never have changed her name or spoken a language other than her mother tongue. She may have lived the rest of her life in or near the African town where she was last parted from her brother. Or she may have gone on to the coast before him. She may have died on the course of the trail of lamentation toward the coast or on that killing Middle Passage and joined the millions of Africans who returned to their homes as ancestors. Or like Isabella de Angola, whose name appears in the log of the first slave ship to arrive in North America in 1619, and the little girl who was named "Phillis" for the slaver who carried her to Boston and "Wheatly" for the family who purchased her as a companion for their daughter in 1751, she may have survived by the grace of an African woman's protection on the passage and her wits in the landing and bought her freedom at great cost. We know that she lived and died during a time when African women had begun to sing and dance an identity woven from the shards of a calabash now broken. At least some of the herstory of the first women of the diaspora is told in performance traditions. Those performances, and the few written records we have, speak of dislocation, dismemberment, and violence; of naming, remembering, embodiment, and resistance; of riding the rain bull winds; and like Juba, of double trouble and conjuring.

One of the first stops of the British ships carrying African people, and goods for trade, into the Americas was Barbados, the Caribbean point closest to Africa and then a place of brutal enslavement. Colonial Barbados was considered by those in the slave trade a "seasoning" ground and a "market" for more lucratively reselling people to the Great Turtle Island North American mainland. The conditions in which kidnapped Africans were forced to work on massive plantations were infamously horrific. People were literally worked to death, and reports of corpses piled at the ports were not uncommon.

Colonial Barbados was also a place where indigenous traditions were being interlaced with a strong Central African, particularly Kongo, presence. Like hundreds of thousands of the African people who were caught in the snares of this massive human trafficking, the enslaved women Tituba and Candy spent their childhoods in Barbados before ending up in Salem, Massachusetts, where both would be tried as witches in 1691.[16] Tituba was separated from her family as a girl and sold into bondage in the household of a "minister." She had considerable husbandry, herbal, and medicinal skills, and those skills were alleged, at trial, as evidence of her witchcraft. Tituba also told stories to her young white charges and the powers of her storytelling were the most damning evidence used against her. Her stories were reported so compelling and enchanting the listeners who became her accusers claimed they had been put under a spell. In court testimony Tituba admitted that her stories and her dreams helped her to "fly home."

Candy, whose story is less well-known, denied culpability for witchcraft, the "black arts." "Me no witch in Barbados. Me mother no witch," the transcript quotes her saying. Yet in court Candy produced a doll, much like a traditional Bakongo charm called *minkisi*, as the vehicle of her magic. Similar "doll-like charms" were made by nineteenth-century Afro-Cubans in order to spiritually resist and "mystically attack slaveholders and other enemies."[17] Both Thompson and Lydia Cabrera describe these figures and the complex statements embedded in their visual forms, and Thompson makes reference to the example of nkisi *matiabo* figures in the Afro-Cuba Kongo constellation, named for, and perhaps used by, communities of fugitives from enslavement, as well as to other iterations of Kongo charms in the diaspora, sometimes known in Haiti and Western Hispanola as *pacquets de congo*.[18] These containers for "strong medine" recall both Ormilla's bag of the Yoruba scripture and the herbal bag of the /Xam woman.

Tituba and Candy may have been two of the three Africans in the town of Salem, Massachusetts, at that time. Unlike many of those accused in the witch hunts, they had no wealth, status, or property, but each of these women carried within her a deep connection to Kongo traditions and knew something about ritual performance, ancestry, journey, history, and transformation.

> She served the meal
> She give me the husk
> Cooked the bread
> She give me the crust
> She fried the meat
> Give me the skin
> That's the way momma took me in.
> Now Juba.

"Juba" offers a glimpse of the portion of enslaved women as well as of the complex truths, and costs, of their resistance. Bondswomen, torn from their own homes, labored as agriculturists, servants, cooks, housekeepers, and nurses and were given the husk, the crust, and "double trouble" in return but, in the collective autobiography, did not simply accept those portions and drew on a range of strong medicines and remembering in acts of day-to-day survival and of epic social transformation.

African women and men foisted into the labyrinth slave labor systems of the Caribbean would have heard the language of home in assemblies of dance and song, ceremony and performance, like this one recorded in Barbados around 1673: "On Sundays in the afternoon their music plays and to dancing they go, the men by themselves and the women by their selves, no mixed dancing . . . their hands having more motion than their feet and their heads more than their hands."[19]

During this period the colonial ruling class complained that the enslaved Africans were "very tenaciously addicted to the rites, ceremonies, and superstitions of their own countries, particularly in their plays, dance, music and burials. And even such as were born here cannot be entirely weaned from these customs."[20] "The manners and customs" of African homelands, already in a great deal of motion in the African world of the seventeenth and eighteenth centuries, returned to common root in the ancestral circles of the diaspora, circles expressing the seamless connection between individual naming and communal survival.[21]

Though over the course of the eighteenth-century African drumming would be outlawed in most precincts, in attempts by colonial legislatures to censure, condemn, or contain the political statements in African performance, performance of African identity echoed throughout the Atlantic region. A description of rings of African song and dance in Jamaica, published in 1797, recalls the assemblies of West and Central Africa and the healing circles of the San as the people embodied the reconstruction of community and identity in a call, a cry, a petition to the divine.

> The song and dance are always united when they associate to amuse themselves; it is on these occasions the Negroes of each tribe or nation assemble in distinct groups with their several instruments. Excellence in dancing is thought to depend on a due performance of certain gestures particular to each class. For persons deemed qualified to exhibit, the others form a circle, observing the time by antic motions of the body, clapping their hands, and rattling their calabashes fixed to sticks; the instruments keeping up a continued sound.[22]

This description of African dance in the Virgin Islands in 1806 is similarly revealing:

> The dance consists of stamping of the feet, twisting of the body ... severe bodily exertion—more bodily indeed than you can well imagine, for the limbs have little to do in it. The head erect, or, occasionally, inclined a little forward—the hands nearly meet before—the elbows are fixed, pointing from the sides—and the lower extremities being held rigid, the whole person is moved without lifting the feet from the ground. Making the head and limbs *fixed points*, they writhe and turn the body upon its own axis, slowly advancing toward each other, or retreating to the outer parts of the ring.[23]

These choreographic inscriptions are familiar ones, the multidimensional gathering, the danced circle as a site of remembering and instruction, the "gravity" of countenance among the practitioners, the "fixed points" of their focus are key aesthetic and symbolic inscriptions in West and Central African dance. The importance of the head as a center of power and the feet as a sculptural representation of connection with the earth and the ancestors is especially notable as a text of performed grammar and is represented wonderfully in the starkly different styles but shared vocabulary of Kongo and Yoruba visual art.[24] From those fixed points of power and the "grounded" connection to the past, practitioners achieve connection with the ancestors and with a longed-for home. The apparent tone of this ring of performance underscores its function as a liminal staging. The Yoruba concept of *itutu*, or "mystic coolness," is an inextricable component of the primal power that they call *Ashe*, the generative power to make things happen.[25] With these movements, practitioners create the space to commune with divinity. And in the circles of women and men creating a theater for metamorphosis, with hand clapping and repetitive motion, the practices of West and Central Africa can again be traced back to the older healing practices of the San.

Another description of an eighteenth-century circle of African performance in the Virgin Islands re-presents endless rings of circles being created in the metaphysical realm:

> For the most part only two enter the ring at a time, but, occasionally, as many as three or four each making a small contribution to the band at the time of stepping into the circle. They circle violently together until one is tired, and when this escapes from the circle another assumes his place, thus continuing to follow, one by one, in succession, so as frequently to keep up the dance, without any interval for several hours.[26]

In another chronicling from eighteenth-century Jamaica these liminal circles were redoubled in polyphonic waves of women's song that rose and fell as they worked the mill in the night, as one voice "and now a second and third chime in, and presently... a full chorus is heard to swell upon the ear, and then to die away again to the first original tone."[27]

But these familiar visions were conjured on a hellish landscape. Historian Nell Painter reminds us that the enslaved African lived, and died, in wartime conditions. Houston Baker aptly describes the central experience of early Africans in the diaspora one of "incarceration."[28] John Stedman, a mercenary in the colonial war against "the revolted Negroes of Surinam," included among his chronicling and "impressions" of Guiana in 1790 a highly stylized drawing of an African woman hanging by her bound hands from the limb of a tree. She is partially unclothed and blood runs from her wounds.

Stedman also chronicles insurrectionary rings of song and dance and the role of women, "Sybils," as prophets of revolt and flight "amongst the Owca and Seramica Negroes." Herskovit's extensive twentieth-century anthropological study of both Surinam and Dahomey underscore African continuities in the role of women's performance in honoring the cycle of life and death, birth and funeral rites.[29] Yoruba lore, Dahomean snake cults, and the even older beliefs represented in the Egyptian uraeus no doubt made their way into Surinam with enslaved Africans.

Juba this and Juba that
Juba killed a yellow cat
And got over double trouble

Much of the record of early diaspora women comes to us from legal documents, ship's logs and invoices, bills of sale, household inventories, and trial transcripts.[30] They too offer a glimpse of the portion of enslaved women that Juba sings, of the "double trouble" she faced, and of the yellow cat, of the conjuring black cat's bone, of her resistance. Eduardo Galeano's *Memory of Fire* recalls the story of two women of Surinam, called Sery and Flora, who were beaten, tortured, and ultimately, beheaded in the year 1711 for their repeated escape attempts and their refusal to reveal the location of fugitive encampments. Galeano also pulls from colonial archives the story of a woman called Zabeth, who never stopped attempting to escape her captivity though she was hunted down, ravaged by dogs, repeatedly branded, brutally beaten, and died chained in the yard of her captors.[31]

From the colonial era into the nineteenth century, written records from North America open a window into lives enveloped by violence and reclaimed, in sometimes killing, often maiming, acts of resistance. In the fall of 1838 antislavery journals followed the case of a woman called Sally whose children had been systemically taken away from her for sale. Sally was accused of murdering the children of the slave owner who testified that she had warned him that "no child of his would live to horsewhip a child of hers."[32] The abolitionist press of the period also followed the story of Margaret Garner, which is retold in Toni Morrison's novel *Beloved*.[33] Garner, a fugitive facing the prospect of recapture, was alleged to have slit her child's throat rather than have her subject to the brutal whims of the slave system. There are many less well-known stories of women rent by and resisting enslavement, among them the story of Celia, a nineteen-year-old woman tried for the murder of a slave owner who had repeatedly raped her and was the father of her two children.[34]

Tragically such tales of horror populate the "deforming mirror" of the history of North American slavery. Juba's invocation of motherhood—"the way Mama took me in"—speaks poignantly to how the "legal status" of children trapped in the North American slave system was legislated to "follow the condition of the mother" and evokes the legacy of psychosexual tortures, the systematic rape and calculated terror, used against women. Many of the "slave narratives" and much abolitionist literature chronicle the legally legislated atrocities of Atlantic slavery aimed specifically at women, including the institutionalized practices of forcefully separating children from their mothers and of beating pregnant women, held face down, with their bellies pushed into a hole dug into the ground. Many of the slave narratives, that of Frederick Douglas among them, recall the image of nursing women beaten until "the blood and milk" flowed mingling down their bodies. Buried within the historical record, but evoked in the song, is the proper and persistent fear that "slave masters" had of being poisoned particularly by women.

On this nightmare terrain Juba's singsong rhyme, storytelling, dance, and song are a remembering embrace of the dismembered bodies of women, a vessel for containing and recording "unspeakable" terror, a sustained and sustaining connection to home, a call, a cry, a keen, a sign, and a warning.

Using the circles of old as sites for healing wounded body and mind, and for longings echoed over geography and generations, the performance of the African diaspora also fueled the fires of perpetual revolt and revolution. Throughout the diaspora ancestral circles of performance often spiraled into acts of resistance, escape, and uprising and were elements of the formation of independent, "maroon" societies, *quilombos, mocambos, palenques, cumbes, ladeiras,* and *mambises*. Documentation of major insurrections against enslavement, including the Haitian revolution, the maroon wars of Jamaica, the battles of Palmares in Brazil, and the revolt associated with Nat Turner in North America, had clear components of ritual performance that provided the transformative spiritual foundations for imagining and enacting liberation. And the herstory, the actual and symbolic role of women, is an essential part of the telling.[35]

From eighteenth-century Jamaica, a site of perennial resistance, African diaspora performance voicing frustration and existential determination in dance and in song resounds.

> Think there is a god on top
> No use we ill, Obisha
> Me no horse, me no mare, me no mule
> No use me ill Obisha.[36]

Song and dance performances were sustaining acts of daily resistance for Africans enmeshed in the killing complex of displacement, occupation, and oppression of colonial slave "society" and in a truly strange land. The Africans' performances were sites for remembering their own humanity, making social critique, and recording witness of their condition in a hybrid language that underscored the journeys sung. "Think There Is a God on Top," recorded in Jamaica by the eighteenth-century traveler J. B. Moreton, is a testimony against the injustice and hypocrisy of the slave system.

The song bears witness to the brutality of the slave economy, the treatment of men and women like beasts of burden, while affirming the divine right of the enslaved person's humanity. "Me no horse, me no mare, me no mule," the song sings, despite the naming of "chattel" slavery. "Me no horse, me no mare, me no mule, no use me ill," the song insists and demands. You can neither own nor "breed" me. The refrain, "No use me ill Obisha," forms a cadenced determination. Louise Bennett points to a twentieth-century revision of these lines in "The Banana Boat Song" (popularly known as "Day-O") in her *Lawd Di Riddim Sweet*, which recalls Equaino's perhaps sardonic expression of a sense of relief on being told that Africans were being carried to "the white people's country to work not to be eaten": "If it were no worse than working, my situation was not so desperate."[37]

> Me come here fe work
> Me nah come here fe idle
> Day da light an me wan go home
> No give me soso bunch
> Me nah hass wit bridle
> Day da light an me wann go home.

Another forerunner in this legacy, a recording from eighteenth-century Jamaica that was invoked in our opening chapter, sings ancestry and journey in rhythmic social commentary.

> If me want to go in a Ebo. Me can't go there.
> Since them thief me from a Guinea. Me can't go there.
> Since them thief me from my *tata*. Me can't go there.
> If me want to go in a Kingstown. Me can't go there.
> Since massa go in a England. Me can't go there.
> If me want to go in a Congo. Me can't go there.
> Since them thief me from my *tatta*. Me can't go there.
> If me want to go to Kingstown. Me can't go there.
> Since massa go in a England. Me can't go there.[38]

Recognizing and recalling the people's Kongo / Central African and Ibo / West African roots, this song reminded the people of their own humanity through a remembering of their homelands. Equiano begins his written narrative by similarly situating his story in geography and ancestry. "That part of Africa, known by the name of Guinea, to which the trade of slaves is carried on, extends along the coast above 3,400 miles, from Senegal to Angola, and includes a variety of kingdoms." Of these "the most considerable," wrote Equiano, "is Benin."[39] The song confirms the sense, again conveyed in Equiano's telling and in later oral and written narratives, that the enslaved were persistently bearing witness to the injustice of their situation and saw themselves not as "slaves" but as people who had been kidnapped or stolen.⁴⁰ Like the African women in sixteenth-century Cuba who sang of "Ma Teodora," these singers remember, recognize, and affirm an identity beyond enslavement in a hybrid tongue. Here they sing of the *tata*, a Ki-Kongo word for "father," they were stolen from, just as "No Use Me Ill" names the slaver *Obisha*. In both lyric and language, in the communal voice of call-and-response, the song recalls the representational modalities of West and Central Africa, of "Congo and Ibo" stolen by "England," enslaved in "Kingstown," and longing for home.

The power and pervasiveness of the displaced Africans' connection to and longing for home and the centrality of that connection to their construction of identity resounds throughout their performances and beyond the physical landscape. Images of Africans walking across the waters or flying back to Africa abound in the folk record, as does death as a metaphor for return and the circle unbroken. "When dancing they form themselves into a circular position, adjoining their huts, and continue all in motion, singing so loud, that of a calm night they may be heard about two miles distance—thus: Hipsaw! My dear! You no do like a-me! You no jig like a-me! You no twist like a-me. / Hipsaw! My dear! You no shake like a-me! / You no wind like a-me! Go-yondaa! / Hipsaw! My dear! You no jig like me / You no work like a-me! You no sweet him a-me!"⁴¹

Patterns of African women's choral performance circles, recorded throughout the eighteenth-century Caribbean, were definitely "saying something." "Hipsaw Me Dear" repeats the circle of ancestral recognition and restates the value placed on precision and memory in lyrics and dance. The structure of the women's performance pays homage to the past and to the "hips like this" signifying of Kongo performance, and the improvisational lyrics bear witness to the present. "Hipsaw Me Dear" testifies to women's consciousness of themselves as women and performers, culture bearers, and laborers and of their determined agency even in enslavement. Black women in the early Americas and the Caribbean constructed and reconstructed old and new definitions of what it meant to be a woman, even as their own beings were under attack.⁴² Do, jig, twist, shake, wind, work, and "sweet" the chosen "him," and each other as well—the public performance of these and other African women, their virtuosic signifying and historicizing across disciplinary and discursive locations, illuminates what would come to be called "Juba."[43]

**Monday's Child**
>Juba this and Juba that
>And Juba killed a yellow cat
>And get over double trouble.
>Juba.

Equiano's sister, her age mates, and her generations to follow were to find themselves in an ontological juggling act. They were not white, and they were not men; they inherited their enslaved status, in the corrupt law of the North American slave system, through their mothers, yet their legacy and condition most truly represented the challenge of social justice and its call to speak out. Answering this call in the coming century, Sojourner Truth would speak of her role as a "cipher," making a stir among the people.[44] That complex tale of experience and survival is compressed in Juba's verse and performance.

The Juba has extensive roots and routes. Katherine Dunham wrote of the plantation era Juba as a circle dance with familiar elements. "In its original African form, the *juba* or *jumba* or *majumba*, as it is called in the West Indies, is primarily a competitive dance of skill. One person steps forward in the circle of dances and begins exhibiting his skill, whereupon he is joined by a member of the opposite sex who joins in this exhibition. The people in the circle may rotate for a certain number or measures, or may remain stationary, all the while clapping rhythmically and encouraging the competitors with song and verse."[45]

Thompson in *African Art in Motion* suggests that the thigh- and chest-slapping dances of the Kongo called *Kamba* became the North American Juba, and one can see its contemporary continuation in the popular fast-moving hand games of urban children and in the formalized step dancing of African American college students. Folklorists Bessie Jones and Bess Lomax Hawes point out the similarity between an Ewe or Ghanaian social dance "that is accompanied partly by drumming and partly by hand-clapping and chest slapping" and the "hand jive" of African American children's play, including early twentieth-century variations of Juba and Ham Bone.[46] The Ham Bone that we learned as kids playing street games. Haitian artist and performance practitioner, dancer, choreographer, and teacher Sheila (Chela) Anozier recently taught me a piece of body percussive dance play from Niger that is literally and metaphorically "strikingly" similar to our North American Ham Bone and Juba. Anozier also points out the bifurcated movement of the Haitian Juba in which the stiffer upper body movements are said to represent European influences and the rhythmic movement of hips is in homage to African roots. Ever the teacher, reviewing this text she wrote, "The dance is Djoumba (sometimes spelled Djouba) and is a work dance connected to cultivation and farming and honoring Azaka—minister of agriculture."[47]

The caldron of converging Pan-African practice appears to be a vast one in which historical documentation is mixed with the articulation of ancestral connection, sacred spiritual practice, incantation, creative act, and conjuring. From the first landings through Equiano's arrival in this region, Africans of the diaspora drew on a constellation of cosmological visions and belief systems to restate and re-create identity and community.[48] Melville and Fran Herskovits's studies among African descendants in Surinam document both the continuity of circle dance in sacred performance and the connection between these performances and the ancestral ring dance of North America called the ring shout, the core movement of which is where we first see the Juba danced.[49] Documentation of African American shout or ring shout performances, comprising sacred circles of singing and movement, including hand clapping and body patting, appear as early as 1819 in a Methodist minister's bitter complaint about African religious song and dance practice: "With every word sung, they have a sinking of one or the other leg of the body alternately; producing an audible sound of the feet at every step, as manifest as the steps of actual Negro dancing in Virginia. . . . If some, in the meantime sit, they strike the sounds alternately on each thigh."

According to Eileen Southern, later in the nineteenth century "the dance would be called a shout and the striking of the body, 'pattin' or 'pattin the

Juba.'"⁵⁰ Not long after this time, performances of the shout would also be outlawed in the United States, and the sacred practice continued only in clandestine gatherings, though their "ancient organizing principles" continued to echo in the clapping, patting, dance, song, and social commentary of the Juba, which, in time would find its way into the foundations of a particularly "American" theater.

The danced record contains many reports of the secular performances incorporating communal art creation and the percussive synchronized hand clapping, foot tapping, and body instrumentation that are called Juba. Solomon Northrup, a professional musician and autobiographer, whose *Twelve Years a Slave*, published in 1853, tells the harrowing tale of being kidnapped from his home in New York into southern plantation slavery, writes of Juba "pattin" during dances on a plantation in Louisiana. Northrup gives the following lyrics:

> Harper's creek and roaring river
> There my dear well live forever
> Then we'll go to the Indian nation
> All I want in the creation
> Is a pretty little wife and a big plantation.⁵¹

In line with Northrup's description are those of William Smith, who wrote of witnessing what was called "Juber pattin" in Virginia some years before the publication of an article called "The Persimmon Tree and the Beer Dance" in 1839. Here Smith recorded participants singing:

> Juber up and down
> Juber all around the town
> Juber this and Juber that
> Juba round the simmon vat
> Hoe corn hill tobacco
> Get over double trouble / Juba boys Juba.⁵²

Each description highlights the synchronized interplay of percussive clapping, body patting, and footwork. Smith's early recording of Juba performance also underscores the essential connection between song practice and allegorical storytelling. He recorded subsequent stanzas of the Juba, including the following:

> Racoon went to simmon town
> To chose the rotten from the sound
> There he sat upon a sill
> Eating of a whip-poor-will.
> Hoe corn! Hill tobacco!
> Get over double trouble,
> Juba boys, Juba.

With history hidden in a ditty, aptly enough, one of the first internationally known African American dancers was a man named William Lane, who went by the stage name "Master Juba" in the mid-nineteenth century. Lane, who was known as an accomplished musician as well as for exceptional handwork and footwork, hailed from the Five Points district of New York, a predominately African American community during that period. Novelist Charles Dickens saw one of Juba's performances in 1842 and wrote a report.[53] Often satirized and, by the mid-nineteenth century, appropriated into racist characterization in the American minstrel theater, Juba's voice, like Equiano's recollection of the woman whose mouth had been locked shut, often comes to us in a muffled scream.

> Harper's creek and roaring river
> There my dear we'll live forever
> Then we'll go to the Indian nation
> All I want in this creation
> Is a pretty little wife and a big plantation
> Up that oak and down that river
> Two overseers and one little n——
> Now Juba![54]

If Equiano's sister's path followed that of her brother into the Caribbean and the North American mainland, performances of her descendants would document waves of cries, of screams, and of motion. By 1819 there were many more of Equiano's countrymen and women in the new United States.

Many of their communal cultural expressions had been either outlawed or severely curtailed. By 1850 it was deemed a criminal offense for an African to read or write, and a range of African discourse had gone underground, into clandestine gatherings, or had become masked in hermeneutic public procession, and the African American generations had begun to articulate new concepts of home. Yet the powerful continuities in African performance remained evident in the gatherings at Congo Square in New Orleans. Famously, Benjamin Latrobe wrote of observing the following scene:

> A crowd of five or six hundred persons, assembled in an open space or public square. All of those who were engaged in the business seemed to be blacks.... They were formed into circular groups, in the midst of four of which I examined (but there were more of them) was a ring, the largest not ten feet in diameter. In the first were two women dancing.... The women squalled out a burden to the playing, at intervals, consisting of two notes, as the Negroes working in our cities respond to the song of their leader. Most of the circles contained the same sort of dances. One was larger, in which a ring of a dozen women walked, by way of dancing, round the music in the center. But the instruments were of a different construction.... A man sung an uncouth song to the dancing, which I suppose was in some African language, for it was not French, and the women screamed a detestable burden on a single note. The allowed amusements of Sunday have, it seems, perpetuated here those of Africa among its former inhabitants.[55]

I imagine herstories resounding in the Juba performance of a woman named Clotilda, which was recorded in the U.S. counties of Maryland in 1832. Clotilda's generation had witnessed cycles of community fragmentation and reconstruction, and her popular anglicized name, and those of the community members she calls to in her song, is a sign of that motion.[56] Clotilda, according to her North American chronicler, who was visiting family on a plantation, was a "Negro girl" who "looked exceedingly strange," "carried herself in a whirling dance-like motion," and spoke in rhymes. The plantation overseer indicated that Clotilda was a child. People in the community appeared to treat her as an adult. One evening, at a dance, played to a fiddler's jig, Clotida took center stage with a complexly bitter performance of calling and patting the Juba. Here is the transcription:

> Laudy! How it make me laugh
> To see the n——s all so safe;
> See um dance de foolish jig;
> And neber min' de Juber rig.
> Juber!
> Juber lef' and Juber right;
> Juber dance wid all yo' might;
> Juber here and Juber dere,
> Juber, Juber ebery where.
> Juber![57]

According to Southern, in her documentary *Readings in Black American Music*, this description is among the earliest to identify African American performance combining banter, percussive body playing, and circles of call-and-response clapping and singing as a "Juba."[58] In it Clotilda entered the circle of performance calling out the action that other dancers responded to in pantomime.

> Guess I knows er n—— gal—
> There she is, her name is Sal—
> And she hab to min' de baby,
> Show us how she rock de cradle.
> Juber!

The transcribing, in addition to the not uncommon wrestling in the representation of African American grammatical patterns, is interspersed with description of the action and the interpretation of surrounding commentary. Clotilda's words here suffice:

> Everybody know Aunt Jinny,
> Nothing can be said against her;
> When she fever n—— take,
> My! How that old lady shake.

Juber!
Uncle Meshach, Uncle Jim,
Once I seed 'em saw er lim',
For to men' the garden palin's,
And to make de post un railin's.
Juber!
Ain't you shame, you lazy n——s?
Wonder if them's the Juber riggers?
Marser Clarry, upon a time
Want ter hear Clotildy rhyme;
One good turn disserb unnudder,
Lemme see him dance de Juber.
Juber!
Try de Juber reed uggin;
Try your bes', un try to win.
Juber forrud, Juber back;
Juber dis way, Juba dat;
Juber in, un Juber out;
Juber, Juber all ubbout.
Juber.

Clotilda's Juba bursts out of the older communal circles, like a Sybil or a mad historian, to testify and bear witness with critical venom. Though still in antiphonal dialogue, her performance articulates another naming in changed locations. Beating her hands against her thighs, patting the ground with her feet, though still within a circle of ancestry—uncles, aunts, and kin—Clotilda no longer sings of Ibo, Kongos, or countrymen. Her song and her life had been tossed about and renamed in a hegemonically racialized language of derision. Her Juba chronicles the labors of enslavement, calls her neighbors out, critiques their turn to the "jig" at the expense of the Juba, laughs at the young lawyer's interest, and teases to shame him. She sings of babies, fevers, work, and failings, and her danced competition speaks of internal explosion. "Try your best and try to win," she calls out.

The winds roared the rain fell.
The poor white man faint and weary
Came and sat under our tree.
He has no mother to bring him milk no wife to grind his corn.
Let us pity the white man no mother has he.

The painful passage of history is all too clear in the poignant comparison between Clotilda's Juba and the improvised song of the Bambara women who could "pity the white man," but Clotilda's bravado also underscores a stunning continuum. Both are revealed in her performance of power imprisoned, magic hidden, in all the Juba variations, a cat she killed to get her over "double trouble." Clotilda's frenzied naming of community in acerbic rhyme is a statement of the first African American generation's complex distillation of the magic and the madness of their time. Struggling between an older communal imagination and a place of extraordinary social and psychosocial dislocation and fragmentation, like the enslaved performance poets of New England, she reaches to speak a new language within an older form. Unlike her mothers, as they are represented by the women Tituba, Candy, Equiano's sister, and the unnamed woman whose head and tongue were chained, Clotilda speaks with a colonized tongue, her voice careening between a mad world's discourses and personal madness. From that precipice she demands, with the force of a contemporary elder (or a modern rapper), that if nothing else and amid the syncretic jigs, her Juba be remembered.

Juba is a river and a city in southern Sudan, a traditional women's day name in some West African languages, a name for Monday's child that continued to resonate in the African diaspora naming—Monday, moon day. Juba is a name possessed, literally by all of this and that. Juba, in the standardization of the rhyme that comes down to us from the early nineteenth century, is momma. She has seen much. She is called on for everything, as in "Juba do this and Juba do that," given a name as in "Juba or Michael or Anthony or Gustavus Vasa's sister" and must serve. She has arrived, not unlike those who would be called Ebo and who were driven from their ancestral city by invading armies and then kidnapped from the coastal refuge by slave traders, via a long route, carrying her gods. From each

3. Sheila (Chela) Anozier, *Bousou*. Courtesy of the artist.

of the places where she worked, serving, cooking, frying, she has pinched some portion. But that portion is the husk, the crust, the skin. Hard parts and black magic are her inheritance and her legacy. Her "double trouble" is no doubt an early articulation of the intersections of multiple identities and oppressions in the lives of African American women. Within them she speaks with the authority of witness.

A woman rides the elemental forces in the form of a bull. She is changed by her journey and saved by her traditional knowledge. The vessel of story is passed down.

Juba Danced

# THE ANCESTORS AND THE LULLABY  3
Passing It On

**Isis and Osiris: Ancient Egyptian Story**

*This is a story found in far-flung fragments. Osiris, progeny of Sky, Sun, and Earth, was captured by stealth, sealed in a crypt, tossed into a river that flows up, found and murdered again, his body dismembered, torn into fourteen sections, then thrown back into the Nile. Isis, sister, beloved, mother, remembers and resurrects him, chanting his magical names, with her incantations. In the cosmological rendering of ancient Egypt, on the text of the tombs of the dead coming forth, Isis, moon goddess, weeps the Nile's fecund inundation, gathers the sacred body in her search, and reconstructs the torn universe to conceive within it eternal life.*

Herstories are, of course, held in cosmologies, and my retelling gathers, like Isis, from many sources. Plutarch, in his *O Isis and Osiris*, describes the tale as a reenactment of the destruction and reconstruction of the universe and, analogously, of the sacred text, inextricably linking the archetypal feminine with night and the cycles of the moon. Images of the ancient Egyptian goddess Isis, crowned with the throne-shape ideogram of her name, Ast, or recalling the animist mother gods of predynastic Sudan, wearing a vulture's wings, the serpent's crown, and the full moon seated between horns, present a constellation of telling. On her cyclical journey down the Nile, gathering Osiris's dismembered body parts and re-membering him with her incantations of his divine names, Isis charts the cycles of life and seasons, of birth, death, and resurrection, in the rites of ancient Egyptian funerary practice. Classical Greek and Roman writers, Plutarch among them, traced their own astrologically named pantheon and the Eleusinian mystery cults back to Isis's celestial, astrological, migrations through Meroe, Nubia, Egypt, and the mythology of African antiquity. This reminder from the past offers new ways of thinking about cultural history today.[1]

**Memory Song**

    Do ba-na co-ba, ge-ne me, ge ne me!
    Do ba-na co-ba, ge-ne me, ge ne me
    Ben d' nu-li, nu-li, nu-li, nu-li ben d' le.

In his magisterial meditation on American history, *The Souls of Black Folks*, W. E. B. Du Bois recalls a lullaby he heard as a child. According to family lore, the song had been passed down, generation to generation, from his grandfather's grandmother who had been seized from her African home and enslaved by Dutch traders. In *W.E.B. DuBois: Biography of a Race*, historian David Levering Lewis notes that Du Bois inserted various versions of the story of this song into others of his major works.[2] Lewis also reprints excerpts from communication between Sulayman S. Nyang, of the African Studies and Research Department at Howard University, and Ms. Denise Williams, a collateral relative of Du Bois. In response to her genealogical research, Nyang writes of "a remote possibility that the song is originally a Wolof song from Senegambia." "If the song is a creolized version of a Wolof song," Nyang writes, it should go like this: "Duga na chi pah, gene ma, gene ma / Duga na chipah, gene ma, gene ma / bena njuli, njuli. Translation: I have fallen into a pit, get me out, get me out / I have fallen into a pit, get me out, get me out / One circumcised boy, one circumcised boy."[3]

Du Bois no longer knew the language and meaning of his family's African lullaby, but the memory of the song remained, and he recognized it as a place to begin talking about the Negro spirituals, or what he calls "the sorrow songs," and what it meant to be an African American at the turn of the twentieth century. Du Bois then goes on to discuss the voice of exiled African music in the spiritual "You May Bury Me in the East."

    You may bury me in the east
    You may bury me in the west

But I'll hear the trumpet sound in the morning.

African American spiritual, eighteenth century[4]

There are radiant threads of connection between these two songs on the African to African American continuum. Du Bois calls both "African," and the epistemological lens of West and Central Africa enrich our visioning. In the Du Bois family lullaby, and in the early spirituals, the structure of the music tells of an African beginning and of performance as a site for multiple conversations and learning. In the antiphonal performance of the three-line stanza, identity is wrought from community in a web of dialogues; between the past and the present, between the lead line's call and the chorus of response, between the rhythm of song and the site of its performance, whether that performance be storytelling, dance, the soothing of a child, or the harvesting of rice. These dialogues fundamentally represent how musical conversation is embedded in traditional West and Central African life and thought.[5] The three-line stanza form itself calls for collaboration and improvisation, as the practitioner "dances" with or against both the leading call and the ritualization of a task.[6] In this way the antiphonal performance also articulates a philosophy of art as inextricable from life. Here, as in older performances of cultural identity, poetry and music are not separate from the telling of stories, the recording of history, the clapping of hands, the moving of feet, or the swaying of baby in arms.

A poetry in motion, the three-line stanzas in the composition of "Do ba-na co-ba, ge-ne me" and "You May Bury Me in the East" function by moving through a geography of loss, search, remembering, and revelation. Both songs perform an unfolding vision, like the quartos of the Western sonnet, and, in an older ritual representation, reenact the symbolic journey of the ancient Egyptian goddess Isis. Paired and viewed in the context of Pan-African tropes, the songs present an "astonishing," and illuminating, juxtaposition. Both "You May Bury Me in the East" and the possible Wolof translation of the Du Bois lullaby articulate buried and emerging consciousness, in an articulation following the cyclical arc of the Bakongo cosmogram, over the darkness in the Yoruba divination text, toward resolution, confident that "I will hear the trumpet sound in the morning."

The "spirit" of the "Negro" spiritual, and of the lullabies within them, is an essential aspect of a root poetics. The lining out of song, composed and learned by singing back and forth in alternating voice, and the multilayered dialogue of this pattern in performance, creates a sung point, a threshold, for conversation over and across space and time. Calling to mind the roots of haiku in ancient conversation with the divine, these songs, spirituals, poems, blues, lullabies, performed in complex call-and-response, were and remain liminal dialogues, sites for both instruction and transformation.[7] African and African diaspora musical practices, according to musicologist Beatrice Landeck, characteristically have a distinctive degree of "rhythmic complexity and syncopation," make use of an "indeterminate pitch of single tones in melody and dissonances in harmony," and engage with predominating "contrapuntal and antiphonal form in dialogue" between a leader's call and a group/choral response and with an "improvisational treatment of all music" and musical composition. Those distinctive characteristics indelibly articulate African and African diaspora epistemology, philosophy, and the passing on of the story.[8]

> Do ba-na co-ba, ge-ne me, ge ne me!
> Do ba-na co-ba, ge-ne me, ge ne me
> Ben d' nu-li, nu-li, nu-li, nu-I, ben d' le

Nyang's suggestion for a possible Wolof-to-English translation of the lullaby's song as one of fall, entrapment, and a call for help offers a fascinating parallel between the roots and route of the telling. The Du Bois family lullaby is a story that was passed down from a woman and given to generations of children. In his own time, Du Bois improvised or signified on its legacy of storytelling by transcribing the performed record, speaking in call-and-response to past, present, and future, in a continuum of witness and improvisational tradition.[9] A tradition in which the historical memory could be embodied and inscribed in a woman singing to her little one in arms.

Following Du Bois's mighty lead, there has been substantial examination of the spirituals and their role in American history and African American cultural reckoning. Mindful that much of our oldest storytelling traditions are intimately connected with birth and death and have been associated, since antiquity, with the phases of the moon, night, women, and the womb, Du Bois's story and his grandmother's song lay fertile ground for an exploration of the lullaby, and the spirituals, generatively intertwined, within them, as a source for an expanded herstorical telling.

The lullaby is a formative rite for a child and an adulthood rite of passage for a woman, a crossroads of experience and a rich articulation of social relations. A daughter's lament and longing, a mother's nuanced and interlaced expression of fear and frustration, love and instruction, the lullaby is a cauldron of storytelling. Like primal sources of art the world round, the repertoire of diaspora lullabies speaks to universal and historically specific themes, and in the African tradition the song memory of a single voice calls to a collective story and a "chorus of remembering" in the recollections of nineteenth-century narrators, twentieth-century informants, and a selection of early autobiography writing by African diaspora women.

**Song Memory**

Swing low sweet chariot
Coming to carry me home
Swing low sweet chariot
Coming to carry me home.

"Swing Low Sweet Chariot," African American spiritual, eighteenth century[10]

When Chaney Mack, a resident of Memphis, Tennessee, recalled her life in slavery for the federal WPA oral history project of the 1930s, she spoke first of her lineage, describing her father as "a full blooded African" and her mother as a woman of indigenous and African American parentage who people called "Big Sarah."[11] Throughout her oral history, Ms. Mack speaks of her sense of a direct connection to African ancestry and to the history of this country. Her father had been taken from Africa at eighteen and told stories of his homeland to his children, bequeathing to Ms. Mack the first name of her paternal grandmother. It was her father, with his homemade fiddle, who taught the young girl Chaney to "dance like they did in Africa." Those fiddling and dance traditions are the tap root, according to musicologists, ethnomusicologists, and cultural historians, of major and continuing streams of American popular music. movement, and theater making.[12]

Chaney Mack's sense of pride in her African ancestry was common among her diaspora contemporaries. Africans in the Americas and the Caribbean maintained an enduring sense of humanity, history, and the imperative for social justice through that heritage. From the earliest period of African presence in colonial North America, both free and enslaved Africans created a profusion of formal and informal social organizations and religious institutions, from burial societies to political, educational, and self-help groups, and engaged in active racial advocacy, support, agency, and activism. Well-known contemporary individuals whose legacies evidenced this spirit of social justice and community work include Elizabeth Freeman, a resident of Barrington, Massachusetts, and an ancestor of W. E. B. Du Bois, who filed suit in American revolutionary era courts for her right to freedom in accord with the Bill of Rights of the U.S. Constitution. Her litigation and victory, in August 1781, established the precedent, in Massachusetts courts, that the Bill of Rights effectively abolished slavery. Freeman, popularly known as "Mumbet," was born into enslavement sometime around the year 1742. She told biographers that her parents were native Africans, and though she could reportedly neither read nor write, her last will and testament bequeathed to her daughter "a black silk gown, gift of her African father" and a "short gown" that had been worn by her African mother.[13]

Another African "activist" whose story appears in the historical records of colonial Massachusetts was a woman called Belinda. In February 1783, at the age of "three score and ten," she submitted a petition for material support to the general court of Boston. After a life in enslavement, increasing the estate of another, Belinda had been abandoned to poverty. Her plea to the legislature paints a romantic picture of an African home "on the banks of the Rio de Volta" and recalls "when she, in a sacred grove, with each hand in that of a tender parent, was paying devotion to the great *Orisa*, who made all things . . . an armed band of white men, driving many of her countrymen in chains, rushed into the hallowed shades!" In her petition Belinda also recalled the horror of the Middle Passage and of bond servitude. Historian Stanley Kaplan speculates that she may have had her story transcribed by a literate African contemporary.[14] This kind of mutual support, between "free" and enslaved, educated and illiterate Africans was a sustaining element of African diaspora community.

Chaney Mack's recollections of her mother, Big Sarah, reflect something of the richly complex web of journey, experience, and cultural locations embedded in the construction of African American identities during this period. According to Ms. Mack, Big Sarah grew up among her maternal Choctaw people in Tennessee and was sold into slavery after a dispute with whites in which her family had been killed. In her daughter's memory, Big Sarah was a woman of Christian faith who also remembered much of her father's language and a woman respected for her pride and her strength within the African American community in Mississippi, where they lived before emancipation. Big Sarah, according to Ms. Mack, cared for and instructed her children in the practical and the magical arts of making a way and surviving. Big Sarah would regularly share her experiences and knowledge with her children, including the prophecies she read in the configurations of the stars.

Big Sarah was a midwife, an herbalist, and a housewife who raised all the children of the household, enslaved and free. "She made her own medicines with herbs," recalled Chaney Mack, "and she taught me to make medicines." Though enslaved, Big Sarah held the keys to the store of the landholding and stood with the child Chaney and the landowner's child when "the Yankees came." She ended her days being called "Grandma Sarah," having lived over one hundred years.

Competence in the domestic arts was a necessity among eighteenth- and nineteenth-century rural women, and African American women's expertise in these areas often drew note. Like Big Sarah, Elizabeth Freeman was also known for her skills as both an herbalist and a midwife and was regularly called on for her services. Tituba of Salem's outstanding knowledge of botany, homeopathy, and healing became evidence in the accusation of witchcraft made against her. The complementary knowledge of astronomy was not unfamiliar to any of these women. As in Ms. Mack's oral history, the narratives of many nineteenth-century African American women, including the abolitionist, itinerant preacher, and women's rights activist Sojourner Truth, recalled their mothers' stargazing, predicting, and pointing out patterns in the night sky.[15]

> Bye-bye baby bunting
> Daddy's gone a hunting
> To catch a little rabbit skin
> To put baby bunting in.
> Nursery rhyme, eighteenth century

Chaney Mack remembered her mother singing the children to sleep with the song "Bye Bye Baby Bunting," which was first published a 1784 edition of Mother Goose rhymes. She also recalled being lulled by the spiritual "Swing Low Sweet Chariot," a song which Du Bois called "the cradle song of death."

> I looked over Jordan and what did I see
> Coming to carry me home
> A band of angels coming after me
> Coming to carry me home.
> "Swing Low Sweet Chariot," second stanza

Chaney Mack, who was reportedly seventy-four at the time of her interview, was like her mother speaking in a lineage of African and indigenous women storytellers whose legacy gives birth to a specifically American literature. Du Bois's great-great-grandmother, coming "to the valleys of the early Hudson and Housatonic, black, little and lithe," shivering in "the harsh north winds," and singing to the child between her knees, is a spiritual and intellectual forerunner in that lineage.[16] Her song and those of Big Sarah suggest a kinship of practice in an adulthood rite of passage into storytelling and witness, a continuum of performance traditions rooted in an old practice of "re-membering."

Black women's public engagement with historical memory during the early national period was widespread as well as deeply rooted. Among the earliest known literary contributions of Africans in North America is the epic poem "Bars Fight," attributed to the storyteller Lucy Terry Prince. Prince's "Bars Fight" is a rhymed recollection of an armed conflict between indigenous inhabitants and settler colonists in Deerfield, Massachusetts, on August 25, 1746. Prince, who was celebrated both as a skilled orator and as a staunch activist for racial justice, was born in Africa, kidnapped as an infant, and sold into slavery in Rhode Island. Her poem was preserved in the oral record until it was published after her death.[17] Another noted storyteller of New England was a woman named Alice who was a recognized retainer and raconteur of the history of her Pennsylvania settlement.[18] Alice, Lucy Terry Prince, Big Sarah, and Ms. Mack herself were kin in the spiraling motion of herstory telling, in traditions embedding myriad meaning and historical documentation that they consciously bequeathed to their children. Black women's cradle songs sing circles of lineage, testimony, formative and transformative teaching.

Writing of African music, musicologist Mildred Green offers a glimpse into how the social performance of instruction is passed on. "A mother may sing a cradle song which entertains her child but which also contains certain expressions of a more mature level. African societies stress exposure to music rather than formal instruction. The mother introduces the child to the music of the culture by rocking him or her to music or singing nonsense syllables that imitate drum rhythms. Mothers carry their children on their backs to public ceremonies and rituals, exposing them to the music and dances performed by adults."[19]

Examples of the stellar range of African women's pedagogical practices in song include the songs of Xhosa women who use nonsense cradle songs to teach children the clicking sounds of their language. Miriam Makeba's Zulu language "Click Song" is one famous recording of this kind of musical art(iculation), which harks back to the Khoisan roots of language itself.

Similarly, the lullabies of indigenous Central Africa, recorded among communities of Mbuti and Ba Benzélé, embrace the expansive soundscape of the forest in a text of richly instructional music and language legacy and present the contemporary listener with other suggestive examples of the layered dialogs of "formative" human practice. The yodeling, hocket, and complex polyphony of indigenous Central African music, and of related

Khoisan language traditions, are apparently of great antiquity. According to Alan Lomax, "forager yodeling," a fundamental sound pattern used by hunter-gatherers and a key component of the music of Mbuti, Ba Benzélé, and San, may trace back to the earliest human sound. This proposal is consonant with linguistic and genetic studies that connect worlds of being back to these locations.[20] These indigenous practices suggest that our earliest "lullabies" may have been performances of throwing the human voice into the cosmos. The daughters of Africa were cradled in vibrant intellectual traditions. The yodels and hockets of polyphonic indigenous "roots" music continue to resound in the griot or bardic traditions of West and Central Africa and in African American "hollers," "moans," and "shouts," a musical vocabulary that many blues practitioners and scholars cite as a root form.

> Attend my lays, ye ever honoured nine,
> Afit my labours, and my strains refine;
> In smoothest numbers pour the notes along,
> For bright Aurora now demands my song
>> Phillis Wheatley, "A Hymn to Morning," eighteenth century

Among the earliest writings that come down to us from African diaspora women is the poetry of Phillis Wheatley, whose book *Poems on Various Subjects Religious and Moral* (1773) was the first published by an African, and among the first published by anyone, in the settler colonial Americas. Wheatley wrote praise songs to nature and poems to the dead or the grieving, songs of remembering and lullabies of the oldest kind. Wheatley enjoyed a moment of international fame, in discourses on both poetry and race, before her death in poverty and obscurity. She was about twenty when her book was published. She was about thirty-one—eleven years later—when she died.[21]

Wheatley had also been kidnapped from an African home as a child and was brought into Boston in 1761, on a slave ship called the *Phillis*, missing her front teeth and with only a scrap of rug wrapped around her against the New England cold. She "inherited" her first name from the slave ship and her last from the people who bought her. According to Wheatley's early biographers, all she could remember of her native land was the image of how "her mother poured out water before the sun at his rising," a performance of libation and veneration. According to the ship's log, Wheatley and the small group of Africans who arrived in Boston with her had come from Senegambia. This region included present-day Senegal and Gambia, areas of centuries-old Islamic traditions, ancient connection to the worlds of Asia and the Mediterranean, and even older poetic griot traditions.[22] The image of her mother and the consistent moral, ontological, and historical themes of her poetry support a more nuanced reading of her memory in her performance.

> Mneme begin. Inspire, ye sacred nine
> Your vent'rous Afric in her great design
> Mneme, immortal pow'r, I trace thy spring
> Assist my strains, while I thy glories sing:
> The acts of long departed years, by thee
> Recover'd, in due order rang'd we see:
> Thy pow'r the long-forgotten calls from night,
> That sweetly plays before the fancy's sight
>
> Phillis Wheatley, "On Recollection," eighteenth century[23]

Bambara, Fulbe, Malinke, and Wolof people, relations to Sundiata's Malian empire and its griot traditions, were among those from the Senegambia region who got caught in the "nets" of transatlantic enslavement. And long before and after the "sun" of the Malian empire, Bambara women sang history. For them the art of storytelling was inseparable from life, a thread of their "manners and customs" and ways of working, like the Bambara women extemporizing on a stranger's presence in their village as they spun their cotton. Though the great griot or *dejali* traditions of that region came to be dominated by male praise singing, we are also aware of the antiquity of the woman song, a lullaby, a song of remembering. Like those of the bards of New England or the diviners of Yoruba land, the Homeric epics or the fables of Aesop, the songs of African women were memorized and performed long before they were written.[24] Traditions of memory and orality remained vibrant among diaspora women, many of whom were orphaned by the labyrinth systems of slavery but remained deeply in connection with a sense of self and lineage, "flying back" to the African home, through poetry, song, and dream.

Their stories bring us back to the image of Du Bois's grandmother. Her voice entwines with Big Sarah's song. At the beginning of an African American literary tradition, at genesis of Phillis Wheatley's songs and Equiano's step into the written discourse, is a Pan-African performance text and a woman's voice singing in ritual and instruction. African women in the Americas used their lullabies to pass on culture and history, telling the story of this and an older time.

**A Chorus of Remembering**

>Bye-bye baby bunting
>Daddy's gone a hunting
>To catch a little rabbit skin
>To put baby bunting in.

There are fragments of a complex narrative in Big Sarah's rendition of "Baby Bunting." In the dancing embrace of soothing a child, the song sings of universal themes, separation and webs of kin, "mothering" and the responsibilities of adult women, the wilderness and the home, dismemberment, reconstruction, and redemption. Big Sarah's revision of an English nursery song takes up the trope of journey by beginning with leave taking. That she has changed the standard "Cry bye" to "Bye-bye" is telling. Separation was a painful dominant reality in the lives of enslaved women and men, and the heartrending trauma of families being torn apart echoes through thousands of narratives. As daughters, sisters, mothers, family and community members, at some point enslaved women would be separated from kith and kin in tragic reproduction of the exilic thrust of the diaspora itself.

In the song memories of people recalling their lives in slavery for the WPA oral history project, lullabies are journey songs that travel across physical and metaphysical, geographical and emotional, distance. While a universal aspect of the lullaby is the journey into sleep, the cradle songs of African American women were sung against demons of lived experience.

Many narrators from the Georgia area, for example, remembered stories and songs about "raw head and bloody bones," which, according to one narrator, kept "children from wandering off" and "scared them to sleep."[25] "We made up sing," recalled Louisa Brown of Murrells Inlet, South Carolina. "We have sing for children. Make them go to sleep. Everyone have his own sing." Ms. Brown recalled singing:

Bye o baby
Go sleepy
Bye o baby
Go sleepy
What a big alligator aiming to catch
This one boy[26]

Her song is kin to the European standard "Rock a Bye Baby," recorded in the 1700s, which some narrators who participated in the WPA project remembered as the only lullaby they had ever heard. Ellen Godfrey, of Georgetown County, South Carolina, who was reportedly a hundred years old at the time of her interview in 1937, remembered singing a threatening variation.

Rock a bye
Rock a bye
Down come the baby cradle and all
Roll 'em roll 'em roll 'em
Roll 'em and boil 'em
And put 'em in the oven.[27]

The narratives of early nineteenth-century women and men affirm the courage and fortitude it took to survive whole and sane in the deranging house of enslavement. Some did not. In 1832 an Antiguan woman named Mary Prince escaped from her enslavement, went to the London Abolition Society, and demanded that her be story be heard and recorded. Her narrative, *The History of Mary Prince a West Indian Slave*, is another of our rare written records of the lives and experiences of African diaspora women in the early 1800s. In her narrative Prince bears witness to back-breaking labor and soul-rending torture. The horror of her tale is otherworldly. Her insistence on the authority of a woman's telling is extraordinary. Prince remembers her own mother dressing her and her siblings on the day they would be separated from each other by "slave" auction, and her mother, holding their clothes, crying "these my babies' shrouds." In Prince's recollection, her mother, torn with grief and lamentation, brought her children before each of the other women on their Bermuda plantation that day, reminding them that their "turn" would soon come. Prince was about twelve at the time and remembers seeing her mother, sometime after their violent separation, among a group of people working off a sloop. Her joy at the reunion soon turned to sorrow when she found that her mother no longer recognized her and was alternately despondent and ranting.[28] Prince also remembers Hetty, a "fellow slave" who cared for her like a parent. After being brutally flogged late in her pregnancy, Hetty gave birth to a dead child before she too passed into ancestry. Hetty's share of tasks, and floggings, were then given to Mary.

Her story is a common one. Frederick Douglass wrote about witnessing the sadistic beating of his aunt by the plantation owner as "the bloody gate" to his own understanding of the system of slavery. Shackled to a stove where she labored, with her head and face in a vise, hung from ceiling hooks and tree, beaten with pans and pushed into ovens—images of the abuse of African women, men, and children repeat ad infinitum through the testimonial bearing of witness to the institution of slavery.[29] Nell Painter's proposal, in her study of Sojourner Truth, that contemporary theory about the developmental effects of child sexual abuse and war induced posttraumatic stress syndrome is useful for understanding the experiences of this generation of diaspora women rings painfully true. Their lullabies tell of navigating a wartime, of embattlement, and of saving graces and sources of sustenance.

Annie Little was born in Springfield, Missouri, in 1856. She remembers "getting all them children to sleep" singing:

Mammy went away—she tell me to stay
And take care of the baby

She tell me to stay and sing this away
Go to sleepy little baby
Shut your eye and don't you cry
Go to sleepy little baby
Cause mammy's bound to come by and by
Go to sleepy little baby.[30]

The lullabies of African American women also sing of ancestry, remembering, community, and kin. Ms. Little's lullaby reveals the voice of an expanded view of mothering, the powerful role of extended family and community in weaving a web of relations to protect children. This too is confirmed by the written record. On large plantations, like the place where Ms. Little was born, very young children or older women often cared for all the community's children during the day, when even nursing mothers did field work, and many narrators speak of the heroism and inspiration of a web of female relations.[31] The survival of children torn from family and home in the upheaval of the *Maafa* and along the "Middle Passage" no doubt depended on the familial embrace of fostering countrymen and women who shared their story and apocalyptic journey. Yet there were few safe spaces for children or adults in a minefield.

We'll stop up the cracks and sew up the seams
The booger man never can catch you
To sleep and dream sweet dreams
The booger man never can catch you
The river runs wide the river runs deep
O bye sweet little baby
That boat rock slow she'll rock you to sleep.
O bye sweet little baby.

Ms. Little's song goes on to describe scenes echoed in numerous testimonies, including Jenny Proctor's vivid description of living quarters that were barely rough shelters and real "booger men" who ripped the peace from the night of bonded women, men, and children.[32] "The wide river" in the song is a distant consolation. The chorus of Annie Little's song was a well-known one, later published in an early twentieth-century collection called *Play Songs of the Deep South* as a "Negro Lullaby." Ms. Little's song is also the chorus of a lullaby sung in the English-speaking Caribbean:

> Go to sleepy little baby
> When you wake you'll get some cake
> And ride a little white horsey.[33]

Louise Bennett's eloquent elaboration on African diaspora cultural documentation in her "Fe We Lullaby," on the *Lawd Di Riddim Sweet* recording, illuminates the continuities and connections. In this piece Bennett recalls the old-time poem that "spoke about things that a happen then," the sacred circles Jamaica's "moonshine baby" songs come from, and a medley of songs these among them.

> Pupa bring cake fe baby alone
> Baby eat all, no give Mama none
> Mama get bex and lick Baby "Bam!"
> Clap han, clap han, till Pupa come home
> Clap han, clap han, till Pupa come home
>
> Don don baby don cry
> U pupa gon a mountain
> Don done baby don cry
> U pupa gona a mountain
> Sweetie water neva done
> E catch it down a fountain
> Sweetie water neva done
> E catch it down a fountain

The challenge of a mother's tale, combining sugary promises and hard realities, was not lost on children. Narcissus Young of Nashville, Tennessee, who also remembered the song "Bye Bye Baby Bunting" in his oral history for the WPA, speaks about losing her mother when she was three.[34] C. B. McCray of Jasper, Texas, juxtaposes his memory of childhood, noting that "Bye Bye Baby Bunting" was his mother's favorite song, with a description of an instrument of slave torture called the "Louisiana shirt."[35] Lorenzo Ezell of Texas gave a similarly stark juxtaposition of recollection. "In those days colored people just like mules and horses," he told WPA historians, "they didn't have no last name. My mama call me after my daddy's master, Ezell. Mama was a good woman and I remember her more than once rocking the little cradle and singing to the baby." The following fable-like song is what Mr. Ezell, born in 1850 in Spartanburg County, South Carolina, remembers his mother singing:

> Milk in the dairy nine days old
> Sing song kitty can't you ki-me-o?
> Frogs and skeeters getting mighty bold
> Sing song kitty can you ki-me-o?
> There a frog lives in a pool
> Sing song kitty can't you ki-me-o?
> Sure he was the biggest fool
> Sing song kitty can't you ki-me-o?
> For he could dance and he could sing
> Sing-song kitty can't you ki-me-o?
> And make the woods around him ring.[36]

In the memory of WPA project oral participants, there were folktales, fables, cautionary tales, allegories, and histories interwoven in the songs their mothers, and grandmothers, sang to them as children. Women, seeking solace for both themselves and their children, drew on this interweaving for moral fortitude and instruction.

John Finney, born in Jackson County, Alabama, was eighty-six at the time of his interview with the WPA slave narrative project. In the course of his interview he recalls what sounds like a traditional lullaby as a corn-husking song:

> The moonlight and the shining star
> The big owl hooting in the tree
> Oh bye bye baby ain't you going to sleep
> A rocking on my knee.[37]

Mary Kindred, who was born in Juniper, Texas, around 1850, remembers a less subtle lesson in the song her grandmother sang to them. The lyrics are similar to those of the English ballad "No John."

> One morning in May
> I spies a beautiful dandy
> A raking away the hay
> I ask her to marry
> She say scornful no
> But before six months roll by
> Her apron strings won't tie.
> She wrote me a letter
> She marry me then
> I say no
> No my gal not I.[38]

Passing it on, Laney Van Hook of Athens, Georgia, remembered singing a fable-like song when her children were young:

> Old Granny Mistletoe
> Lying in the bed
> Out the window
> She poked her head
> She says "Old man
> The grey goose is gone"
> And I think I heard her holler
> "King-can't-you-o."
> The old fox stepped around
> A mighty fast step
> He hung the grey goose
> Up by her neck...[39]

Joanna Thompson of Lafayette County, Mississippi, was born "just before the war." In her oral history for the WPA, she recalls working in a host of occupations by the end of the nineteenth century. She had been a midwife, a nurse, and a washerwoman in the course of her days and recognized that her understanding of a woman's work was informed by the lessons of her grandmother who had cared for children since she herself was a child. It was her grandmother who taught Ms. Thompson this one of the "old slave songs that she said had been used to sing babies to sleep":

> Little black sheep where's your lamb
> Way down in the meadow
> The bees and the butterflies
> A pecking out his eyes
> The poor little black sheep
> Cry ma-a-a-my.[40]

The fable in the folk song mirrors the people's experience in the slaughter of innocents.

The song Martha Richardson of Columbia, South Carolina, remembered her mother singing is an instructive fable in which forest animals convey a lesson about cooperation. One of them, Possum, is a popular character in African American work songs.

> Possum up the 'simmon tree
> Sparrow on the ground
> Possum throw the simmons down
> Sparrow shake them round.[41]

Big Sarah's "Bye Bye Baby Bunting," like the fable-infused lullabies of her peers, draws on symbolic landscapes to cultivate and hold a nurturing space in the nightmare of enslavement. Big Sarah's song begins with leaving, then takes us deep into the forest, the bush. Here the tapestry of philosophical connection is abundant. Tales of hunters are among our oldest, and the wilderness, the forest, or bush is a central trope in African artistic traditions. We were all hunter-gatherers once, and the image of the hunter, moving through the forest, in physical and metaphysical quest, is recognized and restated in myriad texts. In this storied and historical sense the forest is a location both genesis and opposition to the settled town, "civilization," and kingdoms. In the symbolic context the hunter represents the seeker on a vision quest, not just someone out to bring back dinner.

In the cosmological inscriptions of the Kongo and in its pervasive restatement in the African diaspora, the forest (or "bush") is, like the graveyard and the hilltop, a liminal place. Bakongo *minkisi* figures and their descendants in African American visual representation, including mojos, conjure roots, black cats (or in the case of Juba "yellow cats"), and ham bones, incorporate elements from these locations to create protective, guardian magic. These artifacts all fundamentally recognize the power in the spirits of the bush and underscore a continuum between African and African American symbolic inscription.[42] Parallels in Yoruba tradition include the figures of Osanyin, a deity representative of herbalism and medicine and an embodiment of the spiritual bounty of the forest; Ogun, a deity representative of metalworking and iron; and his twin brother, Oshoosi, the hunter—all of whom maintain a potent presence in Afro-Atlantic belief.

> Take your bow, Simbon.
> Take your bow and let us go.
> Take your bow Sogolon Djata.
>   "Hymn of the Bow," Malian epic ballads of Sundiata, eleventh century[43]

The histories of medieval African kingdoms abound with tales of hunter beginnings. In the epic of Sundiata, the griot history Mali, a pair of hunters secure from the Buffalo woman the promise of a future empire. Similarly among the Yoruba, where the hunter god and the god of iron form a divine pair, hunter ballads also tell the story of building a kingdom from far-flung nomadic tribes and recall the connection between the hunter and storytelling. In the Americas, in maroon communities and "slave rebellions," those pairs of hunter and warrior gods lead their people into a new millennium of battle.[44] As the wilderness names a location for transformation, the hunter is a trope for ancestral presence within those sites of ritual performance. Ripples of connection are suggested by the liminal figure of the hunter in Celtic and Greek lore, in which the pig and the wild boar are avatars for divinity in the forest. In the lore of North America Possum becomes a kindred figure. Big Sarah and her contemporaries drew on symbolic lore to speak of ancestry and to look beyond slavery to the lessons of the earth and the stars.

The narrative of Sojourner Truth, named Isabella at her birth in 1797, includes her memory of her mother's perpetual grieving and way of connecting to the children who had been taken away from her. Blending animist and Christian practices, Isabella's parents, Mau Mau Bett and Bomfree, regularly recited the Lord's Prayer below an open sky and told stories of those lost children to Isabella so that the child would remember. Pointing to the stars, as would the peoples of Central Africa and their Brazilian descendants who believe that stars (*Mbwetete*) hold souls, Mau Mau Bett would offer the heavens themselves as an eternal connection. "Those are the same stars, and that is the same moon, that look down upon your brothers and sisters, and which they see as they look up to them, though they are ever so far away from us and each other," her mother told the child Isabella.[45]

Sojourner Truth's recollection remembers ancient notions of moon, star, soul, and being. The classical Greek writer Plutarch links the Greek notion of souls residing among the stars with the myth of *Isis and Osiris*—an embodiment of ancient Egyptian cosmology in the practice and performance representing the cyclical presence of the Sirius star system.[46] Among the astronomer priests of the Malian Dogon, the *Sigui* ceremonies, like those of ancient Egypt, also mark the "renovation" or resurrection of the world in relationship to the Sirius but with a fascinating difference. The Dogon celebration focuses not on Sirius itself but on its tiny, often invisible companion star, which they call *Po Tolo*, "the seed or egg of the world." Among the Bozo, linguistic and regional cousins to the Dogon, the star Sirius is known as the "eye star," and the Bozo describe its moon as "seated" in its orbit, like the pictographic hieroglyph of Isis seated on her throne.[47] Among the /Xam San, in turn, creation myths and cosmovision identify the potency of women in shaping and giving names to the bodies of the heavens. (The next chapter will begin with one of these tales.) /Xam myth also connects falling stars with death. These old and essential connections resonate in contemporary practice and exploration. Ngugi, in his essay "Re-membering Visions" points out that "the oldest and best-known story from African myth," the story of Isis and Osiris, has continued to engage African writers.[48]

In their performances of reconstructing the shattered universe, women like Mau Mau Bett and Big Sarah attempted to construct a barrier between the horrors of slavery and their own lives as well as the lives of children. They did so by drawing on the sources of wealth available to them: webs of kin, ancestry and allegory, recollection and powerful symbolism in nursery story and song.

**Remembering Song**

> If you get there before I do
> Coming to carry me home
> Tell all my friends I'm coming too
> Coming to carry me home
>
>> "Swing Low Sweet Chariot," third stanza

"Swing Low Sweet Chariot," which Chaney Mack and other narrators remember among the lullabies of their mothers, is a song with an abundant history of story. Du Bois called "Swing Low Sweet Chariot" one of "the ten master songs" voicing the experience of the enslaved African in North America, and this song of journey, separation, spiritual presence, and the crossing of metaphysical terrain was also among those inscribed in Richard Allen's African Methodist church hymnal at the turn of the century. According to a contemporary annotation, "Swing Low Sweet Chariot" documents the experience of a woman who was about to be separated from her child and sold from a Mississippi plantation to one in Tennessee. The distraught woman, with no other recourse, was about to drown both herself and her baby in the Cumberland River when, according to the story, an old woman checked her hand, enjoining her to "let the chariot of the Lord swing low."[49] Even the allegorical truth here feels important.

Thousands of narratives of enslavement bear witness to the experiences of African diaspora women navigating a torn physical and spiritual terrain. Many ex-slave narrators, the great orator Frederick Douglass among them, wrote about the essential role women played in providing protection, preparation, and inspiration for family and community. Harriet Jacobs's nineteenth-century autobiographical novel *Incidents in the Life of a Slave Girl*, which presents her experience of and escape from enslavement, and the recently discovered period novel *The Curse of Caste; or, The Slave Bride* by Julia Collins, now considered the earliest extant novel publication by an African American woman, both highlight the separation from parents as a moment of profound spiritual tragedy and transition. Both writers also herald the formative and sustaining role of family, female relations, and adult and elder women. This experience of kin represents the rule rather than the exception. The central role of grandmothers and other female elders is a constant element in African American documents of witness. There is homage paid to the "expected" roles they play in nurturing, but there is also a telling recognition of the role of kindred women as impetus and agent in personal transformation and, often in the case of the fugitive, flight. We will continue to return to these essential relations.

> Swing low chariot! Pray let me in
> For I don't want to stay behind
> Sing low chariot! Pray just let me in!
> For I don't want to stay here no longer.[50]

Deeply resonant stories about the roots and routes of the song "Swing Low Sweet Chariot" abound. Historian Mark Miles Fisher writes that this 1858 version of the song, recorded in Green Mountain, Virginia, was inspired by the rebellion against slavery led by Nat Turner, as well as by the violent racist backlash in response to the uprising, and the heightened concern among Africans about ever getting justice in this land. According to Fisher, "Swing Low Sweet Chariot," this "popular song about . . . reincarnation in Africa," incorporated the image of a French, "sled like vehicle used to transport tobacco in the Carolinas. After Turner's revolt slaves wanted a chariot to swing out of the skies from Africa low enough for their souls to mount and to be carried many miles from North America."[51] Harriet Tubman speaks of "Swing Low Sweet Chariot" as a signal song. In her narrative she talks about how "Swing Low Sweet Chariot," like the song "Steal Away," was used to convey messages among fugitives and activists, helping people to escape from slavery via the Underground Railroad. Du

Bois called "Swing Low Sweet Chariot" a song of the "second generation" of African American articulation.

Aptly, legends surrounding "Swing Low Sweet Chariot" suggest the breath embedded in the spirituals. William Fisher, in his introduction to the Fisk Jubilee Singers' 1871 collection, tells of an American missionary who reported hearing the melody of "Swing Low Sweet Chariot" sung by the natives of Zimbabwe near the area of Mosi-oa-Tunya, which the English renamed Victoria Falls.[52] (Ngugi points to this placing of colonial memory and naming on African terrain as one of Europe's practices of colonial dismemberment.)[53] Some early musical scholars suggest that the song heard in Zimbabwe may have been "The Story of Tangalimlibo," which uses the same response and refrain. It's possible that the indigenous inhabitants of the region near the great Mosi-oa-Tunya were recalling a widespread custom of passing on the patriarchal thrones of antiquity, which is also remembered in Celtic and Greek myth.[54]

According to Fisher's informants, in Zimbabwe the song remembered another story of deliverance as well as a royal history connecting the king of their land with the ancient kings of heaven. Again, although classicists have drawn too sparingly on the stellar bounty of African cosmologies in their comparative mythology study, "Swing Low Sweet Chariot" may be a quintessential example of the trope of the Sun King's ritual death and resurrection. Stories of the golden chariot of the sun come down to us from the cosmological visions of ancient Egypt, which charted the sun god Ra's journey across the sky, from sunrise and birth, to sunset and death. Older texts picture the sky as the body of a woman giving birth to the sun cycling through her. This east-to-west vision of a cyclical universe, represented in a spectrum of African and African diaspora (art)iculation, illuminates webs of connection. The image forges another link between the spirituals "You May Bury Me in the East" and "Swing Low Sweet Chariot" and the celestial text, the tale of Isis, the moon incarnate, and her symbolic performance of historical and metaphorical journey.

Novelist Toni Morrison's reminder about the mythic, the epic, quality of the African American story and, by implication, of the human story comes to mind.[55]

In her oral history for the WPA, Ruby Pickens of Livingston, Alabama, recalls being separated, "sold" away, from her mother. "I recollect mammy said to old Julie 'Take care of my baby child and if I never see her again raise her for god.'" The song Ms. Pickens chose to sing for the interviewer, like Big Sarah's renditions of "Swing Low Sweet Chariot," is a widely known spiritual. It expresses a daughter's sorrow, a mother's lament, and the comfort to be found in an extended web of kinship.

> A motherless child sees a hard time
> Oh Lord help her on the road
> Her sister will do the best she can
> This is a hard world Lord for a motherless child.[56]

It is also reminiscent of the spiritual that became a blues song.

> Sometimes I feel like a motherless child
> Sometimes I feel like a motherless child
> Sometimes I feel like a motherless child
> Such a long long way from home.[57]

James Augustus Holmes of Harrison County, Mississippi, in his oral history for the WPA, remembered "three songs my mother usta sing to me." They are all songs with religious themes: "We Shall Sleep but Not Forever," "All the Way My Jesus Lead Me," and "I'm Pressing on the Upward Way."[58] Julia Woodsbury's recollection of the lullaby as a spiritual puts another twist on the expression "bye-bye." Ms. Woodsbury of Marion County, South Carolina, remembers her grandmother singing:

> Way cross the ocean
> Amongst all the nations
> Master Jesus promise me
> He going come by and by
> He going come by and by.[59]

The goodbye is a leaving, a renting, a tearing. The by-and-by is an opening into becoming. Sojourner Truth brought her mother's story of the stars, the practice of worship below the open skies, and the overarching sense of a cosmology of connection into becoming "Sojourner," an itinerant minister abolitionist and feminist "sojourning" through a harsh land. Harriet Jacobs, who begins her own brave storytelling with the story of her grandmother, drew on the older woman's faith and inspiration and remade herself into a free woman and a writer named Linda Brent, who would publicly challenge the slave system. For Jacobs, her mother's death marked her own coming of age, and at her mother's grave Jacobs determined to set "out into the wilderness" and attempt escape. The dramatic journey of Julia Collin's early African American heroine in the nineteenth-century novel is also animated by a mother's death. Harriet Bailey was separated from her son when he was an infant. He was sold to a plantation twelve miles away, and she remained a field worker on the place where he was born. "Four or five times," under the cover of night, she stole away and walked those twelve miles, and probably suffered severe punishment each time afterward, to lay with her child for a moment in the darkness. Perhaps she sang a lullaby for them both. Her son begins his *Narrative of the Life of Fredrick Douglass* with the story of a mother he barely knew:

> Hush little baby
> Don't you cry
> You'll be an angel
> By and by.

Alec Bostick, born in slavery in Morgan County, Georgia, told WPA interviewers that once children were big enough to work, there was no more time for fun and games. Though he could not have been more than five or six years old at the time of the emancipation, Mr. Bostick remembers "toting water" alongside workers in the fields. He could remember his mother's name and the names of his brothers and sisters, though many of them died while young. He also remembered his mother singing "a little song to the baby."[60] "Hush Little Baby" is a promise, a sorrowful promise.

> I looked over Jordan and what did I see
> Coming to carry me home

A band of angels coming after me
Coming to carry me home

Big Sarah's "Swing Low Sweet Chariot," with its vision of a return and a home in the next life, is an existential song. The river that flows through it, this symbolic water of religious baptism and historical transformation, marks a wide arc of conception. Gathering a world of cosmological proposal, the river water is, like the bush of Africa, a liminal place where the worlds of the living and the dead meet even as, for the enslaved, the water, the river, mark places of departure for both the spiritual and the physical self.[61]

Sometimes I feel like a motherless child
Sometimes I feel like a motherless child
Sometimes I feel like a motherless child
Such a long long way from home

Sometimes I feel like an eagle in the air
Some of these mornings bright and fair
I'm gonna lay down my heavy load
And cleave the air.
   "Sometimes I Feel Like a Motherless Child," spiritual, traditional[62]

The lullabies and spirituals of the African American tradition are a place of departure and critical knowing coming across with the blues line of the griot historian. Big Sarah and other women of her time have left us utterances that are as complicated, layered, and nuanced as their lives and their intellectual lineages and that are, in turn, signposts marking the paths that they made by walking.

4. Carole Byard, *If I Could*. Courtesy of the artist and the artist's estate.

# PUT YOUR HANDS ON YOUR HIPS    4
Rites of Passage in Performance

**The Second San Story: The Girl and the Milky Way**

*Once, before time, among the first people, according to the children of the ancestors who called themselves /Xam, it was the first girl who put stars in the sky and on the hems of the heavens. It happened like this. The little girl was in her hut. She was alone. She was dreaming secrets. Her mothers were gone, and maybe, she was a bit hungry. Surely, she wanted to play. She gathered handfuls of roots from the pantry and cool ashes from the cooking fire. She stole into the night. She tossed the roots into the sky saying, "become the stars," and they became. She tossed the ashes into the sky saying, "Become the Milky Way," and a blanket of light wrapped itself around the starry edges of the universe—heaven's river of celestial footprints.*[1]

**Performing Journey in Rites of Passage**

> We play and dance for you
> That you may remain with us
> That you may bear ten children
> That no bad thing may come upon you
> Let the elephant give you her womb
> That you may bear ten children
> Long live the people of your village
> Long live your relatives and elders
> Who celebrate this festival for you
>
>   Asante rite-of-passage song, twentieth century

The passage from childhood into adult responsibility has, since antiquity, been linked with agricultural cycles, seasons, fertility, the cosmos, and astrological motion, with courtship and reproduction, and with a wide spectrum of creative action.[2] Adult rites of passage traditionally link love with spiritual knowledge, physical maturity, and larger realms of social, historical, and cultural responsibility. These universal themes are essential elements in the African mythos and are dramatized in rites of passage using the circle as a setting for performance.[3]

The centrality of the circle in the song and dance performance of African and African diaspora resounds through the history if not always the renderings. Representations commonly remove half of the dancing ring to show the soloist in the center to the viewer, but the ancestral circle is actually meant to be viewed from above. From the ancient artistic viewpoint of the heavens, circles of women engaged in rites-of-passage performance are altars to the divine, mirroring the motion of the cosmos.

The /Xam San creation story offers us a panoramic vision. There are worlds within worlds, visible from above as well as across the physical terrain, in the picture the story conjures. In his notes to the text, /Xam practitioner and documentary historian //Kabbo explains that the girl's hut is a place of initiation for one about to be "grown," clearly connecting this etiological tale with adolescent rites of passage, fertility, creativity, and the liminality of trance states. From the symbolic architecture of her round house, a small planet in the forest, orbiting the circle of village dwellings, to her simple magical act, the girl's story is rich with cycling celestial imagery. The symbolic elements of this tale wheel throughout the African and Afro-Atlantic universe and are beautifully repeated in the cosmologically influenced architecture of round house dwellings within circular compounds. In his *Flash of the Spirit*, Thompson brings our attention to the Mande round house and its reiteration in the construction of Afro-Mexican communities as statements about the social universe and the individual's place within it.[4]

Aptly, according to //Kabbo, whose name means "dream" and who "dances" in his cultural transmissions, this story was also told to him by his mother, and the way that the first girl combines word and action, sound and movement, in the creation of the stars and the galaxy that we call the Milky Way is central to the telling. Foreshadowing the dream-song dancing of /Xam women, our heroine both speaks (sings) and acts (dances) the creation of the heavens, her movement akin to the dance phrase codified in the outstretched arms and raised palms of ancient Nubian and Egyptian statuary.[5]

> We mold the pot as our mothers did.
> The pot where is the pot?
> The pot it is here.
> We mold the pot as our mothers did.
>   Children's game, southern Sudan, twentieth century

Looking at how daughters of Africa and the diaspora have marked "coming of age" in rings of play and community recognition, performing stages of growing up, social responsibility, and spiritual enlightenment, we wheel from the ancient image into the twentieth century by recalling the Didinga girls' game of pots as a container, a vessel, and a vehicle for transformation.

The Asante song "We Sing and Dance" is, on the other hand, part of a formal rite-of-passage ceremony performed in a ring of girls, singing, dancing, and clapping their hands, within concentric rings of family and community. Those rings of song and dance bear witness to history, geography, and identity in community, as girls mark coming of age, rehearsing the values of their society and preparing for adult responsibility by "acting like a woman" in public performance. The song records and comments on the meaning and experience of womanhood among twentieth-century Asante, including the value placed on good health, fertility, social cohesion and harmony, kinship, and ancestry. The statements are poetic, expansive, and yet prescriptive. Here the elephant's womb, herd, and family loyalty are metaphors for specifically gendered adult behavior, socially encouraged and valued.

The performance models and engages with the use of communal storytelling, its circles within circles a philosophical weaving. Gathering, *you, us, children*, the womb of village, elders, and ancestry in narrative motion, the rite-of-passage performance strengthens the threads of social fabric and, particularly in hierarchal societies, containment. In the metaphysical circles of time represented by the circles of family and community who "celebrate" the festival into being, both the individual and the community are transformed. Little girls step into the magical circle and become young women even as, or perhaps because, the circle is a place of learning and training.

Though /Xam are considered an "extinct" cultural group, their social and cosmic visions live on in a constellation of influence and connection. On the African continent, ethnographic study among groups directly linguistically and culturally related to the /Xam San—including M. Biesele's work among the people called Ju/ hoan or !Kung and Camille Powers's work among other Kalahari Khoisan-speaking people, Hadza people in Ethiopia, and Matoposa people in Zimbabwe—reveals powerful continuities in menarche, medicinal, and agricultural ritual. The chronicles of performance in these ethnographic texts also poetically articulate the egalitarian visions of hunter-gatherer economies. Among the Hadza people, for instance, a girl is said to "have shot her first zebra" at the onset of menstruation, and among Ju/ hoan or !Kung San, first menses rites-of-passage ceremonies include masked dances that collapse gender difference in celebration of adult potency.

In the course of telling stories about their lives, Marjorie Shostak's !Kung San informants reveal the link between trance healing circles and women's rites-of-passage performance, the healing power they call /*Num*, fertility, and the onset of menstruation, which they describe as a woman's "being with the moon."[6] Nisa, Shostak's pseudonymous narrator, also discusses more recent iterations of the trance healing circle in the drum dance ceremonies, a form of trance performance done primarily by women.[7] Her description of the ceremonial hut constructed for her first menstruation makes a lovely complement to //Kabbo's storytelling a hundred years before.[8]

Camille Powers's cross-cultural studies of menarche rites among Kalahari groups, Matopos of Zimbabwe, and Hadza in the north pair well with the stories of Shostak's "Nisa" and with Biesele's work in elaborating a constellation of social and symbolic connections in performance. Powers points out how Ju/wasi rites-of-passage performance, in which circles of masked girls wear representations of the zebra's penis as an emblem, connect to cosmological happenings and to the symbolic renderings of rock art. In a similarly representative and generative creative act, Matopos girls carry images of the crescent moon in their coming-of-age dance. The stellar is a natural metonym in societies based on the economies of hunting and gathering among the Ju/wasi, the onset of menstruation is called "moon sickness."[9] In her narrative report "Nisa" speaks of "living and living," of "seeing the moon," of "being with the moon," and of its passing.

Recognition, and representation, of ourselves within the cosmos and of the connection between the feminine and the moon's cycling is, of course, a literally and metaphorically universal recognition that is wonderfully reiterated throughout what art historian Christine Muller Kreamer and her curatorial colleagues call "the stellar arts" of Africa. Each, and the total, of the essays in their volume *African Cosmos: Stellar Arts*, particularly Karen Milboure's "Moonlight and Clapping Hands," which looks at the cosmic performance of the Lozi of western Zambia, and Allen Robert's "Performing Cosmology," which looks at the potently parallel acts of celestial, geographic, and embodied inscription and representation of the Tabwa of what is now the Democratic Republic of the Congo, suggests to me a widening of the circle of philosophical connection and fills the continental gaps in our wondering and wandering.

African societies, and the people of the African diaspora in turn, have historically reenacted the cycling of heavenly and human seasons in performances that conflate ideas about cosmic and social regeneration. Our first theaters are rooted in these performances. Within that broad continuum, the coming-of-age rite-of-passage plays of African and African diaspora girls and women, like the stories of the little girl who sings and dances the galaxy into being and of Isis who reconstructs the universe in her remembering, represent, and invest participants in, creative action and agency, in performances embodying love, the stars, and their crossings.

The performance of *Njertun* among the southeastern Nubians of Sudan presents a once-complex engagement with this storied embodiment. Years of war and occupation have displaced people long exiled by colonial assaults, and only a glimpse of their traditional practices are inscribed in early twentieth-century photographs and ethnography.¹⁰ Those reports document a rite-of-passage performance in which, after a period of seclusion and training, adolescent girls were presented to the community in a circular dance, within a circle of musicians and male age mates, in the center of the circle of traditional round house reed dwellings. The architecture of the performance, the multiple circles of its staging, is telling and reminiscent of the cosmic curation of the /Xam storytelling. Emblematic of their economy based on cattle herding and husbandry, and a patrilocal social order in which marital arrangements are sealed with gifts of herds, the girls dance with switches of hide and reed indicate their choice of suitors in motion.

As vessels and vehicles of herstory, historicizing, and social commentary, the rite-of-passage performances of African and African diaspora girls and women also embed stories of power and of power contained, of gendered divisions, and of the violent oppression and domination of both ordinary women and the divine feminine. In the late twentieth century, for instance, the masked circles of song and dance of Mende Sande society rites of passage for adolescent girls followed a period of initiation that included training in etiquette, carriage, grooming, dance and song, and genital mutilation.¹¹ Herstory and history may yet judge the bitter parallels between genital mutilation, rape as an act of war, pseudo-religious battles against the education and agency of women, and enslavement. Certainly, feminist readings of the body remind us that hierarchical systems are inscribed on the body politic. We also dance this. We surely benefit from the work of indigenous humanists researching, situating, explicating, interrogating, and putting an end to "traditions" of violation. And then there is the essential power of storytelling. Osmane Sembene's artistic intervention on the issue of genital mutilation in collaboration with a contemporary Malian community is a potent example of the potential in continually reimagining the work of the griot.¹²

**Bridge Suites**

    Brown girl in the ring Tra la la la la
    Brown girl in the ring Tra la la la la la
    Brown girl in the ring Tra la la la la

> She looks like a sugar in a plum...
> Show me your motion Tra la la la la...
>
> "Brown Girl," African American / Caribbean ring game, twentieth century, traditional

J. D. Elder and Alan Lomax recorded this song being sung by children all over the English-speaking Caribbean in 1962 as "one by one" those island nations moved from British colonial rule to independence. The children sang and danced this piece of social commentary in a ring game, clapping their hands to keep time, as each child took her turn "showing her motion" in the center of their circling. One might say they were intuitively "dancing" the African past, the hopes of the present, and the complexity of the postcolonial motion to come.

Restating the far-ranging definition of dance among the Tiv, Thompson offers us a way of understanding "African art in motion" as a holistic practice, inextricably weaving tradition and improvisation:

> The Tiv people of Nigeria use a basic verb which means "to dance." This word, *vine*, unites the dance with further worlds of artistic happening. Thus a person can sometimes "dance" a top, setting the toy in motion, or "dance" a cutlass, twirling the blade artistically, causing it to glitter before the metal bites into the wood. This broad conception of the dance is widely shared in sub-Saharan Africa, *viz* that dance is not restricted to the moving human body, but can combine with things and objects granting them autonomy, intensifying the aliveness an image must embody to function as a work of art.[13]

> He continues: "The phenomenon is fundamentally poetic, it is a means of gaining access to sacred worlds conjured in artistic shapes... time and space. Africa thus introduces a different art history, a history of danced art, defined in the blending of movement and sculpture, textiles and other forms, bringing into being their own inherent goodness and vitality. Dance can complete the transformation of cryptic object into doctrine; dance redoubles the strength of visual presence, dance spans time and space."[14]

> Head and shoulders baby
> One, two, three

> Head and shoulders baby
> One, two, three
> Head and shoulders
> Head and shoulders
> Head and shoulders baby
> One, two, three
>
> "Head and Shoulders," African American street game, twentieth century

Our play performance in 1968 had roots in the southern United States and repeated patterns that have been noted in the Caribbean, throughout the diaspora, and in the performed presence of the ancestors. Players dance it in pairs, two children forming a small circle between them, African style, "dancing apart," in rhythm but not holding hands. The movement takes off from an attentive stance, partners face to face, in which the back is held straight and the knees are slightly bent. Movement begins with a leaning in and a quick, offbeat, raising of arms, elbows bent at tight angles. On the downbeat, following the directions of the lyrics, players tap the temples, then tap the shoulders, clapping on the offbeat and cross-body clapping on the "one two three" count. Restating the circle, the movement continues through a series of subsequent verse, from "head and shoulders" to the ground—"knees and ankles baby"—with ritual bowing and ancestral recognition, before winding "round the world" in the mortal terrain

In introduction to "the way we do," I wrote that we were dancing and singing "ancient canons of speaking." Thompson's dance study of African movement aesthetics provides an extraordinary paradigm for "breaking that down." Drawing on the teachings and commentaries of a stellar body of master practitioners, and a vast body of complementary study, Thompson enumerates some of the essential philosophical qualities of African movement articulation, including an engagement with ancestral communication, and with vitality, suspended beat, multiple meters, and call-and-response, as well as a quality he transmits as "getting down." These elements are powerfully present in the performance of "Head and Shoulders" and provide a translator's gloss for the language of our dancing.

In her longstanding Afro-Caribbean community dance practice, master dancer, choreographer, and educator Pat Hall reminds her students to "feel your feet firmly rooted in the earth" as we move up and to "press deeply into the earth" even as we reach. Her instruction is both practical and philosophical, physically and metaphysically resonant. "Head and Shoulders" begins with an attentive stance, a posture expressing what Thompson calls the "vital aliveness" of West and Central African sculpture and dance. The attitude of the body in the starting position, before the play has begun, is akin to a number of African figurative conventions in the sculptural forms including those of Nigeria, which Thompson discusses in his text. As in those visual texts, the wide-legged stance for "Head and Shoulders" is a technique for lateral movement, a strong place to spring from, and a poetic statement of readiness and alertness. The dance is passing on social and aesthetic values through modeling and teaching. These values permeate West and Central African dance criticism. Again I quote from Thompson's *African Art in Motion*: "Yoruba state that dancers must be prepared for the opening beat of the dance before moving, like a boxer bracing for the punch. The Yoruba dancer is supposed to 'come in' correctly, effortlessly. One with the phrasing of the master drummer. The Cameroon Bangwa judge choreography the same way, looking to see if performers make a proper entrance in relation to the beat. Luba demand that a dancer determine the position of his body, as a quasi sculptural force with bent knees and arms held close to the trunk, before actually dancing."[15] This attitude of readiness, and the sharp coordination it portends, is a key aspect of transformative art practice, the highest accomplishment of which is to become possessed by the spirit.

The first phrase of "Head and Shoulders" is a variation on ritual posturing, opening, and greeting. The motion of touching the temple, then raising the arms into open hands, fingers active and extending, is a basic metaphor for praise and salutation in West and Central African dancing. The opening gesture of the West African *fanga*, or welcoming dance, comes to mind. These "moves" as metaphors are in alignment with the ancient Egyptian hieroglyphs for "rejoicing" and "adoration," which appear throughout the vignettes of their books of "coming forth." Our "Head and Shoulders" revises these conventions, referencing them and the concept of supplication to the divine, with the raising of arms and the quick flutter of our hands, then, rather than opening raised arms in salutation, touching the head and bringing the movement, and the energy, "down" to the shoulders, our danced statement suggesting an ever deepening internal motion, our hands replicating gestures of divine adoration and supplication.

Centered and grounded by disembodied sculptural position, our bent knees, squared torso, and open chest, we danced generatively with a range of African and African diaspora iconography, including that of Bakongo ritual sculpture, or *minkisi*. Wyatt MacGaffey, in "The Eyes of Understanding," reminds us that in the *nkisi* "the head is thought of as the site of communication with the spirits, who were considered able to enter through the fontanele."[16] MacGaffey's work, cataloging an exhibition of Kongo *minkisi* that includes diaspora compositions, highlights the widespread presence and influence of this Central African form in the magical arts of the African diaspora: the use of the gnarled roots of a plant called John the Conqueror, the making of *paquets de Congo*, the practice called *juju*, and the symbolic resonance of "bones" as a potent ancestral force.

Within Yoruba- and Fon-inspired performance practices, the "head" is also a symbolic site for ancestral and divine intervention. The works of Zora Neale Hurston, Maya Deren, and Katherine Dunham, artists who were both anthropologists and practitioners of African and diaspora religion, have demonstrated how the sculptural medium of the initiate's body becomes a vessel for the gods of Africa in the Americas. Their work highlights the connection between the African diaspora's sacred performances of possession, wherein the practitioners greet the divinities who then enter the "head" of an initiate, and the secular enactment of liminality in the ring game, in which, "mounted" by the dizzying swirl of play, the person in the center of the circle becomes the generative complexity of the divine.

Dunham's description of an initiation into the Haitian Vodun practice of Rada Dahomey, in her chronicle *Island Possessed*, is illuminating:

> "*Ah, Bobo! Ah, Bobo!*" we cried in ecstasy perhaps to honor the Bobo-Oule, oldest tribe of the Upper Volta, formerly a part of Western Sudan. Some of the old ones who "spoke language," even when not

delivering messages from the gods, repeated over and over "*Kebiosilie!*" similar to a word used in Dahomey and Yoruba ceremonies in Cuba which might be associated with greeting the Loa Kehiousu or might be an acknowledgment of royalty, I have never known which. All present, whether sitting, standing or squatting began a spasmodic hunching forward and releasing of shoulders, which, when continued for some time, particularly when driven by the piercing beat of the *kata*, enriched by the broken rhythms of the seconde, and eroticised by the deep insistent tones of the mama drums, produces a state of mixed lightheadedness and well being. The forced regular breathing would be auto-hypnotic under any circumstances, and the uninterrupted monotonous shoulder movement engenders an awareness of self, and acts as a catharsis, along with a sensation of equilibrium between head and chest and, eventually, in a Haitian *houngfor*, unless restrained by one convention or another, possession.[17]

Writing, much later, of the "psycho-physiological effects of body emphasis" in sacred dance performances, Dunham returned to description of the repeated patterns of head and shoulder movement, engendering regular rapid breathing, in the creation of a trance state. "Another dance of religious ecstasy is the *zepaules*, which stresses shoulder action," she writes of a form of Haitian dance, in her "Form and Function in Primitive Dance." "It seems that the regular forward-backward jerking of the shoulders and the rapid contracting and expanding of the chest, ensures quick regular breathing. This forced rapid breathing brings about self hypnosis and auto-intoxication, states bordering on ecstasy." Bringing it back "around," Dunham also wrote extensively about the whole body circuit, "the circular flow through spine, chest, and solar plexus," as well as the circular formation as an aspect of the danced technique of Africa and the diaspora.[18]

Knees and ankles baby
One, two, three
Knees and ankles baby
One, two, three
Knees and ankles

> Knees and ankles
> Knees and ankles baby
> One, two, three

Cultural performances are, as James Cone points out in his analysis of the African American spirituals, locations for complex thought. The closed world of the circle girls form is without beginning or end and, as Bess Lomax Hawkes notes, "includes and excludes at the same time."[19] The danced statement is about formal self-presentation ("representing" or "signifying") and the idea that the individual is a vessel and a medium for the historical. The presentation (touching of the head) and salutation (cross-body clapping on the "one two three") pay homage to ancestry while recognizing the role of the individual within the community of art making. In song and movement the dancers speak of tiered worlds and interdependence, rootedness and vitality, flexibility, strength, and agility. Their statement of mutuality and cooperation is redoubled in the refrain as dancers return to salutations, the open palms cross clapping, acknowledging the essential depth of the social bond.

And our play underscores, in its multivalence of presentation, the value placed on memory and precision as, within its act of communal creation, individual girls learn agency in vocality and physical dexterity. These performances require, and teach, quick thinking and coordination, cooperative skill, responsibility, flexibility, and mutuality as well as an epic world vision. The comparison with the Ashanti puberty song is telling. There are no elephants on this new landscape, and its terrain demands different metaphors for female accomplishment. The received values passed on in "Head and Shoulders" translate into the vernacular imperative to keep one's head up and one's shoulders back.

> Round the world baby
> One, two, three
> Round the world baby
> One, two, three
> Round the world round the world round the world baby
> One, two, three

Overarching the specifically African performance phrases in African American girls' play is the universal symbolism of dance. The bow is among our oldest linguistic acts. The poet Basho claps to herald the dawn in a "Summer Moon" in haiku.[20] The head as a source of power is synecdoche in world mythology. The oracular head of Bran the Blessed of Celtic lore or the talking skull of the widespread African tale reverberates throughout this vast storied text.[21] And then, of course, there are the bones:

> Ham bone ham bone where you been?
> Round the world and back again.
> Ham bone ham bone what you do?
> I got a chance and I fairly flew
> Ham bone ham bone where you stay?
> I met a pretty girl and I couldn't get away
>> "Ham Bone," African American ring play, traditional, twentieth century

## Coming of Age and Circles of Ancestry in Shouts and Ring Play

> Come on Mauma, let's go round the wall,
> And that suits me
> Come on Mauma, let's go round the wall,
> And that suits me
> Come on Mauma, let's go round the wall
> Don't want to stumble and I don't want to fall.
>> "That Suits Me," ring shout, early twentieth century[22]

South Carolina, where the "black majority" of the state's population is an old one, is a rich source for recordings of the sacred performance of the ring shout and related secular plays. "By 1740 two-thirds of South Carolina's settlers were Africans, nearly 40,000 people," wrote historian Charles Joyner in his study of the region. Many of those unwilling first settlers were relocated into this area from the slave plantations and estates of the Caribbean, and some were brought in captivity directly from West and Central Africa. The institution of slavery in South Carolina was intense and long lasting and the African cultural presence abiding. Sterling Stuckey, in his *Slave Culture*, reminds us of the bounty of African retentions in the "folk" culture of South Carolina, including the centrality of the circle to ceremonies honoring ancestry and to the communal composition of story and his writing specifically about the role of the circle in girls' rite-of-passage practices of Mende and Temne peoples. The extraordinary linguistic and cultural connections that have been documented between the Carolina and Georgia Sea Island, or Gullah, culture and that of the Mende of West Africa affirm our sense of an ever-wider circle.[23]

Though the powerful sacred circles of the ring shout were outlawed in the early years of transatlantic slavery, and the practices of "African-style" repetitive vocalization and percussion were banned in religious worship, a circular ritual involving rhythmic vocalization, counterclockwise motion, driving repetition, hand clapping, body percussion, antiphonal voice, and lyrical improvisation was carried on clandestinely, in "hush arbors" and secret meetings. Lydia Parrish, a recorder of regional culture and lore, wrote of the difficulty she encountered as an outsider collecting and documenting the song and dance of the Georgia Sea Islands in the early twentieth century. "It took me three winters on St. Simon's to hear a single slave song, three more winters to see the religious dance that called the ring shout, still more winters to unearth the Buzzard Lope and the game song known as ring play."[24] Katherine Dunham, in her *Journey to Accompong*, remembers facing a similar challenge as an anthropology student in the maroon towns of Jamaica.

Parrish did manage, in her forty-year residency in the community, to be invited to witness the wheeling worlds of ring shout performance and to record descriptions and song selections. Describing the movement of one ring shout, Parrish writes of a practitioner who "held her shoulders stiff—at the same time thrusting them forward—kept her feet flat on the floor, and, with the usual rhythmic heel tapping, progressed with real style around the circle." Writing of another practitioner Parrish notes "the pause she makes with head and shoulders slightly bowed slightly forward, arms held close to her body, elbows bent at right angles, forearms thrust out before her, and palms upturned in a supplicating gesture."[25]

> Well I looked up and saw the chariot coming
> And that suits me
> Well I looked up and saw the chariot coming
> And that suits me
> I looked up and saw the chariot coming
> Step on the wheel and the wheel keep turning
> And that suits me.
> "That Suits Me"

The Pan-African movement phrasing of the ring shout, the ancient interlacing of form and function, is familiar. In circles of rhythmic movement and hand clapping, practitioners dance greeting, recognition, generosity, and mutuality. Everyone is welcomed into the ritual experience, called to take the journey, as each person is named in the performed narrative. "Come on Mauma." This is a communal creation. The ring shout "That Suits Me" is also rich in allusion. In the transforming religious experience and in the acts of daily survival, the dancer must move "around the wall" and beyond the "walls" of this reality into divine time. Skill, discipline, dexterity, and community enjoin her not to "stumble" or fall.

In the journey toward spiritual maturity, presenting herself within a circle below the heavens, the practitioner sings of seeing "the chariot coming." "Step on the wheel and the wheel keep turning." This image of an endlessly turning wheel within a wheel broadens our vision of the divine chariot as a symbol in African American articulation. The chariot is the vehicle for "crossing over" earthly bound and its wheels, its wheeling, represents the performance of liberation, the movement of heavenly bodies, and the circle of life. The ring shout marks a religious coming of age through ritual experience of cosmic turning.

> I know moon-rise, I know star-rise
> Lay this body down

> I walk in the moonlight, I walk in the star-light
> To lay this body down.
>> "I Know Moon Rise," African American spiritual ring shout, nineteenth century[26]

The record of earlier ring shouts resonates with the profound essence of this practice. This version of "I Know Moon Light" was recorded among the troops in South Carolina by Thomas Wentworth Higginson, an abolitionist and Unitarian minister who kept a journal during his command of the first African American Civil War regiment. "Often in the starlit evening," wrote Higginson, the men gathered in firelight circles to testify, sing, and shout "without accompaniment but the measured clapping of hands and the clatter of feet."[27]

> O-o-h Moonlight
> Believer what's the matter
> John lay the body down.
>> "I Know Moon Light," early twentieth-century version[28]

Lydia Parrish recorded the above version of "I Know Moon Light," with its subtle reference to forbidden prayer meetings, over fifty years later among the residents of St. Simons Island. Parrish recalled that the response line of "Moonlight Starlight" was "sung with lips closed" when it was performed during a funeral ceremony.[29]

> Hold your light, Brother Robert
> Hold your light
> Hold your light on Canaan's shore
>> "Hold Your Light," African American spiritual ring shout, nineteenth century[30]

"Hold Your Light" was "a favorite" shout among the soldiers of the First South Carolina Volunteers, according to Higginson. The simple verse moved round and round the circle of men, men who had fought for the right to be called men and to join the war for their own emancipation, in hand-to-hand combat, on one of the bloodiest fields of war the world had yet seen. The lead singer began with a call to one man: "Hold your light, Brother Robert." The circle answered in chorus: "Hold your light / Hold your light on Canaan's shore," each man adding his own rhythm, his own voice to the building of song. The simple verse was repeated around and around the circle of men, each time calling one man in turn, the circle responding, adding their voice and rhythm, bringing people back to their humanity in a circle of healing, crossing, hope, and vision.

> Jordan River, I'm bound to go
> Bound to go, bound to go
> Jordan River, I'm bound to go
> And bid them fare ye well.
> "Bound to Go," spiritual shout, nineteenth century[31]

The sacred performance of the ring shout embodied journey and liminality. Silvia King of Marlin, Texas, told WPA interviewers that she had been born in Morocco, kidnapped and enslaved as a grown woman, and lived, in both slavery and freedom, in New Orleans. In her interview she gave her own description of a religious ring shout. "The Black folks get off down in the bottom and they shouts and sings and prays. They gets in the ring dance. It's just a kind of shuffle, then it gets faster and faster and they get warmed up and moans and shouts and claps and dances. Some get exhausted and drop out and the ring gets closer."[32]

Katherine Epps of Uniontown, Alabama, another WPA informant, also looked back over a long lifetime to remember a similar practice, with all the elements of the sacred shout, as a ring play done by children, the circle unbroken: "We usta play 'Sail Away Rauley' a whole lot. We would hold hands and go around in a ring getting faster and faster and them what fall down was out of the game."[33]

> Go round the border Susie
> Go round the border Susie
> Go round the border Susie
> That long summer day
> "Go Round the Border Susie," ring play, early twentieth century

In the sacred performance, adults submit to the swoon of the spirit. In the rites of passage of ring games and courtship play, children mime adult performance and dancers submit to love's embrace. Among Parrish's twentieth-century recordings is "Go Round the Border Susie," a ring play directed by verses that elicit rounds of competition, chase, and flirtation. Like the religious ring shout, this play uses the circle and sculpts a communal composition through calling each participant by name. Perhaps there are more complex histories written in these motions.

In her WPA oral history, Lizzie Hughes, who was born in Nacogdoches, Texas, in 1848, remembered dancing at frolics to the ring play Juba. Her Juba combines elements of trial, magic, and a courting song.

> Juba this and Juba that
> Juba killed a yellow cat
> Juba this and Juba that
> Show your partner where you're at.[34]

Lawrence Evans of Franklin County, Mississippi, who was "too little to work fields" during slavery, could still remember joining the adults playing games by firelight after their "sunup to sun down" days of working. He remembered "one game was to catch hands and go round and round in a circle and sing some song." He also offered a version of the popular "Little Liza Jane":

> Run little Liza Jane and take her home
> Run little Liza Jane and take her home
> Run little Liza Jane and take her home
> Run, run, run.

In her WPA interview Lucy Thurston of Mississippi recalled being separated from her mother at the age of twelve and sold on the auction block to a plantation in New Orleans, where she learned another version of the ring play "Little Liza Jane":

> Oh Lil Liza, Lil Liza Jane,
> Oh Lil Liza, Lil Liza Jane.
> Hair as black as coal in de mine,
> Lil Liza Jane,

Eyes so large and big and fine
Lil Liza Jane.
Oh Lil Liza, Lil Liza Jane,
Oh Lil Liza, Lil Liza Jane.
Mouse in the hole and the cats' going to get it,
Lil Liza Jane,
Cats in the tree and the dog going to get it,
Lil Liza Jane.
Oh Lil Liza, Lil Liza Jane,
Oh Lil Liza, Lil Liza Jane.

The "standard" version, recorded in 1910, also appears in Altona Trent's *Play Songs of the Deep South* as a circle game in which, as in Evans's recollection, the child in the center "steals" a partner from the ring. The song uses the pentatonic scale, and the tune of the refrain is the same as that of a Yoruba welcoming dance song, "Fanga Alafiya," which remains very much alive in the cultural memory of New Orleans and the South Carolina Sea Islands:

Fanga alafiya
ashe ashe
fanga alafiya
ashe ashe
Fanga alafiya
ashe ashe
fanga alafiya
ashe ashe

Its simple words are rich in meaning. *Fanga* is a Yoruba welcoming dance, *alafiya* is a greeting of peace in the Yoruba language, and *ashe* is a Yoruba philosophical concept about the power to make things happen.

I got a bowl you ain't got nothing / Little Liza Jane
I got a bowl you ain't got nothing / Little Liza Jane
I got a bowl you ain't got nothing / Little Liza Little Liza Jane
Oh Little Liza / Little Liza Jane / Oh Little Liza / Little Liza Jane.
   "Little Liza Jane," play song, traditional[35]

"Most folks can't remember many things happened to them when they only eight years old, but one of my biggest tribulations come at that time," Joanna Draper of Mississippi told WPA interviewers. "That was when I was took away from my own Mammy and Pappy and sent off and bound out to another man.... When I was about six years old," she continued, "they take me into the big house to learn to be a house woman, and they show me how to cook and clean up and take care of babies." "I hear tell of them good slave days but I never seen no good times then," said Jenny Proctor of Alabama another WPA informant. "I tended to the children when I was a little gal and tried to clean the house just like Old Miss tell me to. Then soon as I was ten years old, Old Master, he say, "Get this here n—— to that cotton patch."

Mary Reynolds of Louisiana remembered "holding a hoe handle mighty unsteady when they put an old woman to learn me and to scrape the fields. That old woman would be frantic" and warned "you'd better learn it right or Solomon will beat the breath out of your body." "Slavery," Ms. Reynolds testified, "was the worst days ever seen in the world. They was things past telling, but I got the scars on my old body to show to this day." She spoke of running into the slave catchers and their dogs one fearful night; of how the plantation owner "took any on his place he wanted"; of a seamstress, "a yeller gal," who was put up in a house separate from the quarters and had "a mess of white young-uns"; and of her Aunt Cheyney, who had given birth to four of the owner's children.

Coming of age, and into adult knowledge, is an animating dynamic in the written herstories of this period. Harriet Jacobs called the entry into her fifteenth year "a sad epoch in the life of a slave girl.... Soon she will learn to tremble when she hears her master's footfall. She will be compelled to realize that she is no longer a child." In her brave narrative testimony against the injustice of slavery, *Incidents in the Life of a Slave Girl*, Jacobs bears witness to a terrifying coming into adult knowledge. "My master began to whisper foul words in my ear. Young as I was I could not remain ignorant of their import.... He told me I was his property; that I must be subject to his will in all things. My soul revolted against the mean tyranny. But where could I turn for protection?" Mary Prince speaks guardedly of her disgust at the "indecency" of slaveholders. Frederick Douglass spoke and wrote passionately of coming of age through the "blood stained gates" of slavery when he witnessed his aunt being tied "up to a jost" and whipped on her naked back until "she was literally covered with blood." James Curry's 1840 narrative, which was widely reprinted in abolitionist circles, portrays the experience of his own mother, whose person was given as a wedding gift, a not uncommon experience, to "drunkards." She was treated "so outrageously when she came into her teens," wrote Curry, "that it is not proper to be written."[36] James Pennington in his *The Fugitive Blacksmith* also begins his own narrative testimony against the evils of human chattel slavery with a preface recalling the manner in which young girls "in Maryland, Virginia, and Kentucky" were reared "for the express purpose of supplying the market of a class of economical Louisiana and Mississippi gentlemen."[37]

"Run Little Liza Jane" plays on another widely recorded song narrating a fugitive's escape. James Singleton of Simpson County, Mississippi, is among the many WPA informants who remembered it.

Run n—— run, the patroller get you.
Run n—— run, it's almost day.
That n—— run, that n—— flew,
That n—— lost his big black shoe.[38]

This tragically well-known ditty was first recorded by musical scholars William Francis Allen, Charles Picard Ware, and Lucy McKim in their 1867 volume *Slave Songs of the United States*. For many young women and men, coming of age in enslavement was a call to escape, "to run." Those who did were relentlessly pursued by bounty hunters. Many were "caught," killed or brutally assaulted, mutilated, and brought back into bondage. This knowledge was also part and parcel of adult understanding of the institution of slavery. Still captive and enslaved African and African diaspora people, from the time of the their first recorded bondage in the Americas and the Caribbean, "ran" to escape, and we owe the great majority of early African American autobiography to persons who took on tremendous risks for their own liberty and then published their stories as testimony against the system of slavery. Two recently discovered narratives, those of John Washington and Wallace Turnage, like the narratives of Frederick Douglass, William Wells Brown, and Henry "Box" Brown, tell of harrowing fugitive journeys to freedom. Turnage, who made the first of several unsuccessful escape attempts when he was separated from his mother at fourteen, gives his reader a firsthand experience of being tracked down by armed men on horseback, bitten by dogs trained to hunt humans, beaten to bloodied unconsciousness, then chained hand and foot and dragged behind a cart.[39] Mary Reynolds's memory of her Aunt Cheyney's attempt to run away—"just out of bed with a suckling baby . . . some say that was another baby of master's breeding"—is searing. "Old Solomon gets the n—— hounds and takes her trail. They gets near her and she grabs a limb and tries to hoist herself in a tree but them dogs grab her and pull her down. The men hollers them on to her and the dogs tore her naked and ate the breasts off her body."

William and Ellen Craft tell the story of their escape from Georgia slavery in 1848 in a book called *Running a Thousand Miles to Freedom*. They ran those "thousand miles" with Ellen disguised as a young white man and William as her caring slave and attendant. According their joint statement, Ellen was compelled by her own determination not to give birth to children in enslavement. "My wife's first master was her father," Craft writes, and she too was "given away" (her person as a wedding gift) and taken from her mother as a child. Having witnessed the adulthood rites of enslavement, Ellen Craft would not discuss marriage without a plan for liberation from the "wretched system of American slavery."

Black abolitionist writing consistently called out the systematic rape of women at the core of American slavery. Frederick Douglass, whose father may have been the "white man" who sold his mother away, wrote that though the true story of his progeny died with her, the truth was history. "The fact remains, in all its glaring odiousness, that slaveholders have ordained, and by law established, that the children of slave women shall in all cases follow the condition of their mothers; and this is done too obviously to administer to their own lusts, and make a gratification of their wicked desires profitable as well as pleasurable; for by this current arrangement, the slaveholder, in cases not a few, sustains to his slaves the double relationship of master and father."[40] Again, the knowledge reverberates through our texts.

## Playing the Changes

> Little Sally Ann
> Sitting in the sand
> Crying and weeping
> For a precious little man
> Rise Sally rise
> Wipe your dirty eyes
> Turn to the east
> Turn to the west
> Turn to the one
> You love the best.
>
> "Rise Sally Rise," African American play song, nineteenth century[41]

There is little wonder "Little Sally Ann" of the popular play song weeps. Yet like Little Liza Jane, the potentially tragic figure of the young woman coming of age is also a figure called on to take agency in motion. The song instructs the practitioner to "wipe your dirty eyes" and "turn." This history and instruction are represented in early African American literature. William Wells Brown's novel *Clotel; or, The President's Daughter* (1853) and his dramatic writing *The Escape; or, A Leap for Freedom* (1858), alternately the first novel and dramatic publication in African American literary history, revolve around the untold story of race and sex in the national narrative. *Clotel* is loosely based on the life of Sally Hemings, an enslaved African American woman who was the mother of seven of U.S. president Thomas Jefferson's children. Celebrated and abused in the popular tunes of the times, Sally Hemings could be the original character recalled in numerous children's plays. The folk record, and the literature arising from it, recognizes the story of Sally Hemings and Thomas Jefferson as a founding trope in the national narrative.

The early fiction of African American women is animated by contending forces of embodiment, location, dislocation, and abandonment as sites for impossibly wretched "rites of passage." The separation from parents, the death of a mother, the lonely sojourn into adolescence, and the quagmire of color, sexuality, and identity are major themes in the writings of the African American women novelists of the period. Julia Collins's heroine in *The Curse of Caste; or, The Slave Bride* (1865) and Hannah Crafts's heroines in *A Bondswoman's Narrative* (circa 1853–61) are orphans caught in the storm winds of racial and sexual social mores. Like Ellen Craft and Hemings, these early heroines are African American women who appear to be white, and this racial ambiguity, and its ensuing social conundrums, are the dynamic of their tellings. In these novels a woman's fortune, and perdition, turns on racial perception and offers a powerful allegory for the racially constructed tragedy of American history.

Though these early heroines of African American women's novels are troubled and sometimes tragic figures, they are also daring young women who represent a broader collective response to hegemonically constructed racial images, tropes, and "convention." Across the spectrum of their social condition, nineteenth-century African American women turned "to the east" and "to the west" with less assurance than in the old song of hearing "the trumpet sound," but encouraged to wipe their eyes with determination. And in story and performance, those young women nonetheless looked for love.

> Old sweet beans and barley grows
> Old sweet beans and barley grows
> You nor I nor nobody knows
> Where old sweet beans and barley grows
> Go choose your east
> Go choose your west
> Go choose the one that you love best
> If she's not here to take her part
> Choose the next one to your heart.
>
> Ring play, nineteenth century[42]

With lines like "Choose the next one to your heart," the ring plays of the nineteenth century sing shifting perspectives in diaspora communities. By the mid-nineteenth century, though the memory of Africa remained, the performance practices of Africa were being transformed by a young African American population living in a primarily agricultural setting. These second- and third-generation African Americans articulated new ways of signifying within and beyond the witness traditions of their lineage. Their performances are about making home in this country, with all its contradictions; about making "a way out of no way"; and about the continued role of culture in safeguarding an embattled humanity.

> Old Brer Rabbit
> Shake it shake it
> How I love you
> Shake it shake it.[43]

"I'd rather play that game than eat," said Mary Wright of Kentucky recalling a game she played as a girl in her WPA oral history. This game, recorded near the end of the antebellum period, uses distinctively African percussive dance, hand clapping, double entendre, and social commentary but with distinctively African American allegory in the presence of Brer Rabbit, Possum, and Raccoon. Ms. Wright's nineteenth-century lyrics bring to mind another girls performance of the twentieth century.

> Grandma Grandma sick in bed
> Called the doctor and the doctor said
> Grandma grandma you ain't sick
> All you need is a hickory stick
> Hands up,
> Shake shake shake shake
> Hands down.
> Shake shake shake shake
> Do the front do the back do the side side side
> Do the front do the back do the side side side
> I never went to college

> I never went to school
> But I bet you five dollars
> I can shake it like a fool
> Hands up....
>
> Ring play with hand jive, twentieth century

This dance play references the Kongo pose Warner-Lewis describes in her work, with the left hand on the hip, the right hand held poised in the air, and "the Kongo ascription *yaangalala*, in which the hands are thrust above the head with fingers spread wide."[44] According to Warner-Lewis, these and similar formal postures indicate the presence of the spirit in the Bakongo danced lexicon. Our twentieth-century hand jive then turns the Kongo ascription into a jazzy finger wagging and revises Juba's "this and that" in the movement phrase "do the front do the back do the side side side."

> Ebo Dick and Jurdan Joe
> Them two n——s stole my yo
>
> "Nonsense Juba," nineteenth century[45]

This Juba, recorded by Solomon Northrup, the enslaved musician, gives a sense of the hybridity of African identities current by the early nineteenth century. The Ebo and Jordan of the Old World now bear the surnames Dick and Joe, a creole play on the West African day name Cudjoe (Monday), Juba's masculine counterpart.

> This a way you Willowbee
> Willowbee Willowbee
> This a way you Willowbee
> All night long.
>
> "Willowbee," African American play song, late nineteenth / early twentieth century[46]

There is a mapping, a chronology, in the danced play. When Altona Trent Jones recorded the ring plays of her childhood in the American South in the early twentieth century, she documented two versions of "Willowbee." Though the chorus remains the same, in the older version of the play, children danced pantomime and sang a chorus about "stepping through the silent all night long," remembering clandestine meetings and fugitive flight in the same way that the spiritual "Steal Away" signaled imminent escape. Here the "all night long" of the chorus brings to mind nocturnal journeys illuminated and guided by starlight.

Trent's second version of "Willowbee" incorporates the images of the burgeoning postbellum street life in the Northern cities African Americans increasingly migrated to at the end of the nineteenth century. The phrase "strutting down the alley" replaces "stepping through the silent" of the earlier rendition. In the 1960s we, the children of the civil rights movement, in the wake of political assassinations, counterintelligence, and the failure of social integration, again replaced the action verse with "step back Sally." Our plays reminded the bold what we would be told, and then we urged ourselves to jump back into the ring anyhow.

> Ham bone ham bone pat him on her shoulder
> Gimme a pretty girl and I'll show you how to hold her.
> I went to town one day
> I went with my mother too
> My mother bought me a billy goat
> If my billy goat don't butt
> Mama gonna beat my rusty butt.
> Ham bone ham bone pat him on her shoulder
> Gimme a pretty girl and I'll show you how to hold her.
> I went to town one day
> I went with my mother too
> My mother bought me a radio
> If my radio don't play
> Momma gonna beat my NRA
>   "Ham Bone," twentieth century

Poetry and history are also in motion in differing versions of the Juba and the Ham Bone. By the mid-nineteenth century the percussive, synchronized, call-and-response, hand clapping, foot tapping, and body instrumentation had been appropriated into racist characterization in

American minstrelsy and popular culture. Still the plays continued to move in practitioner communities. The above version of "Ham Bone," from Lydia Parrish's Sea Island collection, has Depression-era elements and finds rhythmic play in the solo voice. Parrish's informants were children who "patted" out the rhythm of the play in a circular motion quickly slapping from their thighs to their chests to their bottoms with the palm of one or both hands. Most of Parrish's "Ham Bone" informants were boys, but she includes a beautiful description of a little girl performing "Ham Bone," making of her body an instrument, balanced on her left foot, her right foot placed on her left leg and with one hand deftly holding her skirt hem patting out the rhythms with the other. Those children, circa 1912, still called their dance, body, and song sculpture Juba patting. And "Mama" remains a central figure, both challenging and proposing. By the end of the century, distinct but related performances had been collapsed into one.

> Miss Mary Mack Mack Mack
> All dressed in black black black
> With silver buttons buttons buttons
> All down her back back back
>
> And I love coffee coffee coffee
> And I love tea tea tea
> And I love the boys boys boys
> And the boys love me me me
>
> I went to the river river river
> And I couldn't get across cross cross
> And I paid five dollars dollars dollars
> For the old grey horse horse horse
> And the horse wouldn't pull pull pull
> I swapped him for a bull bull bull
> And the bull wouldn't holler holler holler
> I swapped him for a dollar. . . .
> See that yonder yonder yonder
> in the jay bird town town town

Where the women gotta work work work
Till the sun goes down down down.
> "Mary Mack," hand jive and Juba play, twentieth century[47]

"Mary Mack" is an early twentieth-century game that incorporates rhythmic hand clapping and patting Juba. Mary Mack's tale is a rough one, a tale of moving through serial challenges and strategies for surviving in view of the "jay bird town where women gotta work until the sun goes down." The circle is smaller, just a girl and her partner playing like a shadow who "bears her up" and calls her on. Little girls play it fast, patting the chest, then the hips, breaking with a hand clap, then cross clapping with a partner on the repeating line, as they invoke the transformations that bring Mary Mack to the threshold of the river and the impetus to cross over.

Yemaya hace su
Hace su Yemaya
Yemaya hace su
Hace su Yemaya.
> Orisha song, twentieth century[48]

The river "Mary Mack" is trying to cross flows from and ever returns to the sacred waters of older performance. The songs of the ancient river goddesses "crossed over" many times, sometimes changing names, but being remembered in the motions of hands, in the posture, in the songs, even in a colonized tongue. "Yemaya Hace Su" is a diasporic offering to the Yoruba deity Yemaya, whose divine presence articulates large waters and who, according to the song, when present will "make the waves," troubling the seas in her cyclical birthing.

Maria Mucangue
Washes the lady's clothing
Washes the blouse of chita
It isn't hers it's her lady's

When the Brazilian daughters of the Saint Macumbas or Cambindas enter their trance singing a song associated with the "old slaves" of Rio de

Janeiro, their ritual performance gathers pieces of the same restless dream.[49] It is a story of a woman enslaved whose hidden power as an ancient mother is remembered as it is performed. It is a story of a woman who has taken a perilous journey and a new name that marks the ways she has gone. When her song is sung, when her dance is done, when her journey is performed, her power can be freed again and the collective name can be fully found. The female initiates circle and sing toward the moment of possession, making the way for transformation.

Meditating on these herstories, a Kongo song of Haitian folk tradition, transcribed in Georges Vilson's compilation, comes to mind. It is a song that I am just beginning to learn, but its posture and nuance feel deeply familiar.

Kawolin Akawo mdanse kongo jouk kom fe mwen malo
Kawolin Akawo mdanse kongo jouk kom fe mwen malo
Mdanse kongo, mlaye kongo
Mdanse kongo, mlaye kongo
Kawolin Akawo, negnwe tizo reyan raje
Kawolin Akawo, negnwe tizo reyan raje.

Kawolin Akawo I dance Kongo till my body hurts
Kawolin Akawo I dance Kongo till my body hurts
I dance Kongo I throw down Kongo
I dance Kongo I throw down Kongo
Kawolin Akawo the man with the little ears is crazy

The song is both playful and potently herstorical. Kawolin Akawo, a woman with an African name, dances Kongo, the ancestors, the journey, the rhythms, the movement vocabulary, its meaning, its story, the history, until it hurts. It's so good it's "bad." She "throws down," she gets down, way down, and she gets up, physically and metaphysically, in her dance and song. Her cool, her grace, her grounding, her flight are radiant. And her song, from the tiny Afro-Atlantic nation that took on the imperial armies of European colonialism, is an embodied re-membering, offering, I sense, pointed determination and dismissing social critique to the crazy "man with the little ears" of Western hegemonic discourse.

# ROSY, POSSUM, MORNING STAR  5
Work Songs and the Blues

### Ogboinba: An Ijaw Story

*Among the Ijaw they say that in the beginning God was a woman who sat down, below her tree, with her birthing stone, and shaped the fates of spirits according to their choosing before sending them, along two streams, into the land of the living. They say that, when her spirit came before the creator, Ogboinba asked only for great mystic power, to be a seer and a healer, while another beside her asked for many children, and that those two were afterward born to be women, in the same town, and became close friends. Each year Ogboinba's power grew. She knew the language of all animals and the meanings of dreams and, in time, touched and healed legions. They say that in time both women married, but while her friend gave birth to many children, whom she cared for like her own, Ogboinba gave birth to no children, though she deeply wanted them. So, they say, Ogboinba packed her most powerful medicines and set out to return to the place of beginning, to re-create herself, to have children. On her journey Ogboinba met and battled kings, sorcerers, deities, and magicians. In each meeting and contest Ogboinba declared her name, her story, and her determination, sang her incantations, circling round and round, countering her fabled opponents and gaining greater power so that when she came to crossing the primal sea, her bag of medicine was heavy with all she had won. They say that when, despite all warnings to turn back, she came, as no living being had ever come, to the place of beginning, God cursed her boldness for challenging fate and would have struck her down had Ogboinba not hidden in the eyes of a pregnant woman, where, according to the story, she remains, watching.*[1]

Our closing story telling begins with a journey of creation and the liminal figure of a woman in motion, stories within stories within her own. Countering the fragmentation of the broken calabash of Asante story, Ogboinba, the seer and healer, undertakes a journey embracing tropes of earth, tree, branch, and water crossing, stream and ocean. She is pounded and shaped, like grain into flour, below the communal gathering tree, by the water twice crossed. She remakes herself in the journey back and becomes a part of the endless cycle of being and transformation. Like early cosmological inscriptions of the mythical /Xam San woman, she rides the bull wind of her opponents and gathers power and knowledge. Like the Egyptian goddess Isis, she walks the cosmological terrain re-composing the torn body of the human migration. In this telling Ogboinba crosses deeply contested ground, brandishing her bold testimony and her circles of song as weapons and augmenting her power in her peregrinations.

**Journeys of Experience, Work, and Imagination: Playing Possum**

This West African story of Ogboinba's journey from the goddess/mother's womb into the vision of her womanhood transformed is a wonderfully suggestive allegory for the performance of blues-singing women and, closer at hand, the trails of women's songs of work and imagination that lead to them. African American women's work and play songs, and the blues that come out of them, engage with characteristically African modalities of storytelling, improvisational "bantering," and historical documentation, pairing song and dance in percussive, multi-metered, polyphonic call-and-response performance, to engage in circles of ancestry, articulation of journey, acts of witness, transformative pedagogy, and communal art making. These performances, in the African tradition, chronicle the diaspora's legacy, expressing both received values and cumulative historical knowledge.

Countering what novelist, critic, and theorist Ngũgĩ wa Thiong'o has called the "dismembering practices" of the European colonial "project," these performances are part of the dynamic lineage of linguistically subversive acts of agency, construction of identity, and cultural survival, of Africans kidnapped, brutalized, enslaved, and yet in perpetual vibrant resistance to slavery and dehumanization. In their performances African

American women who had been called "nigga," "heifer," "bitch," "sow," "breeder," "hoe," "hand"—less than fully human in the killing metonymy of "chattel" slavery—name themselves daughters, sisters, lovers, dreamers, dancers, workers, and survivors.

African Americanist theorists have identified "black culture" as a vessel of "black consciousness": the "signifying" acts and signal circle forms of African diaspora oral, performed, and literary tradition; the "flash of the spirit" of African art; and the shining continuum of "African art in motion," as well as the "reconstruction of womanhood" and "conjuring" in African American women's storytelling.[2] This final chapter begins with a look at performances of working that form a bridge into a blues closing. We pick up where we left off in the last chapter, with the voice of a little girl singing, dancing, and acting like a woman.

> Put your hand on your hips and let your mind roll forward.
> Back, back, back, back until you see the stars.
> Skip so lightly, shine so brightly,
> That is the Possum-a-la.
>
> "Possum-La," play song, twentieth century[3]

Skipping or shuffling around in a circle, "chugging" to the side with a deep knee bend on the word "Possum," clapping, patting, and heel tapping throughout, a little girl in Alabama performed the "Possum-La" for folklorists John and Alan Lomax in 1937. Her movement and song recalled the work songs, ring shouts, and Juba patting of the nineteenth century, as well as the older ritual theater forms they drew on, in a rite-of-passage play highlighting both continuity and change in diaspora performance. Hands on hips, arms akimbo, in her circling dance song storytelling, the little girl's Possum-La leads the way on a journey, in the African tradition, to "see the stars" and shine "so brightly," engaging beautifully with fable and allegory. Yet where African girls' rite-of-passage plays evoked the potter, the hunter, the snake, the zebra, the elephant, "Possum-La" plays with the phrase "playing possum," alluding to a creature who "plays" dead (or unconscious) when threatened and to a practice of feigning ignorance in self-protection. What a resonant image for cultural hermeneutics, the story within the story, from Alabama, a Creek place name that means "we may rest here."

> Possum up a that 'simmon tree
> Possum up a that 'simmon tree
> I don't see nothing but the 'simmon seed.
> Possum-la, possum-la, possum-la
> I don't see nothing but the 'simmon seed.
> I want you to catch that possum for me
> I want you to catch that possum for me
> I don't see nothing but the 'simmon seed.
>    "Possum-La," play song, twentieth century[4]

The little girl's performance had plenty of contemporary roots and branches. A "Possum-La" was "introduced" in an African American traveling show in 1895 and storyteller Bessie Jones recorded a related verse and play performance forty years later with a "focus on the fat possum" enjoying the fruit that is out of the singer's reach. The trickster possum and its partner Raccoon, a pair of small tree-dwelling animals who between them work night and day, appear often in the songs nineteenth-century African American women sang while working, songs that quickly entered the American popular "song book."

> Raccoon has a bushy tail Possum's tail is bare
> Rabbit's got no tail at all but a little bunch of hair.
> (Chorus)
> Bile them cabbage down, down
> Bake that hoe cake brown brown
> The only song that I can sing is
> Bile the cabbage down.
>    "Bile the Cabbage Down," work song, nineteenth century[5]

Work songs document the central experience in the lives of most Africans in the early history of the Americas who worked "from sun up until sundown," recognized the true extent of their worth, and despite the pervasive and horrific violence, brutality, and trauma of enslavement, drew sustenance from their own strength and accomplishments. When asked about source of a plantation owner's great wealth, an enslaved woman lifted and held out her lacerated arms, telling the story in a gesture.[6] Both Jacqueline Jones, in her *Labor of Love, Labor of Sorrow*, and Angela Davis, in her *Women, Race, and Class*, bring our attention to enslaved women's particular oppression and forms of resistance. Black women were mercilessly violated as women and exploited as workers and as the mothers of children who also would be consumed by the slave system, and they bore the weight of their bondage throughout the cycles of their lives. Yet they often met the challenges of their condition with incredible imagination and resilience, cultivating extraordinary internal resources, as they cultivated the world around them. Jones's history of black women's work paints a vivid description of the cycles of their physical labor.

> The rhythm of the planting-weeding-harvesting cycle shaped the lives of almost all American slaves, 95% of whom lived in rural areas. . . . Dressed in coarse osnaburg gowns; their skirts 'reefed up with a chord tied tightly around the body, a little above the hips . . . with their fathers, husbands, brothers, and sons, Black women spent up to fourteen hours a day toiling out of doors, often under a blazing sun. In the cotton belt they plowed fields; dropped seed; and hoed, picked, ginned sorted, and moted cotton. On farms in Virginia, North Carolina, Kentucky, and Tennessee, women hoed tobacco; laid worm fences; and threshed, raked, and bound wheat. For those on the Sea Islands and in coastal areas, rice culture included raking and burning the stubble from the previous year's crop; ditching; sowing seed; plowing, listing, and hoeing fields; and harvesting, stacking, and threshing the rice. In the bayou region of Louisiana, women planted sugar cane cuttings, plowed, and helped to harvest and gin the cane. During the winter they performed the myriad of tasks necessary on nineteenth century farms: repairing roads, pitching hay, burning brush, and setting up post and rail fences.[7]

The comments of an unnamed but deeply well-spoken WPA informant bring home the recognition of knowledge brought to and drawn from working:

> I am no mathematician, no biologist, neither grammarian; but when it comes to handling the Bible, I knocks down the verbs, breaks up prepositions and jumps over adjectives. I am a God sent man. All the education I got, it was out in the fields. That was my fountain pen and pencil. The blade of my hoe was my pen, and my slate was the ground. Now the law says "Black and white shan't mix." Who made that law? They made it. I made a law with my hoe, that all weeds must die that I hit.

African labor, knowledge, and vision laid the foundations for the European colonial settlements and "occupying" nations of the Americas and the Caribbean. Regional examples abound. Journalist Tim Hashaw, in his *The Birth of Black America*, draws on the Virginia historical record to show how the agricultural and husbandry skills of kidnaped and captive, and subsequently freed, *Malunga*, Africans were essential to the "success" of what had long been a failing colony. Before the arrival of the Africans, the settler colony of Virginia simply could not feed itself. In his *Black Majority*, historian Peter Wood writes that in South Carolina, as elsewhere, Africans were "the source of rice agriculture, new forms of cattle breeding and herding, boat building, inland water navigation, hunting and trapping, medicine and other innovations." According to Wood, "no development had greater impact upon the course of South Carolina history than the successful introduction of rice," a crop that European colonists had no familiarity with but that had long been cultivated in Africa, primarily by women. In his study Charles Joyner points out that the desire to "acquire" the rice cultivation skills of the people of the Senegal/Gambia region is clearly reflected in the records of colonial South Carolina's human trafficking and notes that "African and Afro-Carolinian methods of planting, hoeing, winnowing, and pounding (de-husking) persisted through slavery and on into recent years."[8]

> I got a rainbow
> Huh!
> Round my shoulder
> Huh!
> It ain't gonna rain

Huh!
It ain't gonna rain
Huh!

"Rainbow Round My Shoulder," work song, traditional

African diaspora performance records both physical and metaphysical labors in the dance of song. The "success" of the colonial project was due, in no small part, to the work ways of black men and women, in and despite their enslavement. A powerful component of those work ways was the role of communal song. This story is intrinsic to the interpretations offered by African American historians dating back to George Washington Williams's work in 1881 and is recorded in the histories the people sang.

Come on Mr. Tree
You almost down
Huh!
Come on Mr. Tree
Hit the ground
Huh!

Work song, traditional

The African tradition of communal work song was a tool for the survival and achievement of Africans laboring in the diaspora, and its performance is a recording of their historical contribution. The black sailors and pilots of eighteenth-century Caribbean and North American sea islands built boats, navigated them, and reportedly, "trained the boat hands to the oar" within rich performance traditions.[9] On land the practice of field hollers, whoops, and yodeling formed the basis of communication and coordination of work across distant rural locations and call-and-response singing coordinated the pace and spirit of group agricultural work in the sowing and harvesting of cotton, tobacco, and rice; the processing of grain; and the construction of buildings. That work was, in turn, chronicled in the songs the people were singing.

Work songs indelibly connect African American performance with ancestral and historical recognition, "bantering," social commentary, and communal articulation traditions of Africa.[10] The extemporaneous songs of Bambara women and the work songs of the diaspora live on a vibrant continuum. Africans, on the continent and in the diaspora, "danced" with work, composing histories of their journeys, their past and present, in these performance traditions. Work songs assisted the people in sustaining a sense of transcendent identity, agency, and authority and, as deeply pedagogical sites, are vessels of vision.

While most discussion of African American work songs is concerned with the experience of men, there is much to be learned from the experience told in the songs and narratives of women, which seamlessly blend stories of their particular journey, witness, and acts of transformation with folkloric allusions. From their lullabies to the songs they sang while working in the fields or cooking, women's performances of work are as much about story as about rhythm and pacing, intricately interweaving questions of work and freedom with ideas about love and relationships. And yes, her songs are about race, class, identity, "playing possum," domestic arts, cleaning, and cooking.

> Raccoon and the Possum
> Racklin cross the prairie
> Raccoon ask the Possum
> Do she want to marry
> Bile them cabbage down, down
> Bake that hoe cake brown, brown
> The only song that I can sing is
> Bile the cabbage down.[11]

One of the many women who recounted their experiences in slavery for the WPA remembered singing the above verse while working. The lines of this version of "Bile the Cabbage Down" alternate between a contemporary fable and a chorus that brings us back to the kitchen, staple foods, and cooking. Black women did the work of men and the work traditionally done by women and recorded that range of work, and how they felt about it, in their songs.

Work songs in a woman's voice narrate, in Zora Neale Hurston's words, "everything they don't want to forget" and pass on experience and instruction in their chronicling. Work and craft were important to these women. You got to brown that hoe cake and the cabbage needs to be thoroughly boiled "down." The narratives of many women who were enslaved give detailed descriptions of the consuming tasks of day-to-day rural life and of how they were done, properly. In her reminiscences Silvia Dubois, who served in a tavern, described how to make all kinds of brandy. Jenny Proctor and Millie Evans, two WPA informants, gave painstaking descriptions of how dyes were made from barks and plants, perfumes from flowers, winter sage gathered for brooms, wool corded, and cooking done "in swing pots" over a fireplace. Landscape and larder come together in these women's chronicles—the big picture and the microcosm. While Possum plays at marrying, our narrator keeps work on the domestic front going.[12]

In her oral history for the WPA, Jenny Proctor recalled folks "going to the cotton patch 'way before day a-singing 'Peggy Does you Love me Now.' One old man he sing":

> Saturday night and Sunday too
> Young gals on my mind
> Monday morning 'way for dau
> Old master got me going.
> Peggy does you love me now?
> Possum up a 'simmons tree,
> Rabbit on the ground.
> Lord, Lord possum
> Shake them 'simmons down.
> Peggy does you love me now
> Rabbit up a gum stump
> Possum up a holler.
> Get him out little boy
> And I'll give you half a dollar.
> Peggy does you love me now?

The sexual allusions in women's songs are a little different from those recorded in songs sung among men but do express the values women and men shared in recognition of work, kin, community, and testimony.[13]

Antebellum work songs in a woman's voice contain recollection, moral lessons, adult observations, social commentary, joke, and lament. And they play possum.

> Possum up in a 'simmon tree
> Raccoon on the ground
> Raccoon say to possum
> Won't you shake that 'simmon down.
> Bile them cabbage down
> Bile them cabbage down
> Look here gal don't want no fooling
> Bile them cabbage down.
> Went to Susy's house
> Bile them cabbage down
> Susy wasn't home
> Look here gal don't want no fooling
> Bile them cabbage down.
> My old missus promise me
> When she die she going to set me free.
> She live so long till her head got bald
> She give up the idea of dying at all.
> "Bile the Cabbage Down," twentieth century[14]

This version of "Bile the Cabbage Down / Possum and Raccoon" was recorded on St. Simons Island in the 1920s. It sings of women's work and community ties and of how, with mutuality, webs of kin, strict discipline, and a sense of humor in the telling, African American women attempted to navigate the fundamental injustice of their "historically" constructed situation. There is playful sexual connotation in the image of "shaking" the fruit down (which would surely be redoubled in accompanying motion), but the persimmon that is out of reach also represents a greater goal. Alternating verses, and lines, of allegory, instructional injunction, and reference to a web of female relations with the ditty about "missus" and her promise of manumission for the enslaved "when she die," the song plays smartly with history and double entendre. The often-unfulfilled promise of granting freedom to "a loyal servant" or "illegitimate" child in the last will and testament mirrors the refusal of the slave-owning class to let the system "die" with emancipation and belies the narrative of "benevolence" in structures and institutions of social domination. This note on the stubborn persistence of the iniquity of slavery brings the song poignantly into the early twentieth century, when the death grip of white racial and economic terror, violence, and institutionalized segregation continued to hold folks captive.

> We are the valiant soldiers, who've enlisted for the war,
> We are fighting for the union, we are fighting for the law
> We can shoot a rebel farther than a white man ever saw
> As we go marching on . . .
>
> (Chorus)
> Glory, glory hallelujah! Glory, glory hallelujah!
> Glory, glory hallelujah! As we go marching on.
>
> We are done with hoeing cotton, we are done with hoeing corn
> We are colored Yankee soldiers, as sure as you are born
> When massa hears us shouting, he will think its Gabriel's horn
> As we go marching on . . .
>
> They will have to pay us wages, the wages of their sin
> They will have to bow their foreheads to their colored kith and kin
> They will have to give us house-room or the roof will tumble in
> As we go marching on . . .
>
> We bare the proclamation, massa hush it as you will
> The birds will sing it to us. Hopping on the cotton hill
> The possum up the gum tree couldn't keep it still.
> As he went climbing on.[15]

In 1863, as African and African American men fought to enter "the fight" in uniform, Sojourner Truth rallied the troops of the First Michigan Regiment of Colored Soldiers by galvanizing historic banter, journey, witness, and transformative song traditions in her improvised "We Are the Valiant Soldiers." Her ballad, to the tune of "John Brown's Body," plays on folk references and revels in a pride of place drawn from experience. Like the antebellum song "No More Auction Block," her rhetorical performance revises the work songs of slavery toward an era of freedom and paid labor. "We can shoot a rebel farther," she sang, and "we mean to show Jeff Davis how the Africans can fight." In Truth's performance the people's work is the work for social justice and national as well as personal liberation. The possum, who can't keep still the echo of proclamation, "climbing on" as the soldiers "go marching," is clearly a political being.

**"I recollects just as bright as the stars be shining."**

> Shoo, fly don't bother me
> Shoo, fly don't bother
> Shoo, fly don't bother me
> Cause I belong to somebody.
>
> I feel, I feel, I feel
> I feel like a morning star
> I feel, I feel, I feel
> I feel like a morning star.
>
> "Shoo Fly," play/work song, late nineteenth century[16]

The work songs of nineteenth-century women, and men, chronicle the labors and imagining of people, old and young, often children, subverting the system of enslavement with the magic of dreams. Recollections from written narratives offer context for a complex reading of the line "cause I belong to somebody." "I played with the two children all day, then set the table," recalled Francis Black, who was born in Grand Bluff, Mississippi. "I was so small I'd get a chair to reach the dishes out of the safe. I had to pull a long fly brush over the table while the white folks ate."[17] Other women of Ms. Black's generation remembered similar chores as very small girls. In her oral history, Fairy Elkins told WPA interviewers, "After Miss come, I had to stay in the house with them and mind the flies off the table while the white folks eat. I had to do other things around the house too. We didn't have time to learn to read and write and I never went to school until after the war."[18]

Having small children fan flies was apparently common on the large estates of the slave economy. The young Equiano's first assignment on a Virginia plantation was the weird task of fanning the flies from the body of a sleeping man. Another unnamed but highly articulate storyteller whose oral history is recorded in Botkin's *Lay My Burden Down* remembered moving into the "big house" as soon as he was "big enough to step around."[19] He recalled how young girls were put to work gathering feathers and making fly brushes and how he, as a little one, was put to the task of fanning the table while perched in a swing suspended from the ceiling. In his recollection he was so young he "took to going to sleep up there." The exploitation and abuse of children as personal servants, sleeping at the foot of the bed or standing ready at the kitchen sideboard, was another painfully common feature of "the particular institution." In time, the informant continued, "they took down the swing and got a little gal to stand behind the missus chair and fan the flies. The missus allow to Master Johnson that the style done change, when he wants to know how come she took the swing down."[20] "Shoo Fly," a ditty that became a popular twentieth-century child's play, remembered by some WPA informants as a ring play or dance song and by others as a children's ring game, recalls the chore-laden childhoods of many nineteenth-century African American women and men who "never had time for any games."[21] The second stanza speaks to the unstoppable dreaming of small children fanning flies, though they were often under threat of severe punishment. A song of work rather than, strictly speaking, a work song (though it may well "dance" with the task of fanning flies), "Shoo Fly" bears witness to the conditions and the consciousness of children working. Might the morning star Venus in the east, an ancient point of metaphor and reference, also be a reference to the stellar pathways, like following the North Star, leading to freedom?

The lullabies their mothers sang to them were quickly passed on as little girls worked as nurses while they were still children themselves. Ellen Betts of Louisiana recalled of her childhood:

> I don't do nothing all my days but nurse, nurse, nurse. I nurse so many children it done went and stunt my growth.... When the colored

women had to cut cane all day till midnight come and after, I has to nurse the babies for them and the white children, too. Some of them babies so big and fat I had to tote the feet while another gal tote the head. I was such a little one, about seven or eight years old. When late of night come, if the babies wake up and bawl, I set up and out screech them till they shut they mouth.²²

Joanna Draper of Mississippi told WPA interviewers a similar story of a childhood spent taking care of other children. "When I was about six years old," she recalled, "they take me into the big house to learn to be a house woman, and they show me how to cook and clean up and take care of babies."²³ These were common childhood experiences among enslaved and free African American women, most of whom, as their songs remind us, had to attend to multiple shifts of domestic work, including field work, child care, and cooking. The narrative of Silvia Dubois and the fictionalized autobiography of Harriet Wilson, two nineteenth-century African American women who lived in the northeastern region of the United States, tell of childhoods bound out into domestic service, of cooking, sewing, washing, house cleaning, and taking care of white infants in return for meager room and board.

The work songs that coordinated group work, like field clearing, wood cutting, rowing, planting, and harvesting, also "danced" with the tasks, like cleaning, cooking, and childcare, that were usually done by small groups or individual women. "There was a song we usta sing about hoecake when we were making them," recalled WPA informant Harriet Jones, who had lived in both North Carolina and Texas as a young girl before the emancipation. Hers is a song of satire not very subtly masking rage:

> If you want to bake a hoecake
> To bake it good and done
> Slap it on a n——'s heel
> And hold it to the sun
> My Mammy baked a hoecake
> As big as Alabama
> She throwed it against a n——'s head

> And it ring just like a hammer
> The way to bake a hoecake
> The old Virginia way
> Wrap it around a n——'s stomach
> And hold it there all day.[24]

Ms. Jones also remembered songs, sung by women and men together in work gangs, that chronicle the complex oppressions of day-to-day history.

> It's a cool and frosty morning
> And the n——s goes to work
> With hoes on their shoulders
> Without a bit of shirt.[25]

Another song Ms. Jones recalled offers playful yet critical comment.

> I goes up on the meat skin
> I comes down on the pone
> I hits the corn pone fifty licks
> And makes the butter moan.

Her song echoes of the chronicling of economic injustice in the Juba and the spiritual "No More Auction Block"—the hard work, the peck of corn, the crust of bread, the meat skin—and expresses this recognition of injustice with humor and defiance.

"Women worked in the fields the same as the men," recalled George Fleming of Spartanburg, South Carolina, "some of them plowed just like the men and boys. Couldn't tell them apart in the field as they wore pantlets or breeches. They tied strings around the bottom of their legs so the loose dirt wouldn't get in their shoes."[26]

> Sometimes I feel like a motherless child
> Sometimes I feel like a motherless child
> Sometimes I feel like a motherless child
> Such a long long way from home.
>
> "Sometimes I Feel Like a Motherless Child," spiritual, traditional[27]

Throughout the antebellum period and into the post-Reconstruction era, African American women worked with men and as hard as men but were articulately conscious of the difference. The image of the "motherless child" far from home resounds through their storytelling as does the complexity of being powerful but constrained, "homemakers" in the homes of others, and nurses to children who were not their own, in addition to doing, as equals, the work "of men." Mary Kincheon Edwards was born in Baton Rouge, Louisiana. She recalled an average workday in the course of which she "wet nurse the baby son, what name was Elijah. Then I knit the socks and wash the clothes and sometimes I work in the fields and I helped make the baskets for cotton." Her story is illustrative: "I pick two and three hundred pounds in one day and one day I picked four hundred.... I so fast I take two rows at a time. The women bring oil cloths to the fields so they make a shady place for the children to sleep but them what's big enough has to pick. Sometimes they sing: o-he I's going home and cuss the old overseer."[28]

Exuberant or light, their song was resonant. John Moore, also of Louisiana, remembered picking corn, making molasses, and hearing the "corn hollers... my mother would jump up and sing."

> Sugar in the gourd
> Sugar in the gourd
> If you want to get
> The sugar out
> r-o-o-l-l the gourd over.[29]

Mr. Moore's memory illuminates a root poetic. Vocal elaborations, "moans," "field hollers," "whoops," and "shouts," which musicologists trace to the hockets and yodeling common to Central African and Khoisan languages, embellish a range of diaspora performance, including the work song. These song modalities and vocal techniques, rich with ostinato and onomatopoeia, come from a long history of casting sound—"throwing the voice"—against the canopy of tree and sky, over the distances of veld and forest, in calls to community, ancestry, and the divine. Those vocalizations continued to resound in the sacred hush arbors and over the fields of the diaspora. In these "talking drum" vocal forms, Africans in the diaspora sang yet another mapping of their journey, bearing witness to trials and sweetness, in performances fully embracing the dialectical possibilities of testimony and prayer. This sound play enlivens the work songs (in the emphatic "Huh!" at the end of a line) and later the blues and jazz "scatting," creating, in an ancient tradition, sites of expression, meditation, reflection, and power beyond words.

Wayman Williams of Mississippi recalled an aunt who split rails alongside men during the Reconstruction era. The song she sang "when she come down on a rail" plays in a familiar way with breath, vocal technique, and the turning of hard work into transformative song.

> Times are getting hard. (Biff)
> Money's getting scarce. (Biff)
> Times don't get no better here. (Biff)
> I'm bound to leave this place.[30]

The nature of African American women's work did not change significantly with the move from slavery to freedom. In the U.S. South, women continued to labor in agriculture as had their foremothers while struggling to locate themselves in relationship to mainstream concepts of gender and womanhood. Nineteenth-century African American women certainly recognized what we have come to call intersectionality and multiple oppressions. In her WPA oral history, Pauline Grice, who was born on a large plantation near Atlanta, Georgia, remembers, as did many informants, singing about cotton.

> Old cotton, old corn, see you every morn
> Old cotton, old corn, see you since I was born
> Old cotton, old corn, hoe you till dawn
> Old cotton, old corn, what for you born?[31]

Like the riddle of the sphinx, "Old Cotton Old Corn" narrates the parallel courses of a day, a life, and the cycles of agricultural seasons. The staple crops of North American slavery and industrialization were sung in many songs of both slavery and freedom, including the Juba songs and the monumental epic of liberation "No More Auction Block," which is also known by the line "Many Thousands Gone." The tonal burden of its rendering poignantly represents the physical and psychic weight of this work done in bondage. Songs about working cotton chronicle a labor history written by men and women who worked the crop from July through December and harvested it "carrying a bag strapped around the neck."[32]

Lydia Parrish recorded the following song in the Georgia Sea Islands in the 1920s:

> Way down in the bottom
> Where the cotton boll is rotten
> Won't get my hundred all day
> Before I'll be beated
> Before I'll be cheated
> I'll leave five fingers in the boll.
> Black man beat me.
> White man cheat me.
> Won't get my hundred all day.[33]

Observation and metaphor enrich these lyrics. Parsing the rich metonymy of the song, Parrish's informant explained that the five fingers referred to the compartments holding the bolls at the bottom of the cotton stalk. The "hundred" refers both to the 150 pounds of cotton a field worker, a field "hand," was "required" to pick in slave times and to the false promise of a living wage after emancipation. The rotten boll "down in the bottom" was both a real source of lost income as well as a symbol of systematic social disintegration and corruption. "Way Down in the Bottom" chronicles the multiple wages of new, and old, forms of slavery after emancipation, in which the people continue to be beaten in the fields and are now also cheated in the marketplaces of paid labor. Sea Island residents have a particular relationship to the "mainland" culture and economy, and this too is evident in the song. These were, in all cases, hard times. "I, as a colored woman have had in this country an education which has made me feel as if I were in the situation of Ishmael, my hand against every man and every man's hand against me," Francis Ellen Harper wrote of her experience within this crucible of crisis and exploitation.[34]

> Where do you come from
> Where do you go
> Where do you come from
> My cotton eyed Joe?
> If it hadn't been for, if it hadn't been for
> My cotton eyed Joe
> I'd have been married a long long time ago.
> Well I come from the east
> And I come from the south . . .
>
> "Cotton Eyed Joe," ballad, work song, traditional[35]

The folk ballad and work song "Cotton Eyed Joe" is akin to the songs of John Henry that were sung by workers on the railroad lines. "Cotton Eyed Joe," a lament of love unrequited and of a woman "waiting," tied to work at the expense of self-fulfillment, is also a symbolically rich song of disillusionment with the land's promise. African American women had been carried through the fields in their mother's wombs and on their backs and laid swaddled at the end of crop rows as infants, before taking up work in the fields themselves. They had a deep relationship to the crop, to the land, and to the nation that they had built. Gathering working knowledge in a woman's narrative, the song is a commentary on race, sex, and the failure of American democracy set in a story of love's betrayal. "Cotton Eyed Joe" is also a song of transcendence, a song that charts a journey in order to keep moving, a song that sings of the experience, work, and imagination, that brings a young girl into adulthood knowing, and motion, at the turn of the twentieth century.

## Poor Rosy, Trouble and Transformation

> Poor Rosy, poor gal
> Poor Rosy, poor gal
> Rosy break my poor heart
> Heaven shall be my home.
> I can not stay in hell one day
> Heaven shall be my home

> I'll sing and pray my soul away
> Heaven shall be my home.
>
> "Poor Rosy," work song, nineteenth century[36]

"I like 'Poor Rosy' better than all the rest but it can't be sung without a full heart and a troubled spirit," a woman of Port Royal told song collector Lucy McKim, dismissing children's performances of the song as mere copying.[37] McKim was an abolitionist and a trained musician working among the newly emancipated African American community of Port Royal, South Carolina, at the beginning of the American Civil War. McKim reports that her informant was "a respectable house servant who had lost all but one of her twenty two children." "Poor Rosy" was known on many stages. Du Bois speaks of this lament of love as "among the oldest" of the sorrow songs and closes his classic study, *The Souls of Black Folks*, with its refrain. The collective song memory, including the oral histories of WPA informants, remembers "Poor Rosy" as a reel, a ring play, a love song to a dance tune, a spiritual, and a work song.

Carolina and Georgia boat men sang "Poor Rosy" as they rowed barges along the vast island channels, and women sang versions set to the pace of a hominy mill's grinding stone.[38] Several variations on this antebellum song to "Rosy" were still sung, shaped to the cadences of hard labor on southern prison work gangs, when John and Alan Lomax recorded the voices and folklore of men incarcerated in the American penal system in 1933.[39]

> Hard trials on my way
> Hard trials in my way
> Hard trials in my way
> Heaven shall be my home
>
> "Poor Rosy," second stanza

"Poor Rosy" was among the first of the African American songs to be chronicled in what was to become a growing popular recognition of the cultural heritage of American song, and its publication in *Dwight's Journal* during the Civil War marks a milestone in North American musicology and cultural documentation. Within the song are echoes of the old work songs of Africa, remnants of sacred circles, rings of play and transformation, and the lullabies of women with babes in arms, as well as the genesis of the blues. Most of the early Port Royal chroniclers marveled at the versatility of song in a community where day-to-day tasks were all accompanied and coordinated by singing. African practices of coordinating group work, communal creation, teaching, and documentation in work songs are a powerful component of the African diaspora legacy.[40] "Poor Rosy" in its multiple incarnations reminds us of the African conception of absolute webs of connection between the sacred and the secular, the living and the dead, art and life, philosophical constructs sufficiently different than prevailing Western notions.[41] At its heart "Poor Rosy" is a performance of journey and motion, a journey toward freedom and a motion toward home.

> When I talk I talk with God
> When I talk I talk with God
> When I talk I talk with God
> Heaven shall be my home.
> "Poor Rosy," third stanza

Like all work songs, "Poor Rosy" artfully engages with dualities, with "hard trials," with dreams and visions, and composes new locations within. The song bears witness to the overwhelming "hell" of the present and to its own power, to "talk with god" and "sing and pray my soul away," as a vehicle for transformation. The singer calls to mind the Bakongo understanding of a god in which the petitioner is in direct contact. "When I talk," according to the song, "I talk with God. Heaven shall be my home." In concentric circles of dialogue, the singer expresses frustration with the limitations of this world and knowledge of a divine one. From the interconnected stages of daily experience, "Poor Rosy" sings of both the overwhelming reality of slavery and the inexorable human presence within it.[42] Interweaving questions of self and relations, personal and community mobility, work, love, and freedom, the complex antiphony of "Poor Rosy" recalls the voice of "Cotton Eyed Joe" in its existential expression. As

McKim's female informant underscores, the true performance of "Poor Rosy" is wrought from adult understanding.

> I don't know what people want of me
> Heaven shall be my home
>> "Poor Rosy," fourth stanza

One story, published by Northerners who lived and worked among the people of Port Royal during the Civil War, connects "Poor Rosy" with the story of an enslaved man named Caesar.[43] According to this chronicle, Caesar related his experience of the early 1820s some forty years later. Caesar claimed to have been the author of the song or at least its partial subject. He said he had been in love with a woman named Rosy who broke his heart. Subsequently, Caesar became interested in an African colonization project but was unable to purchase his freedom and take leave of the "hell" he was in without his love.

The anecdotal story of Caesar touches on some essential quests and questions in the lives of African Americans during the period of Civil War and Reconstruction. Their existential quest was for a place to call home. The question was how to navigate political condition, history, distance, and time. Some were still reaching, as did the earliest Africans enslaved in these regions, for a return to an African motherland. Others were struggling to make, to claim, a home in these lands. For all African Americans, the question of "home" sat beside the question freedom. In literary narrative and vernacular performance forms, people wondered about the meaning, and range of motion, of their "emancipation," and the economic requirements of living as free men and women composing "home." "Poor Rosy," like many songs of women's sacred, work, and play performance, necessarily complicates the question of freedom by asking about love and its fetters or wings. Caesar, according to the story, can neither be with the woman he loves in these United States nor buy his freedom from bondage in this place to reconstruct an African homeland. His conundrum is analogous to that of African Americans of the period, free or enslaved, and this conundrum is at the root of a performance of lament, of witness to "trouble" and hard times, which is also a performance of agency and, in the telling, an act of transformation.

## Blues Opening

> Nobody knows the trouble I see. Nobody knows but Jesus.
> Nobody knows the trouble I see. Glory hallelu!
>
> "Nobody Knows the Trouble I See," spiritual, traditional, nineteenth century[44]

In "Of the Sorrow Songs," W. E. B. Du Bois called "Nobody Knows the Trouble I See" one of the "ten master songs," a work "of undoubted Negro origin, and wide popular currency," a work "particularly characteristic of the slave."[45] "Nobody Knows the Trouble" is known widely throughout the Americas and the English-speaking Caribbean. According to one strand of North American lore, "Nobody Knows the Trouble I See" was also composed as the lament of an enslaved black man.[46] Having been torn from his family by slavery, the anonymous bard "poured" his story into this song.[47] His "slave song" weaves its way through the oral tradition, singing a universal journey.

> One morning I was a-walking down,
> O yes, Lord!
> I saw some berries a-hanging down,
> O yes, Lord!
>
> "Nobody Knows the Trouble I See," second stanza

A complementary history comes from the South Carolina and Georgia region. Between 1861 and 1865 the people of Port Royal in the Georgia Sea Islands participated in one of the nation's first democratic experiments. Self-emancipated upon the arrival of Union troops and the total exodus of a fleeing white planter class, the African American people of Port Royal cast off slavery and immediately applied themselves to fully active citizenship. They stepped into the civic vacuum in their war-liberated city, took up the work of governance, created institutional structures to support the polity and a civil society, and began to "imagine freedom." Visited upon by Northern teachers, politicians, abolitionists, song chroniclers like McKim, "carpetbaggers," missionaries, and government agents of a nascent Freedmen's Bureau, the people of Port Royal engaged in an extraordinary experiment with the possibilities of free labor and reconstruction of the torn body politic. During this brief period, they composed and began to implement an agenda of land redistribution, labor organization, governance, and educational reconstruction—a model for liberty and democracy after the war.

> I pick the berry and I suck the juice.
> O yes, Lord,
> Just as sweet as the honey in de comb.
> O yes, Lord.
>> "Nobody Knows the Trouble I See," third stanza

The people of Port Royal and their progressive allies focused their energies on education and land, but soon, at the war's end, their plans and hopes, and those of a nation, for "radical reconstruction" were dashed. The "hostilities" were over, Lincoln had been assassinated, and by the fall of the year of general emancipation, the U.S. government was refusing to continue to meet its promise of land and protection for freedmen. With the old planter class re-enfranchised and returning, the newly freed people would be again landless. Given the extent and authority of this community's political accomplishment, a U.S. general came to speak before a Port Royal town meeting to present the current government rulings. Some no doubt argued this betrayal. The residents of Port Royal knew that their labor had given the land value and that, in this sense, the land was rightfully theirs. But this was the final word from the government. There would be no more money, federal troops, or legislative support to protect the freed people's citizenship.

According to reports from this historic gathering, on the outskirts of the crowd a woman began to sing the sorrowful chorus of "Nobody Knows the Trouble I See" and soon the meeting house was enveloped in communal voice.[48] A voice of deep and long experience that was also prophetic:

> Sometimes I'm up
> Sometimes I'm down

Sometimes I'm almost on the ground.
"Nobody Knows the Trouble I See," alternate third stanza[49]

"Nobody Knows the Trouble I See" is history written in song. Its three-line stanzas, its flat third, its blue notes, and its worldly concern restate traditions of communal witness and a lineage of testifying. Its words bear witness to a journey, to a knowing, and to a recognition that the question of freedom was and remained in the people's own hands.[50]

What makes Satan hate me so?
Because he had me once and he let me go.
"Nobody Knows the Trouble I See," alternate fourth stanza[51]

The song sings of personal "trouble" and situates the trouble within a larger struggle, a struggle represented in mythic terms. Speaking to political debates on the war, the Union, and the role of the African American, as well as to the still ongoing discourse about race in the United States, the song recognizes that the singer alone knows and can tell the entire story of this troubled American history.[52] The singer, the Africans, and the carpenter Jesus, whose birth, journey through life, and crucifixion mirrored the experience of African Americans, and whose resurrection symbolized the endless cycling of the seasons and the promise of redemption.[53] "Sometimes I'm up, sometimes I'm down, sometimes I'm almost on the ground," the song sings, like the motherless child, of flying "like an eagle in the air" and of falling "a long way from home." Or "like a morning star"—brilliant with a vision wrought from the long lonely journey. "Nobody Knows the Trouble I See" represents the African American journey as universal experience.

The woman who stood in the Port Royal assembly stood as a witness, a cipher, to sing of trouble, of knowledge, and like the fabled Ogboinba the healer, of being baptized by the waters she has crossed over. In Port Royal, as the people wrestled to turn from slavery to freedom, the woman called and the community responded in song. Those strains, her solitary lead to that of the voices gathering, forms a bridge between a folk past of communal work and communally articulated narrative to what would be a future of life and work, a blues song, composed of old identities constantly transforming in motion.

### Making and Moving Knowledge

> Now I'm troubled in mind! I'm so troubled in mind!
> I ask good Lord to show me the way to ease my troubled in mind!
>
> "Troubled in Mind," spiritual, traditional, nineteenth-century version[54]

> Trouble in mind I'm blue
> But I won't be blue always
> Cause the sun's gonna shine
> In my back door someday.
> I'm gonna lay my head
> On a lonesome railroad line
>
> "Trouble in Mind," blues, traditional, twentieth-century version[55]

The movement from "I'm So Troubled in Mind" and "Nobody Knows the Trouble I See" to the lonely refrain of the blues song "Trouble in Mind" begins with the transplanted epistemology of an African home and takes root in fragmentation and reintegration of the African diaspora. The arc of performance moves from a communal voice, displaced and yet rooted, to a solo voice, singing its own strophe and antistrophe, in motion. At every point along this journey, the performance is about making and moving knowledge, from experience and work, toward home and freedom. And this journey in song sings the Great Migration, a historic mass movement and demographic shifting of the African American population.

The postwar period was marked by industrialization, protracted civil and economic strife, and violence against black folks. This period was also marked by extraordinary determination on the part of African Americans to re-create themselves as free women and men. Their new renditions of the old songs sing that the way to ease the trouble in mind, in slavery and freedom, had everything to do with embracing continuities and change and continuing to produce knowledge in performance while transforming and moving that knowledge.

> If I live
> Sangaree

Don't get kill
Sangaree
I'm going back
Sangaree
To Jacksonville
Sangaree
If I live
Sangaree
See next fall
Sangaree
Ain't going to plant
Sangaree
No cotton at all.

"Sangaree," ring play, late nineteenth / early twentieth century[56]

The vast majority of African Americans remained tied to the land during this period, planting and harvesting crops in the North American south as they had under slavery. The fundamental economic relationships remained the same. Black people worked, enriched, but had been and remained systemically excluded from ownership of the land. African Americans knew that there were other possibilities and were determined to seize the ring of opportunity by migrating to cities like Jacksonville in search of another way of life. The songs tell this story and remind us that the people saw sharecropping, tenant farming, and trying to make some money with their crop as the first step in a longer process. This version of the ring play "Sangaree" mimics the cadence of the work song, remembering the old ways of working and the dreams that would carry the people onto new horizons. The repeated line "If I live and don't get killed" gives a nod to the formidable odds against them.

According to Parrish, whose Georgia Sea Island informants provided several verses of the song, "Sangaree" can be dated from its refrain. The "julep sangaree," a Caribbean recipe mixing wine, sugar, nutmeg, and water, was popular among antebellum planters before the 1840s. The close colonial ties between the British West Indies and South Carolina, including the role of the West Indian planters and the sugar industry in fostering North American slavery, are infamous. Parrish also notes linguist Darwin Turner's belief that the term "sangaree" was derived from *sangari*, a Mende word for ring dance.

> Times getting hard
> Times getting hard
> Money getting scarce
> Soon as I sell my cotton and corn
> I'm going to leave this place
> Going down town
> Going down town
> Going down to Lynchburg town
> Take my tobacco down.
>    "Lynchburg Town," work song, nineteenth century[57]

"Lynchburg Town," according to Alan Lomax, draws from folk roots. It was first published in prewar minstrel songbooks and had a popular resurgence during the period of postwar migrations.[58] After the Civil War, work remained a central issue in the lives of African Americans, and people navigated between the economies of different labor forms, the ability to define their own work, and the ever-present threat of racial, and sexual, violence. The songs sing the conundrum of their situation. Black families saw sharecropping, primarily in cotton and tobacco, as one of the few available means of working toward economic independence. Despite tremendous odds, as the song sings, people held on to the hope that, with the next crop, they could buy themselves out. No doubt some imagined themselves "inching along" as in the song.

> Keep inching along, inching along
> Jesus will come by and by
> Keep inching along like a poor inch worm
> Jesus will come by and by.
> When I get to heaven, be able to tell

Two archangels gonna toll the bell.
When I get to heaven, ain't I gonna shout.
Nobody there to put me out.
Ever since my lord set me free
This world's been a hell to me.
   "Keep Inching Along," spiritual, traditional, nineteenth-century version[59]

Progress on these goals was slow and long in coming. With few other viable options, many families continued to farm shares of rented land in return for a percentage of their harvest, though the corruption of the sharecropping and tenant-farming systems are legend. From the war years and the emancipation on, a clear priority for the newly freed men and women was breaking free of the gang work system of slavery and extricating African American women from field work and domestic work in white households.[60] Increasingly African American women turned to self-employment alternatives like marketing, cooking, and laundry work in their own homes. These economic juggling acts fed into the migrations of African Americans who joined in the "exodus" of 1881 to 1915 by seeking better deals at the end of each contract and moving a little at a time toward the southern cities and "up north."

Black women attempted to use the new possibilities to remove themselves psychology as well as physically from the "hell" of racial violence, economic disenfranchisement, and the sexual abuse of white men. In her *Reconstructing Womanhood* Hazel Carby examines the roots and branches of a new imagination of female identity in nineteenth-century America. By the 1890s African American women channeled their traditions of community service into public political engagement, and activists like Francis Watkins Harper and Ida B. Wells moved the feminist abolitionist legacy of women like Harriet Tubman, Sojourner Truth, and Maria Stewart into the crafting of the public, capable, and community-serving presentation of a new womanhood. Black women were reconstructing ideas of womanhood and reimagining themselves through work and migration. The realities they faced, and their imagined flights, are poignantly expressed in song.

> They tell me Joe Turner's come and gone
> They tell me Joe Turner's come and gone
> Got my man and gone.
> He come with forty links of chain
> He come with forty links of chain
> Got my man and gone.
> They tell me Joe Turner's come and gone
> They tell me Joe Turner's come and gone
> Done left me here to sing this song.
> Come like he never come before
> Come like he never come before
> Got my man and gone.
>
> "Joe Turner," blues, nineteenth century

A substantial body of African American song bears witness to both the man-made and the natural disasters that compelled the movements of the Great Migration. Among these histories in song is "Joe Turner." "Joe Turner" is among the oldest recorded blues songs and, according to a number of musicians and musicologists, the musical basis for much of the classical blues.[61] It was recorded in the early 1890s, just seven years after the Supreme Court of the United States ruled the Civil Rights Bill of 1873 unconstitutional, right around the time of the fabled death of John Henry. "Joe Turner" is a song in a woman's voice and remembers African Americans' continuing experience of institutionalized racial violence and of families being torn apart by systemized racialized incarceration.

When newly emancipated African Americans attempted to flex the power of their citizenship and their capacity as laborers, as had the citizens of Port Royal, the forces of racial hegemony lashed out with increasing vengeance against the freedmen and women. W. E. B. Du Bois wrote of a "return to slavery" in the "black codes," forced labor, debt peonage, massive incarcerations, labor gang conscription, and unbridled racial and economic terrorism exacted, by the state itself, against African Americans during this period. Chain gangs, Jim Crow laws, lynchings, and other forms of mob violence were the weapons of a despotism that did not want to die.

In 1892 Memphis-based journalist Ida B. Wells reported that there had been more mob murders of African Americans the first year of the 1890s than in any previous year on record. In a series of articles that was later published as a booklet titled *Southern Horror: Lynch Law in All Its Phases*, Wells pointed out that lynching was a tool of white economic and social domination and called out the shameful history of the rape of African American women by white men. Black men, Wells wrote, were being accused of crimes that they had not committed in order to further a system of disenfranchisement and exploitation and to distort a long history of white supremacist violence and abuse. Wells was run out of town, her press was looted and burned down, and her life threatened.[62]

Southern's *The Music of Black Americans* recounts the history of "Joe Turner."[63] In the early 1890s a white man by the name of Pete Turney was governor of Tennessee and made his brother Joe the "long chain man" for the prison work gangs that had become a specter of the rule of race in the turn-of-the-century American South. The job of the long chain man was to transport men incarcerated on work gangs from one state to another. The men on those work gangs, many of whom had been arrested on fictitious, trumped up, politically motivated charges, were hired out to the highest bidder and forced to labor at the hardest and least socially desirable tasks while chained together hand and foot.

Though "he come like he never come before" the chain gangs were all too similar to the "slave coffles" of an earlier era.[64] And there is a troubling contemporary commentary in the way that the songs of slavery have survived into the modern era in the penal camps and on the work gangs of Louisiana, Texas, and other southern states.[65]

> The first time I saw boll weevil
> He was sitting on the square
> The next time I saw boll weevil
> He had all his family there
> They looking for a home
> Just a-looking for a home . . .
> If anybody asks you

> Who was it wrote this song
> Tell them it was a dark-skinned farmer
> With a wild pair of blue ducklings
> A-looking for a home
> Just a-looking for a home
>
> "The Boll Weevil," ballad, early twentieth century[66]

"The Ballad of the Boll Weevil" also sits at the crossroads shaping the blues tradition and documents the historical factors that got a rurally based people moving. The African American ballad, a multi-verse song form, developed in an interactive relationship with some of the European ballads and similar African epics, combines storytelling with social commentary in continuing the lineage of witness. The many versions of the song "Boll Weevil" are work songs with clear connections to historical events. Just after the turn of the century an infestation of a pest called the boll weevil swept across the southern states, destroying cotton crops and putting already hard-pressed tenant and sharecropping farmers out of home and work. The song's verses approach the life story of a plague with vernacular wisdom, comment derisively on "scientific" methods used against the insect, and identify with the boll weevil's migratory search for home. Lomax's informant on the song explains with a ditty: "The cotton bush his shade / Its roots his cook kitchen / The boll his dining room / where he do all his eating."[67]

> When I was young I used to wait
> On master and give him his plate
> And pass the bottle when he got dry
> And brush away the blue tailed fly . . .
> Old massa's dead and gone to rest
> They things is for the best
> I'll never forget till the day I die
> Old massa and the blue tailed fly.

In the popular ballad "The Blue Tailed Fly" the servant has outlived the master to sing the praises of an even "lesser" creature. Lomax reports that "The Blue Tailed Fly" was written by an abolitionist and that the popular chorus, "Jimmy crack corn and I don't care, my master's gone away," is said to be of "slave origins."[68]

While there is much apparent truth in the comment that "the blues has always been around," the proliferation of the form from the late nineteenth century into the twentieth sings of the motions of African American consciousness and imagination.[69]

> Riding in a buggy, Miss Mary Jane
> Miss Mary Jane Miss Mary Jane
> Riding in a buggy, Miss Mary Jane
> I'm a long way from home
> Who moan for me
> Who moan for me
> Who moan for me my darling?
> Sally got a house in Baltimore
> Baltimore, Baltimore
> Sally got a house in Baltimore
> And it's ten stories high.
> Sally got a house in Baltimore
> Baltimore, Baltimore
> Sally got a house in Baltimore
> And it's full of chicken pie.
>
> "Miss Mary Jane," African American game song, nineteenth century[70]

In their search for a home, thousands of African Americans migrated to cities, taking the cries of the country with them. Pre–Civil War folkloric reels like "Lynchburg Town" followed African American performers into the earliest American theaters and into the street culture of urban African American communities, and the testimonies and instructional tales embedded in lullabies and rite-of-passage plays reappear in girls' street games and women's blues. While retaining their African markings, the performances of women in the twentieth century sing and dance shifting perceptions, bearing witnesses to both old problems and new conundrums. Though Miss Mary Jane may ride in a buggy and Sally has a house in Baltimore, the refrain of the song grieves and wonders who will moan for the "poor girl a long way from home."

Rosy, Possum, Morning Star

**Blues Closing**

> Poor gal a long ways from home
> Poor gal a long ways from home
> I'm a poor gal a long ways from home.[71]

Asked for her memories of North American slavery, Lucy Galloway of Harrison County, Mississippi, recalled:

> One gal that come from Africa. She was a poor African that had long hair and plait it in two long braids down her back and tie it with a red ribbon bow. She say that they put her on a block to sell, they told her to dance for them. She sure was a good dancer. She dance the same way what she did in Africa and what she had learned there. She was fifteen when they bring her over here. They bought her in South Carolina from a speculator. She said she was a slave in Africa. Lucy (the girl) was smart and clean as a pin.[72]

"Poor Gal" that she was Lucy could dance. If we could see her dance, on an auction block, in a strange country, speaking at least two languages at once, knowing what we know, we would know infinitely more. At least some of the possibilities for looking back through the lives between Lucy's and our own are in our ability to recognize and hear her storytelling. Was Lucy's movement a precursor to the "Possum-La"? Might we see her footprints in the "morning star" and "the motherless child," in "Cotton Eyed Joe," in "Poor Rosy's" song, and in the articulation of the Port Royal woman who inscribed the complexity of U.S. Reconstruction when she stood up in a meeting house, in 1865, to sing "Nobody Knows the Trouble I've Seen"? Surely her blues dance was shaped by the currents of Ogboinba's epic journey, witnessing, and transformation, which would continue to ebb and flow in the performance of women's work and play songs and into the oft-repeated refrain of "The East Coast Blues."

"The blues have always been," an old school fiddler in New Orleans is reported to have "scoffed" when asked about the music's origins.[73] He surely could have been speaking of Lucy's hard trials, and determination, of the trouble in mind as a kidnapped woman stands before a cannibalizing crowd, dancing. In this spirit our story ends where it began. From African women a long way from home to African American women wresting home from a stony ground, what we have come to call the blues is a way station in the journey toward remembering.

> I live four miles out of town
> I am gone to glory
> My strawberries are so sweet and sound
> I am gone to glory
> I brought them four miles on my head
> I am gone to glory
> My child is sick my husbands dead
> I am gone to glory
> Nows the time to get them cheap
> I am gone to glory
> Eat them with your bread and meat
> I am gone to glory
> Come sinner get down on your knees
> I am gone to glory
> Eat these strawberries when you please
> I am gone to glory.[74]

The journey of that "poor gal" was a constant refrain in early twentieth-century African American performance, and this strawberry vendor's song, recorded by novelist William Wells Brown, sings and dances her trails, trials, and tribulations. African American women who were women identified, women on their own, single, divorced, or widowed women made up an overwhelming percentage of those who moved into cities on the current of the Great Migration, and their songs dominate the early blues record. The street vendor's song is an illustration and example of how, in the bantering traditions of old, women were imagining, constructing, and reconstructing their lives in performance. The fragmentation of loss, through war and displacement, is the warp of her song. Yet the weave is her transforming recognition that "I'm gone to glory" and the agency expressed by her bold testimony at work. In this tapestry the singer takes the shards of her experience of work and migration, ancestry and journey, and redefines herself in song.

The performances of the early blues-singing women drew on the wandering epics of street vendors and traveling bards moving the songs of the country into an urbanizing century. Their twentieth-century histories in song revise the trope of the "poor gal," the "motherless child" a long way from home, the lone star and the solitary eagle in the air. As some made their way, and their living, performing on the African American theater circuit, on the "formal" concert stage, and with the traveling theater companies of the late nineteenth and early twentieth centuries, these women signified the changed construction of African American identity and community in professional performance while continually remembering and representing the folk roots of their narratives. Despite the fact that, with the exceptional nod to the classic blues-singing women, the blues has been often understood as a male form, the female voice is also at its genesis.[75] For while it was generally understood that, in the oft-used refrain, "when a man gets the blues he jumps a train and rides, when a woman gets the blues she just hangs her head and cries," women *moved* in a number of ways between 1880 and 1930, and their performances contain the record of these currents of motion.

> House catch on fire and ain't no water round
> If your house catch on fire ain't no water round
> Throw your trunk out the window building burn on down.
> Gertrude "Ma" Rainey, "Southern Blues"

Gertrude "Ma" Rainey, the premier blues singer of the early twentieth century, first heard the form she would call the blues being sung by another woman performer in Missouri in 1902. Like the spirituals and folk performance of "home," it was a strophic song, built from musical phrases of three short lines. Like "Poor Rosy" and "Cotton Eyed Joe," the song sang of failed love in a woman's voice. Rainey remembered it as both familiar and strangely new and haunting. W. C. Handy, who is often called "the father of the blues," recalls a similar experience in 1903, recognizing the music of his Alabama home in the "weird" song of a man playing his guitar in a

Mississippi train station.[76] In the juke joint, in the train station, unhinged from their rural roots, the familiar field hollers, work songs, whoops, moans, spirituals, and shouts bore a new patina of sound.

Rainey's own life and oeuvre embodies the motion of African American cultural migration and the journey of song. Rainey was born Gertrude Malissa Nix Pridgitt in Columbus, Georgia, in 1886. She began to perform in southern traveling shows, "tent shows," carnivals, and minstrel shows when she was fourteen and was popularly acclaimed, before ever recording, for her deep connection to folk traditions. The poet Sterling Brown wrote, in his often-cited paean to Rainey, about how she "get way inside of us . . . keep us strong . . . jes' catch a hold of us somekindaway."[77] Rainey sang of journey and, inherently, of ancestry, and her songs bear witness to the act of wresting agency and authority from "hard luck roun' our do.'" In her *Blues Legacies* Angela Davis notes that Rainey's turn-of-the-century song titles are "permeated with travel themes: 'Leavin' This Morning,' 'Traveling Blues,' 'Walking Blues,' and 'Runaway Blues.'"[78] Rainey sang of the experiences of African Americans and offered biting commentary on some of the concerns of women.

The metaphors in Rainey's "Southern Blues" encourage a layered reading, from the image of the burning house to the unrequited love to whom she sings "let me be your rag doll till your chiny come." Rainey's lyrics play with the idea of the "house" of conventional domesticity, and her warning, despite her self-effacing invitation, is to get out before the building burns down. For African American women the concept of domestic safety had always been, at best, an elusive one. "City women" and blues women had left even the idea of the safety of the hearth, and the protection of a man, behind. Referencing and revising a long tradition of work songs, "Southern Blues" also alludes to the burning house of the American South. When Billie Holiday recorded "Strange Fruit" in 1939, the allusion to the horror of mob violence and lynching was clear. The racial violence and economic disenfranchisement of the American South frames "Southern Blues" for Rainey's African American audiences. Those audiences also knew that the North was not the hoped-for land of promise and were aware of the experiences of the "poor gal" making her way without conventional social and material support. Rainey sang of the poor gals' situation in a form that was cathartic and liberating.

> I'm going away and it won't be long
> I know you'll miss me from singing this lonesome song
> Lottie Kimbrough, "Going Away Blues," 1927[79]

The women and men who left the burning house of the South did so in response to personal, political, and economic struggles that had everything to do with race and sex. The performances of the early blues-singing women are full of bravado and daring that breaks away from dominant race and gender ideologies. As Davis points out, there are few if any references to marriage or children in women's blues.[80] Their reclaimed griot's songs are itinerant, "lonesome" but potent, representations of the polyphonic music, the antiphonal dialogue, essential to African traditions.

> One John in the city one lives up on the hill
> But the man I love lives in Jacksonville.
> Nellie Florence, "Jacksonville Blues," Columbia, 1928, last stanza[81]

Nellie Florence's "Jacksonville Blues" begins with a farewell that revises the lullabies of slavery, then goes on to incorporate folk play with adult sexual allusion and the self-actuating performance of girls' circle games to articulate a vision of female sexuality and identity that plays hard against the norm. Florence is of course also playing off other texts singing of disillusionment and a determination to keep moving. The traditional "Third Alley Blues" is one of these songs.

> I just want to get back to Birmingham . . .
> I'd rather be in third alley without a dime . . .
> Than be in Chicago wasting my time.
> Ivy Smith, "Third Alley Blues," Document Records, 1927[82]

The blues sing of sorrow toward transcending. Like the ring shouts and the healing circles of old, blues performance engages with the creation of liminal space, through formal strophic acts of witness, and provides a forum for recognition and transformation. Contemporary scholars Angela Davis and James Cone, in their studies of the form, underscore the intersection between the blues and the spirituals. Blues-singing women wrest transformational space, for themselves and their audiences, with their storytelling. African American audiences in particular recognized how, in the words of the poet, Ma Rainey "jes' catch a hold of us somekindaway." Meditating on the phenomena brings to mind Federico Garcia Lorca's writing about the concept of Duende.

> Nobody knows my name . . .
> See that lonesome road? Lord you know its gotta end.
> Bessie Smith, "Young Woman's Blues," Columbia, 1926, first and last stanzas[83]

The collective autobiography written in performance is told anew in the blues of the twentieth century. Bessie Smith's "Young Woman's Blues," recorded in 1926, brings us back to the challenge posed at the end of the Civil War in "Nobody Knows the Trouble I See." The loneliness she sings of is the price of forging a path and coming into a new knowledge.

> I woke up this morning couldn't even get outta my door
> There's enough trouble to make a poor girl wonder
> Where she want to go
> Bessie Smith, "Back Water Blues," Columbia Records, 1927[84]

Smith's "Backwater Blues" takes us back to the primeval waters and the mountaintop of vision and witness in African American performance traditions, back to the Middle Passage and the endless search for home in the diasporic imagination. The song recounts the story of the Great Mississippi Flood of 1927, a natural disaster exacerbated by the human tragedy of racism and mob violence. The historical memory sets the song in epic terms. "When it thunders and lightening and the wind begins to blow. . . . There's thousands of people ain't got no place to go." Witnessing this crisis Smith "went and stood up on a high lonesome hill . . . and looked down on the house where I usta live," bemoaning that now "I can't live there no more," though "there ain't no place for a poor girl to go."

5. George "Geo" Smith, *Dance Sister*. Courtesy of the artist and the artist's estate.

# CODA
Circling Back Around

*Scene. Predawn. Central African village. From a darkened stage we hear the voices of women punctuated by the rhythmic pounding of their mortars. Lights up on a woman and a girl working. Pounding corn.*

> Lilo ntwe Mama (I am pounding corn today Mama.)
> Milo ntwe (I am pounding corn tomorrow.)
> Lilo ntwe Mama (I am pounding corn today Mama.)
> Milo ntwe (I am pounding corn tomorrow.)
>   "Corn Pounding Song," Zambia, twenty-first century[1]

When prompted to bring her native language and song into our study with very young children, Mbachi Kumwenda, a Zambian woman in one of my learning communities at the Hayground School, shared first a lullaby and then taught us this corn-pounding song. The lullaby was pure onomatopoeia, and the children and I immediately recognized her Nyanga rendition of the sound of a baby crying. Our group of four- and five-year-olds, and two women, intuitively connected with the song's simultaneous presentation of sound and meaning. Nahki presciently began singing the lullaby to the child he understood was in his teacher's womb. We similarly learned the corn-pounding song, though without the necessary stampers or corn, as is traditionally the case, through its rhythm.

**Storyteller Calls "Crick!"**

Black girl engaged in the song and dance of ring games, in a contemporary North American city; the welcoming performances of sixteenth-century "old Guinea" women; the documentary performances of eighteenth-century

Bambara women; the public occasional performances of an eighteenth-century African chronicler's Niger delta homeland; the cosmological altars of Bakongo; the performed journeys of Yoruba; the danced circles of San; the legacy of an African-language lullaby in nineteenth-century New England; the persistent presence of African, and subsequently African American, women merging art and life in the eighteenth- and nineteenth-century record of diaspora experience; and the songs, in the last century, of blues-singing women: these cultural artifacts form a tapestry, a whole cloth of text, a weaving of history and poetry, in sound and motion. That text, that weaving, can be seen as a tapestry of collective autobiography, depicting experiences and dreams, troubles and triumphs, geographies, journeys, lineage, and flight, recalling anthropologist Clifford Geertz's image of culture as a vast web, as well as the older Asante story of the web-weaving spider Anansi.

Linguist, translator, and poet A. K. Ramanujan, introducing a collection of *Folktales from India*, reminds us that "cultural traditions of every kind, whether they are plays, rituals, or games, contain texts, written and oral" and that as part of the rich dialogic web of relations, the "interactive continuum" of conversation that is the human narrative, these texts "are also contexts and pretexts for other texts."[2] The voices of African and African American women intricately thread this elegant intertextuality. This vast spectrum of the text, textile, contexts, and pretexts situating the performance practices of African American women echo, a song, a dance, an image, in our refrain.

This journey of inquiry into the texts of African diaspora women's cultural performance opened with a musing on the roots of these practices in our shared human beginnings and the visual record of the female figure as symbol and sign. As an example of this root and record, a pretext for our subject, we pondered the image, meaning, and inscription of a profusion of small clay figurines in the shape of women, with birdlike heads and long upwardly extending arms, excavated from predynastic Egyptian and Nubian grave sites. In these concluding notes I return to that image and to the Brooklyn Museum, where one of these figurines, a work of painted pottery no taller than my own forearm, is housed in the Egyptian antiquities collection.

Removed from the sacred theater of the grave site, housed in a square glass case near the collection's entrance, she stands on her post-like base, her chest fully extended, her raised arms flung behind her head, her long slender fingers slightly curved and tapering off, feather-like, into a fan of fingertip. Her feet and what would be her footsteps, hidden by her long white skirt, descend seamlessly into the earth, in the form of a post. While she is presented as "a mystery," what we know about ancient Egyptian cosmologies, and the wider constellation of African performance tradition they sit within, provides informing context. The art of ancient Egypt arises, of course, from the knowledge, belief, and understanding that by crafting the sacred performance of the tale of Isis and Osiris, one could achieve immortality. The performance of ancestry, journey, witness, and liminality is embedded in ancient Egypt's monuments, its vast body of funerary texts. The figure of the woman is a liminal one.

The presence of our female figure within the museum's re-presentation of the visual narratives of human discourse also underscores our telling. In the collections of the Brooklyn Museum (as has been the colonial legacy of "exhibition" and academic convention), the art and artifact of Nubia and Egypt, of African antiquity, are housed separately from those of "Africa." Belatedly acknowledging the critical interrogations of generations of thinkers, from the anonymous "folk" to Frederick Douglass and W. E. B. Du Bois, and including contemporary radical historians, among them John Henry Clarke, Yosef Ben Jochannan, Walter Rodney, and Ivan Sertima, new language has been added to the introductory curator's statement leading into the collection now called "Eternal Egypt." The statement, aptly situated as a backdrop to our female figure, now recognizes that the division of "the birthplace of civilization" from its sub-Saharan nest is an artificial one, a racist invention, arising from the Atlantic slave trade, the building of empire, and the colonial project and traceable, in "the academy," to writings from 1840. The separation of Egypt from Africa in the Western intellectual heritage, whether understood as "Eurocentric," racially constructed, or "isolationist," is modern, and we are still wrestling with all its implications. A hegemonic vision has become, over time, the fragmenting essentialism at the foundation of a history that has plucked its own eyes out.

The collections remain separate, and like many of us, much of the museum's "African" art collection has been displaced or dispersed. Yet downstairs, where the work was formerly housed, or in the archives, though pulled from its geographical and living performance contexts, the visual narrative of the "Arts of Africa" collection, and the sacred worlds gathered in its "artistic shapes," offered and offers still a telling dialogic continuum. At the lip of what was for many years the entrance to the "Arts of Africa" exhibit at the Brooklyn Museum, amid a circle of Malian masks and sculptural objects, stood a Dogon *Togu No* post, a house support in the shape of a woman, a sturdy but slender, staff-like, architectural work recalling the female figure of Egypt.

*Togu No* are "shelters consisting of carved posts which support wooden beams piled with layers of millet stalks" that provide a cool building for men's gatherings, a site for community decision making, in which ancestral presence and counsel is understood to permeate the space. The *Togu No* post is carved from a single block of wood that gradually widens from its base into a branching "Y" shape. Above its midsection the post bears four breasts. Its upper supports suggest outstretched arms, and instead of a bird head, on its open neck one imagines the spiritually permeable roof of the *Togu No* house.

The *Togu No* post beautifully articulates the circle unbroken.[3] The connection between Dogon and ancient Egypt is fairly apparent, and interestingly enough, the new curator's statement for "Eternal Egypt" refers in example to the correspondence between a headrest from the Egyptian Middle Kingdom (circa 1818–1630 BC) and one from eleventh- or twelfth-century Malian Tellem or Dogon cultures that match in craft, shape, and form and, in turn, recall the figure of both the liminal woman and the *Togu No* post.

The structural consonance between these works repeats the liminal woman's compositional lines and reminds us of the web connections linking Dogon, Bozo, and Egyptian (and later Greek) ceremonial observations of the Sirius star system and "resurrection" of the universe in the appearance of its rarely visible moon. The ancient Egyptians called it Ast. The Bozo called it an "egg star." The Greeks reimagined it as a goddess of grain and harvest. It seems no coincidence that the *Togu No* post is understood by Dogon as "honoring" the feminine.

A series of other deeply articulate works encased in museum glass, in an artificial dome of silence, once circled the *Togu No* post. A *Katanga* funeral mask, festooned with a series of complex crosses, which customarily performs the creator god Amma's construction of the world, and the figure of a musician, now playing a broken kora, sing their reliquary praise songs across distance and time. An Ivorian percussive stamper, the musical version of a grain-pounding instrument, in the form of a three-foot carved sculpture of a woman, stands with arms akimbo, round belly marked by scarification. Another inscription, and a *Nodli*, the *Jowei* helmet masks of the Liberian Sande society, opens her wide mouth in a perpetual "O."[4] Freed to sing and dance as they were made to, these works of art are text, context, pretext, hypertext, in an orchestral performance of storytelling and their relocated visual narratives echo poignantly in the inscriptions of violence and hope within early African American women's performance, in their Jubas and lullabies, in their sacred circles and rite-of-passage plays, in their children's games and work songs.

**Community Responds "Crack!"**
Black women's performance texts remind us of the essential role of women as both creators and bearers of cultural articulation. It is a text that is the necessary complement to the written documents of Africans who took the journey and told the story of the Middle Passage into the black Atlantic, a text that in its ritual form re-members the architecture of the torn universe as the practitioner engages, like Spider, in weaving the shattered fragments of the calabash of knowledge into ever-new coherence, and it is a text that may assist us in taking up the urgent current challenge of re-imaging ourselves as we re-imagine the mother tongue as that of an African woman.

An African woman once named in the full geography of the human narrative. An African woman, like Eurydice, in liminal migration. A woman who was kidnapped, perhaps as a child, wrenched from her story and the resplendent naming of her own history and brought into a vision, a construction of the world and knowing, that would deny her both history and voice. An African woman who may have had a brother, like Olaudah Equiano, whose name means "he who has a loud voice." An African woman who, on the shard-strewn terrain of the Western historical imagination, in the master narrative of hegemonic racial construction, had no name. A woman who, though in bondage, nonetheless made a mark, in body and voice, singing to her children or plaintively through the night, alone or collectively at work, and in ritual circles marking birth.

An African woman who, in the enduring motion of the human spirit, renamed herself. A woman like Ma Teodora, who according to the sixteenth-century Afro-Cuban ballad held on to her African musical instruments though laboring, in enslavement, "chopping sugar cane." A woman like Isabella de Angola, who arrived, with a small group of kidnapped Africans, on the shores of the colony Virginia in the year 1619 and later appears in the census records as a "free" woman having given birth to the first so recorded "African American." A woman like "Poor Rosy," whose lament of love and freedom became an emblematic nineteenth-century song. A pretext to the blues. Once Yoruba, Fon, Ibo, Ijaw, Akan, Bambara, Bakongo, Teme, Mende, Mande, Luba, once, long ago San, with the shards of history, this woman reinvented herself African and American. In her lullabies, in a spiritual, in ring shouts and courtship rites, in the songs she sang while working and the songs that were her prayers, this woman made new coherence of those shards, made her own name, and created a vessel, a vehicle, for its unsubduable inscription.

We return, in refrain, to pairing the evolutionary biologist's image of human history as a "long line of women, holding hands" with the novelist's image of the whirling circle of a children's game. In this ancestral line of spiraling movement and song, a blues-singing woman of the twentieth century, bearing witness to a flood in Mississippi, holds hands with a Zambian woman pounding her corn in the twenty-first. This continuum composes a shining circle, in call-and-response, charting and engaging individual and collective journey, testimony, and transformation, and in the center of that circle of performance is the liminal figure of a woman in motion. This image reverberates from the grave figurines of Egypt and the *Togu No* posts of the Dogon, from the healing circles of hunter-gatherer / Xam women, to the circular ritual of Yoruba, Fon, and Bakongo and their restatement in the circles of the African diaspora.

Bessie Smith, "standing up on a high lonesome hill," in the transcendent vision of her "Backwater Blues," does not really stand alone. Reaching across a generative lineage of dialogue and composition, "Backwater Blues" is in kinship and conversation with a constellation of texts, including numerous historic renderings of waters crossed and "waded in"; troubles "in mind," seen, and known; an old spiritual's injunction to "go tell it on the mountain"; the magical arts and "double trouble" of a representative figure called "Juba"; a cradle song that rocks with the vision of a chariot "swinging low"; the bright "morning star" of a children's song; and a world of ring plays that enjoin a "poor gal" to dust herself off, put her hands on her hips, and step into the center of a circle of a transformative rite of passage. And yes, "Backwater Blues" is in conversation, in dense intertextual relation, to the performances of the twenty-first-century Zambian women whose corn-pounding song sets the stage for the final notes in this storytelling.

> Lilo ntwe Mama (I am pounding corn today Mama.)
> Milo ntwe (I am pounding corn tomorrow.)
> Lilo ntwe Mama (I am pounding corn today Mama.)
> Milo ntwe (I am pounding corn tomorrow.)

When contemporary Zambian women sing, "I am pounding corn today Mama / I am pounding corn tomorrow," as they hand mill their corn, they are weaving multiple dialogs in composition. Singing back and forth, as they turn cereal grain into foodstuff, they weave a web of text in the continuum of a particularly female figuration of history and poetics in performance. Like the songs of eighteenth-century Bambara women, the corn-pounding song of Zambian women offers document and social comment, history and philosophical statement, in incisive, economical, and embracing poetry. Their polyphonic performance, inextricably pairing voice and movement, inscribes a journey in an unrestricted concept of time and articulates their recognition of the value of women's work as central to both physical and social survival even as, in the doing, they embody the communal essence of cultural creation. In the dialog between each woman's voice and the work that she is doing, in the dialogic dancing of the pounding instrument, as movement is coordinated by song, in the dialog between the lines of the song, between women singing back and forth, between today and tomorrow and, by implication, the ancestral time, the women offer discursive weaving.

> Lilo ntwe Mama
> Milo ntwe

Performance, the song reminds us, is knowledge. In this case, the knowledge of cultivation, communal creation, mutuality, and the role of women, in the endless weaving of the work of today and the work of tomorrow, and the web connecting the present, the future, and the past from which this performance has sprung. Like the paintings of classical Eastern traditions, their images cast no shadow, their verb tense is continuous, their performance is timeless. What is known here is being reproduced for tomorrow as it has been passed on from an older time. What is known here is wrest from the journey that the performance is re-presenting. What will be known is to be found in the doing. When Zambian women pound their corn and sing this song, their performance marks a crossroads where circles of ancestral recognition, historical documentation, and the communal construction of dynamic new space move hand in hand.

The performance keeps moving as young women join in the work and the learning of work and song. "I am pounding corn today Mama / I am pounding corn tomorrow" is a site of coming of age into a woman's work, of learning, and of engagement. Together, girls and women embody the dialog and cooperation so necessary in agricultural society. Together their pounding instruments percussively keep time recalling, perhaps, the first drum. Sonorous as the sacred song, they sing, "This is who I am." Soft as a lullaby, they whisper dream. Moving from a grounded position, they teach agility, readiness, and timely entrance into the circle of life's performance. And in the nexus of creation, pounding corn into flour, placing line over line in call-and-response, the voices of women and girls at everyday activities swelling into the majesty of song, the performance is an act of transformation. On the most fundamental level, hard work becomes art that feeds us.

That artful articulation inscribes the geography of journey and transcends the confines, the trouble, the limitations, of its location.

Call (Last Time) "Crick!"
Lilo ntwe Mama
Milo ntwe

The performance practices of African American women articulate widespread rhizomes and deep roots with exciting implications, in their sprawling intertextuality, for invigorating interdisciplinary humanist study. The performed journey of this work only begins to envision the potential extent of that terrain. The "stellar" geographies of Afro-Atlantic lullabies; the byways that carry Juba, the ancient name of a city in southern Sudan, a West African woman's day name, into the sacred and secular dances of Africans in North America who subsequently called emancipation "the Jubilee; the generative relationship between the sound and movement vocabularies of African women's rites of passage and the sacred circles and ring games of the African diaspora; the fluid poetry of work songs and their restatements in multiple locations—each of these paths opens into fertile and fecund epistemological landscapes on which history is sung with an eye on the heavens. And on each of these paths we are reminded that work songs arise also from the songs of women and of the essential connection between women's work and culture, between culture and, for women who were traditionally agriculturists, cultivation.

The web of physical and metaphysical connection linking female sexuality, the fertility of land, and cultural production is, of course, ancient and inscribed in a world of "performance." The Chinese character for "art," for one old and resonant instance, is itself a metaphoric performance that begins with the botanical radical, the sign or symbol for flower and leaf, followed by a pictograph that depicts agricultural instruments. A thrasher. A digging stick. The final element of the character is the image of a woman, on her knees, engaged in cultivation. The character recalls parietal images of San women, with their digging sticks and bird headdress, the liminal woman, in trance dance, her digging stick becoming a percussive instrument, her hand clapping, rhythmic pounding, and singing creating the stage for community healing. These hunter-gatherer women were the repositories of vast botanical knowledge, and the traditional role of African women in agriculture, culture, and cultivation, in turn, brings to mind the words of the seventeenth-century Japanese poet Basho, who wrote, "The beginning of art is a rice planting song."

Lilo ntwe Mama
Milo ntwe

The comparative terrain is compelling, potential connections are like the Latin name Eurydice "wide ranging." Finally, this journey holds within a compelling story about the role of women as storytellers and the figure of the liminal woman as a metaphor for knowledge, made in experience and embrace, re-composed from dismembering and fragmentation. The proposal is an expansive one. The first story in Ramanujan's Indian folktale collection, a Tamil tale that he calls "Tell It to the Walls," closes with an image wonderfully akin to that of Bessie Smith's "poor girl" on a hill overlooking the ruin of her town in "Back Water Blues." In this tale "a poor widow" who is literally swollen and filled to bursting with her experience of domestic trials, abuse, and oppression finds herself walking outside her town, entering a deserted house, and safely alone within, enumerating her woes to the four walls. One by one the walls collapse with the weight of her sorrow and complaint, and the woman walks off, liberated from her wretchedness. Like the songs of the blues-singing women, the poor widow's stories echo across the scene of devastation, opening a path in the telling. The moral in this story about storytelling is metaphorically fitting. The widow whose presence upheld an oppressive patriarchal household brings the house down with her performance.

I close reflecting on another of the stories retold in Ramanujan's collection, which he calls "A Story in Search of an Audience." This tale is directly related to a Telugu women's ritual in which the retelling of a story of the telling of a magical story imparts a blessing, a tale type recalling the mysteries of Egypt. The Telugu story begins with the ritual ablutions of an "old woman" who, on a Sunday, the appointed day of the appointed month, as the temple chariot is taken on procession through the streets, sets out in search of someone to hear her ritual storytelling in order to fulfill the observation of her religious practice. The old woman appeals to family, then neighbors, moving from her home through the town, but can find no one willing to take the time to hear her tale until she meets a poor pregnant woman, gives food to her, and is able to tell the story to the child in the woman's womb. The old woman happily relates the story of the sun god and then sings a lullaby both bestowing and foretelling the blessing that child will bring to all she encounters on her life journey. According to the lullaby, wherever the child may go, poverty will become prosperity, cotton seeds will become pearls, dry trees bear fruit, old cows give milk, barren women give birth, lost jewels be found, and dead men come to life again. The second part of the story is that of the journey of the baby into a young woman who fulfills the blessed destiny bequeathed and foretold in the lullaby.

The multiple ritual journeys and the prophetic lullaby of the Telugu story are in radiant alignment with the creative performance in the Ijaw story of Ogboinba the healer, who also embodies the divine and a tale foretold in the womb. In the Ijaw story the womb is the birthing stone of the female deity and her prophetic "lullaby" shapes the circular journey of Ogboinba, who sings and dances her power before, returning to the divine to reside in the eyes of a pregnant woman. Ogboinba's powerful incantations, her bag of medicine, the knowledge she has made on her journey are all inscribed on the child in the womb, and hence, on all of us in the story's performance.

Ogboinba the healer, and the blues-singing women who follow her, takes a journey of self-creation that revises the astral storytelling journey of Isis (Ast) and the San story of the little girl who creates the stars and the Milky Way in her sung and danced play, as well as the cautionary "recreation" tale of the young woman who rides the rain bull. This symmetry is striking but not surprising given the "network of intertextuality" the performed record illuminates. This recognition of narrative correspondence is at the core of what Ngugi called "an African re-membering project," which might gather the shattered fragments of knowledge from Spider's broken calabash, deconstruct isolationist hegemonic constructions of difference, and begin to welcome a full imagining of shared human beginning and being. In the dream song dance tradition.

# Notes

**Past and Prologue as Prelude**

1. "Female Figure," El Ma'mariya, fourth millennium BCE, Brooklyn Museum of Art, New York. See also Brooklyn Museum, *Africa in Antiquity*.
2. Budge, *Book of the Dead*; Budge, *Gods of the Egyptians*; Ellis, *Awakening Osiris*; McKinney-Johnson, "Egypt's Isis." See also Bernal, *Black Athena*.
3. Jeffries, "Image of Women in African Cave Art"; Williams, *Stories That Float from Afar*; Williams, *Cosmos in Stone*; Williams, *Mind in the Cave*; Williams, *Rock Art of Southern Africa*; Williams and Clottes, *Shamans of Prehistory*; Dowson, *Rock Engravings of Southern Africa*; and Coulson and Campbell, *African Rock Art*.
4. Some of this scholarship includes Turner, *Africanisms in the Gullah Dialect*; Abrahams and Szwed, *Discovering Afro-America*; Bastide, *African Civilizations in the New World*; Cabrera, *El monte*; Stuckey, *Slave Culture*; Thompson, *Flash of the Spirit*; Gates, *Signifying Monkey*; Levine, *Black Culture Black Consciousness*; Herskovits, *Myth of the Negro Past*; Herskovits and Herskovits, *Surinam Folklore*; Hill, *Theater of Black Americans*; Hill and Hatch, *African American Theater*; Holloway, *Africanisms in African American Culture*; Karasch, *Slave Life in Rio de Janeiro*; Hurston, *Mules and Men*; Hurston, *Tell My Horse*; Hurston, *Sanctified Church*; Gonzalez-Wippler, *Rituals and Spells of Santeria*.
5. Popular writing on this topic includes Nicholas Wade, "Genes Help Identify Oldest Human Population," *New York Times*, January 8, 2002; "In Click Languages, an Echo of the Mother Tongue," *New York Times*, March 18, 2003; "What We Spoke When the World Was Young," *New York Times*, February 1, 2000; and "Languages Grew from a Seed in Africa, Study Says," *New York Times*, April 14, 2011. Disciplinary texts in linguistics include Greenberg, *Language, Culture, and Communication*; Greenberg, *Languages of Africa*; Chomsky, *Language and the Mind*; and Ruhlen, *Origin of Languages*.
6. Thomas, *Old Way*, 8–9.
7. Cooper, *Voice from the South*; Washington, *Invented Lives*, xxvii.
8. Cooper, *Voice from the South*, 123; Gates, *Collected Black Women's Narratives*, xi.

### 1. The Way We Do

1. For Anansi stories in Africa and the Caribbean, see Bennett, *Anansy and Miss Lou*; Bennett, *Anancy Stories and Dialect Verse*; Bennett, *Yes Me Dear*; Courlander, *Treasury of African Folklore*; McClusky, *Art from Africa*. For Great Turtle Island stories, see Allen, *Grandmothers of the Light*. For an introductory gloss of Yoruba and Fon cosmologies, see Thompson, *Flash of the Spirit*; Bennett, *Anancy and Miss Lou*, 2; Davidson, *Black Mother*; Davidson, *African Past*, 220.
2. From memory and Jones and Lomax Hawes, *Step It Down*, 31–33.
3. See Elder, Lomax, and Lomax Hawes, *Brown Girl in the Ring*; Abrahams, "Jump Rope Rhymes of South Philadelphia"; Brady, "Gonna Shimmy till the Sun Goes Down"; Brady, "This Little Lady"; Jones and Lomax Hawes, *Step It Down*.
4. Nunley and Bettlheim, *Caribbean Festival Arts*, 183–87.
5. Nunley and Bettlheim, *Caribbean Festival Arts*, 17–29.
6. The vast literature on African performance continuities in the diaspora this narrative draws on includes Warner-Lewis, *Central Africa in the Caribbean*; Dunham, *Island Possessed*; Dunham, *Journey to Accompong*; Deren, *Divine Horsemen*; Charters, *Roots of the Blues*; Cohn, *Nothing but the Blues*; Leacock, *Spirits of the Deep*; Bastide, *African Civilizations in the New World*; Bascom, *Sixteen Cowries*; Turner, *Africanisms in the Gullah Dialect*; Gates, *Signifying Monkey*; Herskovits, *Myth of the Negro Past*; Herskovits and Herskovits, *Surinam Folklore*; Hill, *Theater of Black Americans*; Hill and Hatch, *African American Theater*; Homer, *Iliad*; Homer, *Odyssey*; Herodotus, *History of Herodotus*; Holloway, *Africanisms in African American Culture*; Lomax and Lomax, *Folk Song USA*; Martinez-Ruiz, *Kongo Graphic Writing*; Thompson, *Aesthetic of the Cool*; Thompson, *Face of the Gods*; Thompson, *Flash of the Spirit*; Stuckey, *Slave Culture*; Karasch, *Slave Life in Rio de Janeiro*; Cabrera, *El monte*; Hurston, *Barracoon*; Hurston, *Mules and Men*; Hurston, *Tell My Horse*; Hurston, *Sanctified Church*; Gonzalez-Wippler, *Rituals and Spells of Santeria*; Gonzalez-Wippler, *Santeria Experience*; Gonzalez-Wippler, *Tales of the Orisha*; and Deren, *Divine Horsemen*, among so many.
7. See Southern, *Music of Black Americans*, 333–34; and Southern, *Readings in Black American Music*.
8. Southern, *Music of Black Americans*, 333–34. See also Courlander, *Negro Folk Music USA*; Cone, *Spirituals and the Blues*; Baraka, *Blues People*; Baker, "Blues as Literature"; and Baker, *Blues Ideology*.
9. Elder, Lomax, and Lomax Hawes, *Brown Girl in the Ring*, 202–3; Warner-Lewis, *Central Africa in the Caribbean*, 235; Marilyn Worrell, interview by the author, February 18, 2008; and Thompson, *African Art*, 47–73. See also Nettleford, *Dance Jamaica: Cultural Definition and Artistic Discovery*; Nettleford, *Dance Jamaica: Renewal and Continuity*; and Nettleford, *Inward Stretch Outward Reach*.
10. Thompson, *African Art*, 4–67.

11. Thompson, *African Art*, 47.
12. Thompson, *African Art*, 54.
13. Parrish, *Slave Songs of the Georgia Sea Islands*, 114–15.
14. Ralph Ellison, "Shadow and Act," in Ellison, *Collected Essays*, 229; Southern, *Music of Black Americans*, 361–65. See also Jackson, "If He Asks You Was I Running."
15. Bascom, *Ifa Divination*, xii.
16. Hurston, *Barracoon*, 45–46.
17. See Franklin, *From Slavery to Freedom*; Quarles, *Negro in the Making of America*; Clarke, *African People in World History*; Huggins, *Black Odyssey*; Harding, *There Is a River*; Palmer, *Passageways*; Feelings, *Middle Passage*; Gilroy, *Black Atlantic*; and Stuckey, *Slave Culture*, 3–97.
18. Tables on the regional origins of African people enslaved in the sixteenth, seventeenth, and eighteenth centuries are in Curtin, *Atlantic Slave Trade*. Following the lead of linguists, I attempt to refer to regional or linguistic grouping in my narrative.
19. Bascom, *Ifa Divination*, 163.
20. Bascom, *Ifa Divination*. See also Willet, *Ife in the History of West Africa*; and Willet, *Sculpture of Western Nigeria*.
21. Drewal, *Yoruba Ritual*, xiii.
22. Du Bois, *Souls of Black Folk*, 734–35.
23. Dixon, *Ride Out the Wilderness*, 5.
24. Du Bois, *Souls of Black Folk*, 736.
25. Lomax and Lomax, *Folk Song USA*, 470.
26. Du Bois, *Souls of Black Folk*, 735.
27. Parrish, *Slave Songs of the Georgia Sea Islands*, 168–71.
28. Thompson, *Flash of the Spirit*; McClusky, *Art from Africa*, 201; Gonzalez-Wippler, *Rituals and Spells*; Gonzalez-Wippler, *Santeria Experience*; Deren, *Divine Horsemen*, 119–30; and Dunham, *Island Possessed*.
29. Williams, *Cosmos in Stone*, 54–68.
30. Hughes, *Collected Poems*; Nettleford, *Dance Jamaica: Renewal and Continuity*; Nettleford, *Dance Jamaica: Cultural Definition and Artistic Discovery*; Cliff, *Harder They Come*; Robeson, *Odyssey*; Ngũgĩ wa Thiong'o, "Dismembering Practices," in Ngũgĩ wa Thiong'o, *Something Torn and New*, 3–29; Reagon, *If You Don't Go*. See also Feelings, *Middle Passage*.
31. From Hughes and Bontemps, *Book of Negro Folklore*, 305.
32. See Stuckey, *Slave Culture*; and Gilroy, *Black Atlantic*.
33. Boone, *Radiance from the Waters*; Phillips, *Representing Woman*; McClusky, *Art from Africa*, 197–215.
34. Niane, *Sundiata*, 1.
35. See Davidson, *African Past*; Chomsky, *Language and the Mind*; and Greenberg, *Language, Culture, and Communication*.

36. See Laye, *Guardian of the Word*; and Niane, *Sundiata*.
37. See Hill, *Theater of Black Americans*; Bascom, *Ifa Divination*; Beckwith and Fisher, *African Ceremonies*, vol. 2.
38. See Beckwith and Fisher, *African Ceremonies*, vol. 1.
39. Bascom, *Ifa Divination*; Gates, *Signifying Monkey*; Curtin, *Africa Remembered*; Turner, *Africanisms in the Gullah Dialect*; and Dalphinis, *Caribbean and African Languages*.
40. See Ellison, "Shadow and Act."
41. Niane, *Sundiata*. See also Laye, *Guardian of the Word*.
42. Davidson, *African Past*, 13, 63–100. See also Courlander, *Treasury of African Folklore*; Gonzalez-Wippler, *Tales of the Orisha*; Gonzalez-Wippler, *Santeria Experience*; Gonzalez-Wippler, *Rituals and Spells*.
43. See Andrews, *To Tell a Free Story*; Starling, *Slave Narrative*; Gates, *Classic Slave Narratives*; and Gates, *Norton Anthology of African American Literature*.
44. See Norton, "Afro-American Family," 12; McKim, "Negro Songs," 1–2; and Du Bois, *Souls of Black Folks*, 734.
45. See Quarles, *Black Mosaic*; Curtin, *Atlantic Slave Trade*; Davidson, *African Slave Trade*; and Kolchin, *American Slavery*.
46. See Wood, "It Was a Negro Taught Them," 26–45; and Wood, *Black Majority*. See also Sobel, *World They Made Together*.
47. Foner, *Short History of Reconstruction*, 254–60.
48. Rose, *Rehearsal for Reconstruction*; and Rose, *Slavery and Freedom*. See also Botkin, *Lay My Burden Down*; and Levine, *Black Culture Black Consciousness*.
49. McKim, "Negro Songs," 1.
50. Cohn, *Nothing but the Blues*, 13.
51. Bascom, *Ifa Divination*, 221.
52. Bascom, *Ifa Divination*, 3–5.
53. Janzen and MacGaffey, *Anthology of Kongo Religion*, 25–32.
54. Thompson, *Flash of the Spirit*, 101–60; Thompson, *Face of the Gods*, 48–49. See also Warner-Lewis, *Central Africa in the Caribbean*.
55. Thompson, *Face of the Gods*, 48–49.
56. Thompson, *Flash of the Spirit*, 103–16; quoted text, 108–9.
57. Thompson, *Flash of the Spirit*, 108–9.
58. Thompson, *Flash of the Spirit*, 188–89.
59. Thompson, *Flash of the Spirit*, 188–90, 108–16; Warner-Lewis, *Central Africa in the Caribbean*, 166–67; Ms. Wendy Johnny, interview by the author, September 1997; Ms. Carol Francis, interview by the author, September 1997. See also Bastide, *African Civilizations in the New World*; Leacock, *Spirits of the Deep*; Deren, *Divine Horsemen*; Dunham, *Island Possessed*; and Hurston, *Tell My Horse*.
60. Parrish, *Slave Songs of the Georgia Sea Islands*, 117.

61. Turner, *Africanisms in the Gullah Dialect*; Stuckey, *Slave Culture*; and Parrish, *Slave Songs of the Georgia Sea Islands*.
62. See McClusky, *Art from Africa*, 210.
63. Frederick, "Singing Freedom into Being."
64. Lomax, *Folk Songs of North America*, 470.
65. Thompson, *Face of the Gods*, 38.
66. Thompson, *Face of the Gods*, 34–45.
67. See Bleek, *Specimens of Bushman Folklore*; Williams, *Stories That Float from Afar*; Williams, *Cosmos in Stone*; Williams and Clottes, *Shamans of Prehistory*; Greenberg, *Languages of Africa*.
68. For historical discussion of this song, see Lovell, *Black Song*, 308.
69. Equiano, *Interesting Narrative*, 20.
70. Equiano, *Interesting Narrative*, 26.
71. Equiano, *Interesting Narrative*, 34.
72. Equiano, *Interesting Narrative*, 39.
73. Carretta, *Equiano the African*; Byrd, "Ebo, Country."
74. Equiano, *Interesting Narrative*. See also Phillip D. Curtin, "African Travelers of the Eighteenth Century," in Curtin, *Africa Remembered*; and G. I. Jones, "Olaudah Equiano of the Niger Ibo," in Curtin, *Africa Remembered*; Carretta, *Equiano the African*.
75. Hughes and Bontemps, *Book of Negro Folklore*, 290.
76. Huggins, *Black Odyssey*, xii–xiii.
77. Gates, *Norton Anthology of African American Literature*, contains introductory and explicative discussion of this well-known song text.
78. Landeck, *Echoes of Africa*, 63.
79. See Bastide, *African Civilizations in the New World*; Curtin, *Atlantic Slave Trade*; Warner-Lewis, *Central Africa in the Caribbean*, 264–339. See also Gutman, *Black Family*; Cody, "Naming Kinship and Estate Dispersal"; Kilson, "Ga Naming Rite"; and Ndoma, "Kongo and Personal Names Today."
80. Davis, *Women, Race and Class*, 3–29.
81. Moreton, *Manners and Customs in the West Indies Islands*, in Abrahams and Szwed, *After Africa*, 290–91.
82. See Gates, *Signifying Monkey*, on "hermeneutics" of African American oral histories.

**2. Juba Danced**
1. Bleek, *Specimens of Bushman Folklore*; Bleek, *Reynard the Fox*. See also Beier, *Origins of Life and Death*; Williams, *Cosmos in Stone*; Williams, *Stories That Float from Afar*; and Thompson, *Face of the Gods*.
2. Wade, "What We Spoke"; Williams, *Cosmos in Stone*.
3. Driberg, *People of the Small Arrow*, 45.

4. Southern, *Music of Black Americans*, 6–9.
5. Thompson, *African Art*, 29.
6. See Davidson, *African Past*, 122–27. See also da Gama, *Journal of the First Voyage*.
7. See Thompson, *African Art*, xiv. See also Davidson, *African Past*.
8. See Dunham, "Notes on the Dance," and "The Negro Dance," which are anthologized in Clarke and Johnson, *Kaiso*.
9. Park, *Travels in the Interior Districts*. See Southern, *Readings in Black American Music*, 4–7.
10. Thompson, *African Art*, 37.
11. Stuckey, *Slave Culture*, 3–97.
12. Thomas, *Old Way*, 8–9.
13. Thompson, *African Art*, 37.
14. Thompson, *African Art*, 37.
15. Parrish, *Slave Songs of the Georgia Sea Islands*, 116.
16. See Petry, *Tituba of Salem Village*; Conde, *I, Tituba*; Drake, *Witchcraft Delusion in New England*; Burr, *Narrative of the Witchcraft Cases*; Starkey, *Devil in Massachusetts*; Hanson, *Witchcraft in Salem*; Demos, *Entertaining Satan*; Karlsen, *Devil in the Shape of a Woman*; Boyer and Nissenbaum, *Salem Witchcraft Papers*; Piersen, *Black Yankees*; and Miller, *Crucible*.
17. Thompson, *Flash of the Spirit*, 125.
18. Thompson, *Flash of the Spirit*, 117–31; and Cabrera, *El monte*.
19. Richard Ligon, *A True and Exact History of the Island of Barbados*, in Abrahams and Szwed, *After Africa*, 51–69.
20. Griffith Hughes, *The Natural History of Barbados*, in Pierson, *Black Yankees*, 75.
21. See Williams and Clottes, *Shamans of Prehistory*; Williams, *Believing and Seeing* and *San Spirituality*.
22. "Characteristic Traits of Creole and African Negroes in Jamaica," *Columbia Magazine*, April–October 1797, in Abrahams and Szwed, *After Africa*, 293.
23. George Pinckard, *Notes on the West Indies*, vol. 1, in Abrahams and Szwed, *After Africa*, 293–94.
24. See Warner-Lewis, *Central Africa in the Caribbean*, 199–263; and Thompson, *Flash of the Spirit*, 3–17.
25. Thompson, *Flash of the Spirit*, 11–17.
26. Abrahams and Szwed, *After Africa*, 290–91.
27. Beckford, *A Descriptive Account of the Island of Jamaica*, in Abrahams and Szwed, *After Africa*, 287.
28. Baker, "Blues as Literature."
29. See Herskovits, *Dahomey*; and Herskovits and Herskovits, *Surinam Folklore*. See also Stedman, *Narrative of a Five Years Expedition*, 364.

30. See Lerner, *Black Women in White America*.
31. Galeano, *Faces and Masks*, 8, 42. See also Gale Jackson, "Fugitive Slaves," in Jackson, *Bridge Suite*.
32. Starling, *Slave Narrative*, 114.
33. See Morrison, *Beloved*.
34. See McLaurin, *Celia*.
35. See Price, *Maroon Societies*; Cone, *Spirituals and the Blues*, 30–31; Deren, *Divine Horsemen*, 62–63; Aptheker, "Maroons within the Present Limits"; and Diegues, *Quilombo*.
36. Moreton, *Manners and Customs*. See Abrahams and Szwed, *After Africa*, 289–90.
37. Equiano, *Interesting Narrative*, 34.
38. Abrahams, *African Folk Tales*, 290–91.
39. Equiano, *Interesting Narrative*, 12.
40. Warner-Lewis, *Central Africa in the Caribbean*.
41. Thompson, *African Art*, plate 42; Abrahams and Szwed, *After Africa*, 289–95.
42. See Angela Y. Davis, "Standards for a New Womanhood," in Davis, *Women, Race, and Class*. See also Washington, *Invented Lives*; and Carby, *Reconstructing Womanhood*.
43. See Gates, *Signifying Monkey*; Brathwaite, *Development of Creole Society*; and Berlin and Hoffman, *Slavery and Freedom*.
44. Truth, *Narrative of Sojourner Truth*.
45. Clarke and Johnson, *Kaiso*, 223.
46. Jones and Lomax Hawes, *Step It Down*, 22.
47. Sheila Anozier, personal communications with the author, 2011–19.
48. See Bastide, *African Civilizations in the New World*.
49. Herskovits and Herskovits, *Surinam Folklore*; and Herskovits, *Dahomey*.
50. Southern, *Readings in Black American Music*, 62–63.
51. Northrup, *Twelve Years a Slave*, 167.
52. Abrahams and Szwed, *After Africa*, 37.
53. Southern, *Readings in Black American Music*, 95.
54. Northrup, *Twelve Years a Slave*, 167–68.
55. Abrahams and Szwed, *After Africa*, 386–87; and Southern, *Readings in Black American Music*, 50–51.
56. See Brown, *Clotel*; Gutman, *Black Family*; Abrahams and Szwed, *After Africa*; Norton, "Afro-American Family"; Weischhoff, "Social Significance of Names"; Ndoma, "Kongo and Personal Names Today"; and Kilson, "Ga Naming Rite."
57. From James Hungerford, *The Old Plantation*, in Southern, *Readings in Black American Music*, 71–81.
58. From Hungerford, *Old Plantation*, in Southern, *Readings in Black American Music*, 71.

## 3. The Ancestors and the Lullaby

1. Plutarch, *Moralia*; Budge, *Book of the Dead*; Budge, *Gods of the Egyptians*; Bernal, *Black Athena*; Ellis, *Awakening Osiris*; McKinney-Johnson, "Egypt's Isis"; Adams, "African Observers."
2. Lewis, *W.E.B. DuBois*, 14–15.
3. Du Bois, *Souls of Black Folk*, 734; Lewis, *W.E.B. Du Bois*, 585.
4. Du Bois, *Souls of Black Folks*, 734–35.
5. Green, *Black Women Composers*. See also Southern, *Music of Black Americans*; and Oliver, *Savannah Syncopators*.
6. See Thompson, *African Art*, xii–xiv.
7. Landeck, *Echoes of Africa*, 13–15.
8. Landeck, *Echoes of Africa*, 13–15.
9. See Du Bois, *Souls of Black Folk*, 732–40.
10. Gates, *Norton Anthology of African American Literature*, 13.
11. Rawick, *American Slave*, Supplement Series 1, vol. 5:1415–27.
12. See Southern, *Music of Black Americans*; Lomax, *Folk Songs of North America*; and *Black Banjo Songsters of North Carolina*.
13. For documentary history of Elizabeth Freeman and other Revolutionary-era African Americans, see Kaplan, *Black Presence*, 244–48.
14. Kaplan, *Black Presence*, 243–44.
15. Truth, *Narrative of Sojourner Truth*, 18.
16. Du Bois, *Souls of Black Folk*, 733–34.
17. See Norton, "Afro-American Family," 137.
18. See Kaplan, *Black Presence*, 241–42.
19. Green, *Black Women Composers*, 27.
20. Ba Benzélé of Central Africa, *Anthology of World Music*; Mbuti of Central Africa, *Mbuti Pygmies of the Ituri Rainforest*. See also Cohn, *Nothing but the Blues*; Eileen Southern, "The Blues," in Southern, *Music of Black Americans*. Lomax, quoted from Thompson, *Face of the Gods*, 34.
21. Wheatley, *Poems on Various Subjects*; Wheatley, *Memoir and Poems*; Robinson, *Black New England Letters*; Robinson, *Phillis Wheatley in the Black American Beginnings*; Richmond, *Bid the Vassal Soar*; O'Neale, "Slave's Subtle War," 144–65; and Sistrunk, "Phillis Wheatley," 391–98.
22. See Equiano, *Interesting Narrative*, 14.
23. Wheatley, *Poems on Various Subjects*, 62.
24. See Robert Fagles, introduction to Homer, *The Odyssey*.
25. For full text and discussion, see Rawick, *American Slave*, 12:222, 100.
26. Rawick, *American Slave*, 2:117.
27. Rawick, *American Slave*, 2:165.

28. Prince, *History of Mary Prince*; Gates, *Six Women's Slave Narratives*.
29. See Starling, *Slave Narrative*.
30. Rawick, *American Slave*, 5:21.
31. See Botkin, *Lay My Burden Down*; and Lester, *To Be a Slave*.
32. Proctor's reports have been reprinted in a number of texts. For the full text of Proctor's recollections, see Botkin, *Lay My Burden Down*, 89–93.
33. Trent-Jones, *Play Songs of the Deep South*, 20–21; Bennett, *Yes Me Dear*; and Bennett, *Lord de Riddim Sweet*.
34. Rawick, *American Slave*, 16:80.
35. For full text of the interview, see Rawick, *American Slave*, 4:89.
36. Rawick, *American Slave*, 4:27.
37. Rawick, *American Slave*, 4:38.
38. Rawick, *American Slave*, 4:285.
39. Rawick, *American Slave*, 13:89.
40. Rawick, *American Slave*, 8:19.
41. Rawick, *American Slave*, 3:96.
42. See Janzen and MacGaffey, *Anthology of Kongo Religion*; MacGaffey, *Art and Healing*; MacGaffey, "Eyes of Understanding"; MacGaffey, *Religion and Society*; Hurston, *Dust Tracks on the Road*; and Hurston, *Tell My Horse*.
43. See Niane, *Sundiata*, 21. See also Laye, *Guardian of the Word*.
44. See Diegues, *Quilombo*.
45. Truth, *Narrative of Sojourner Truth*, 8.
46. Plutarch, *Moralia*.
47. Havalin, "The Sirius System," in Van Sertima, *Blacks in Science*. See also Kreamer, *African Cosmos Stellar Arts*.
48. Ngũgĩ wa Thiong'o, "Re-membering Visions," in Ngũgĩ wa Thiong'o, *Something Torn and New*, 33.
49. Maude Cuney Hare, "The Source," in Patterson, *International Library of Negro Life and History*, 19–33.
50. Fisher, *Negro Slave Songs*, 145.
51. Fisher, *Negro Slave Songs*, 45.
52. Patterson, *International Library of Negro Life and History*, 21–22.
53. Ngũgĩ wa Thiong'o, "Dismembering Practices," in Ngũgĩ wa Thiong'o, *Something Torn and New*, 3–29.
54. See Bauer and Peyser, *Music through the Ages*. See also Graves, *Greek Myths*.
55. See Morrison, *What Moves at the Margins*, 65–80.
56. Rawick, *American Slave*, 6:73.
57. This well-known song is anthologized widely. See Fenner, *Cabin and Plantation Songs*, 115.

58. Rawick, *American Slave*, 8:1027.
59. Rawick, *American Slave*, 3:239.
60. Rawick, *American Slave*, 13:111.
61. See Dixon, *Ride Out the Wilderness*. See also Anderson and Kreamer, *Wild Spirits Strong Medicine*.
62. Hughes and Bontemps, *Book of Negro Folklore*, 10.

### 4. Put Your Hands on Your Hips

1. //Kabbo in Bleek, *Specimens of Bushman Folklore*, 72–79.
2. See Graves, *Greek Myth*. See also Walker, *Woman's Encyclopedia of Myths and Secrets*; and Allen, *Grandmothers of the Light*.
3. See Jones and Lomax Hawes, *Step It Down*; Elder, Lomax, and Lomax Hawes, *Brown Girl in the Ring*; and Beckwith and Fisher, *African Ceremonies*.
4. Thompson, *Flash of the Spirit*, 195–206.
5. See Campbell, *Masks of God*, introduction.
6. Shostak, *Nissa*, 149–50, 376.
7. Shostak, *Nissa*, 297–98.
8. Shostak, *Nissa*, 163–64.
9. Powers, "Woman with the Zebra's Penis," 53–57.
10. See Rodger, *Village of the Nubas*.
11. See Phillips, *Representing Woman*; and Boone, *Radiance from the Waters*.
12. See Sembene, *Moolade*.
13. Thompson, *African Art*, xii.
14. Thompson, *African Art*, xii.
15. Thompson, *African Art*, 20.
16. MacGaffey, "Eyes of Understanding," 65.
17. Dunham, *Island Possessed*, 131.
18. "Form and Function in Primitive Dance" is reprinted in Clarke and Johnson, *Kaiso*, 502–6.
19. See Jones and Lomax Hawes, *Step It Down*, 87.
20. "Summer moon / clapping hands / I herald dawn." Basho, *On Love and Barley*, 9.
21. See Bascom, "African Folktales"; Abrahams, *African Folk Tales*; Gautz, *Mabinogion*; and Graves, *White Goddess*.
22. "Ham Bone" text in Parrish, *Slave Songs of the Georgia Sea Islands*, 115. "That Suits Me" text in Parrish, *Slave Songs of the Georgia Sea Islands*, 137.
23. Joyner, *Down by the Riverside*, 15; Stuckey, *Slave Culture*, 14–15.
24. Parrish, *Slave Songs of the Georgia Sea Islands*, 20.
25. Parrish, *Slave Songs of the Georgia Sea Islands*, 55–56.
26. Katz, *Social Implications of Early Negro Music*, 16. See also Du Bois, *Souls of Black Folk*.

27. Higginson, "Negro Spirituals," in Katz, *Social Implications of Early Negro Music*, 11–21.
28. Parrish, *Slave Songs of the Georgia Sea Islands*, 76. See also Work, *American Negro Songs and Spirituals*; Cone, *Spirituals and the Blues*; Frederick, "Singing Freedom into Being"; and Fisher, *Negro Slave Songs*.
29. Parrish, *Slave Songs of the Georgia Sea Islands*, 76.
30. Katz, *Social Implications of Early Negro Music*, 12. See also Zwick, *Glory*, for visual depiction.
31. Katz, *Social Implications of Early Negro Music*, 13.
32. Rawick, *American Slave*, 4:2.
33. Rawick, *American Slave*, 6:120.
34. Rawick, *American Slave*, 4:167.
35. Nina Simone, "Lil Liza Jane," on Simone, *Don't Let Me Be Misunderstood*. See also Hughes and Bontemps, *Book of Negro Folklore*, 424–25.
36. Jacobs, *Incidents in the Life*, 27; Prince, *History of Mary Prince*; Douglass, *Narrative*, 25. For Curry, see Starling, *Slave Narrative*, 118.
37. Pennington, *Fugitive Blacksmith*, in Bontemps, *Great Slave Narratives*.
38. See Southern, *Music of Black Americans*, 120.
39. See Price, *Maroon Societies*, 1. John Washington and Wallace Turnage narratives in Blight, *Slave No More*, 213–60.
40. Douglass, *Narrative*, 23.
41. For musical notation and play illustration, see Trent-Jones, *Play Songs of the Deep South*, 24–25.
42. For song, see Hughes and Bontemps, *Book of Negro Folklore*; Jones and Lomax Hawes, *Step It Down*; and Trent-Jones, *Play Songs of the Deep South*. See also Rawick, *American Slave*, 6:256.
43. Rawick, *American Slave*, 16:63.
44. Warner-Lewis, *Central Africa in the Caribbean*, 202.
45. Northrup, *Twelve Years a Slave*, 168.
46. Trent-Jones, *Play Songs of the Deep South*, 16.
47. See Hughes and Bontemps, *Book of Negro Folklore*, 430.
48. See also Gonzalez-Wippler, *Tales of the Orisha*.
49. João do Rio, *Religioes no Rio*, in Karasch, *Slave Life*, 240.

### 5. Rosy, Possum, Morning Star

1. Ulli Beier, "The Woman Who Tried to Change Her Fate," in Beier, *Origins of Life and Death*.
2. See Levine, *Black Culture Black Consciousness*; Gates, *Collected Black Women's Narratives*; Stuckey, *Slave Culture*; Thompson, *Flash of the Spirit*; Thompson, *African Art*; Carby, *Afro-American Women Novelists*; Spillers, *Conjuring*.

3. For musical notation and play description, see Jones and Lomax Hawes, *Step It Down*, 127.
4. Jones and Lomax Hawes, *Step It Down*, 127.
5. Lomax, *Folk Songs of North America*, 493.
6. Litwack, *Been in the Storm*, introduction.
7. Jones, *Labor of Love*, 14–16.
8. See Hashaw, *Birth of Black America*; Wood, *Black Majority*, 33; and Joyner, *Down by the Riverside*, 14. See also Wood, quoted in Abrahams and Szwed, *After Africa*, 24; and Wood, "It Was a Negro Taught Them." See also Epstein, *Sinful Tunes and Spirituals*, 68–75, on work songs.
9. Epstein, *Sinful Tunes and Spirituals*, 69–70. See also Wood, *Black Majority*, 124; and Jones, *Labor of Love*.
10. See Epstein, *Sinful Tunes and Spirituals*, 68–75; and Abrahams and Swzed, *After Africa*, 22–26.
11. Rawick, *American Slave*, 3:96.
12. Botkin, *Lay My Burden Down*, 61–65, 89–93.
13. Courlander, *Negro Folk Music USA*. See also Jahn, *Neo-African Literature*; and Levine, *Black Culture Black Consciousness*.
14. See Parrish, *Slave Songs of the Georgia Sea Islands*, 121.
15. Truth, *Narrative of Sojourner Truth*, 126.
16. Hughes and Bontemps, *Book of Negro Folklore*, 343.
17. Rawick, *American Slave*, 4:87.
18. Rawick, *American Slave*, 11:115.
19. Botkin, *Lay My Burden Down*, 141.
20. Botkin, *Lay My Burden Down*, 141.
21. Rawick, *American Slave*, 3:193.
22. Botkin, *Lay My Burden Down*, 125.
23. Rawick, *American Slave*, 8:160.
24. For complete interview, see Rawick, *American Slave*, 4:233.
25. Rawick, *American Slave*, 4:233.
26. Rawick, *American Slave*, 11:130.
27. Hughes and Bontemps, *Book of Negro Folklore*, 290. Listen to Billie Holiday.
28. Rawick, *American Slave*, 4:15–16. See also Landeck, *Echoes of Africa*.
29. Rawick, *American Slave*, 5:127.
30. Rawick, *American Slave*, 5:185.
31. Rawick, *American Slave*, 4:127.
32. Jones, *Labor of Love*, 17.
33. Parrish, *Slave Songs of the Georgia Sea Islands*, 247.
34. Foster, *Brighter Coming Day*, 218.

35. Nina Simone, "Cotton Eyed Joe," on Simone, *Don't Let Me Be Misunderstood*.
36. See Southern, *Music of Black Americans*, 164; "Poor Rosie," in Lomax, *Prison Songs*.
37. Katz, *Social Implications of Early Negro Music*, 9–10. See also Allen, Ware, and McKim Garrison, *Slave Songs of the United States*.
38. "Poor Rosy," in Parrish, *Slave Songs of the Georgia Sea Islands*.
39. "Poor Rosie" and "What Makes a Good Song Leader," in Lomax, *Prison Songs*.
40. See Katz, *Social Implications of Early Negro Music*; Southern, *Music of Black Americans*; Work, *American Negro Songs and Spirituals*; and Krehbiel, *Afro American Folk Songs*. See also Lomax, *Prison Songs*.
41. See Katz, *Social Implications of Early Negro Music*; Lomax, *Folk Songs of North America*; Work, *American Negro Songs and Spirituals*; and Southern, *Music of Black Americans*.
42. See Cone, *Spirituals and the Blues*; Baraka, *Blues People*; and Frederick, "Singing Freedom into Being."
43. See Fisher, *Negro Slave Songs*, 48.
44. Fisher, *Negro Slave Songs*, 94. See also Southern, *Music of Black Americans*, 194–95; and Lovell, *Black Song*, 232.
45. Du Bois, *Souls of Black Folk*, 268.
46. See Baker, *Blues Ideology*; and Baraka, *Blues People*.
47. See Lovell, *Black Song*, 122.
48. See Rose, *Rehearsal for Reconstruction*, 353.
49. See Southern, *Music of Black Americans*, 195.
50. See Foner, *Short History of Reconstruction*; Quarles, *Negro in the Civil War*; and Du Bois, *Black Reconstruction*. See also Taylor, *Reminiscences of My Life in Camp*; and Grimke, *Journals Charlotte Forten Grimke, 1862–64*. See also Litwack, *Been in the Storm*.
51. Southern, *Music of Black Americans*, 195.
52. See Lovell, *Black Song*, 304–6; and Work, *American Negro Songs and Spirituals*, 14–27. See also "Get Thee Behind Me Satan," in Silverman, *Folk Blues*, 43.
53. See Cone, *Spirituals and the Blues*; Fredericks, "Singing Freedom into Being"; Baraka, *Blues People*; Lovell, *Black Song*; and Stuckey, *Slave Culture*.
54. See Katz, *Social Implications of Early Negro Music*, 97.
55. Nina Simone, "Trouble in Mind," on Simone, *Don't Let Me Be Misunderstood*. See also Gates, *Norton Anthology of African American Literature*, 29.
56. Parrish, *Slave Songs of the Georgia Sea Islands*, 13, 99.
57. Lomax, *Folk Songs of North America*, 507.
58. Lomax, *Folk Songs of North America*, 494.
59. Lomax, *Folk Songs of North America*, 45.
60. See Jones, *Labor of Love*.
61. See Silverman, *Folk Blues*, 29; and Southern, *Music of Black Americans*, 334–35.

62. Ida B. Wells, "Southern Horror," *New York Age*, June 5, 1892. See also Giddings, *Where and When I Enter*, 17–39.
63. Southern, *Music of Black Americans*, 334–35.
64. Du Bois, *Black Reconstruction*, 670–708. See also Bennett, *Before the Mayflower*, 239.
65. See Silverman, *Folk Blues*; Jackson, *Wake Up Dead Man*; and Alan Lomax, "Work Songs," in Lomax, *Folk Songs of North America*.
66. Lomax and Lomax, *Folk Song USA*, 236.
67. Lomax and Lomax, *Folk Song USA*, 225.
68. Lomax, *Folk Songs of North America*, 505.
69. Southern, *Music of Black Americans*, 330.
70. Lomax, *Folk Songs of North America*, 498.
71. Hurston, *Mules and Men*, 262.
72. Rawick, *American Slave*, 8:804.
73. Southern, *Music of Black Americans*, 330.
74. Brown, *My Southern Home*, 211.
75. See Davis, *Blues Legacies*.
76. Lieb, *Mother of the Blues*; Harrison, *Black Pearls*; and Davis, *Blues Legacies*. See also Southern, *Readings in Black American Music*, 202–16, on Handy.
77. Sterling Brown, "Ma Rainey," in Gates, *Norton Anthology of African American Literature*, 1220–21.
78. Davis, *Blues Legacies*, 141.
79. For musical notation, see Sackheim, *Blues Line*, 34.
80. Davis, *Blues Legacies*, 12.
81. See Sackheim, *Blues Line*, 40, for musical notation.
82. See Sackheim, *Blues Line*, 42, for musical notation.
83. Originally released 1926, Sony BMG Music Entertainment. See Davis, *Blues Legacies*, 356. Listen to Smith's recordings.
84. Originally recorded 1927. All rights reserved by Columbia Records, a division of Sony Music Entertainment. See Davis, *Blues Legacies*, 263–64.

**Coda**

1. Mbachi Kumwenda, personal communication with the author, 2005.
2. Ramanujan, *Folktales from India*, xviii.
3. Brooklyn Museum of Art.
4. Unknown Dogon Artist, *Togu Nu* post, Mali, 1800s–early 1900s, sculpture; *Katanga Mask in Three Pieces*, Mali, 1900s, mask; *Figure of a Seated Musician*, N'duleri style, Mali, 1700s, sculpture; *Rhythm Pounder*, (Deble) Ivory Coast, 1800s, instrument; and *Ndoli Jowei Helmet Mask for Sande Society*, Grand Bassa Region, Liberia, early 1900s, mask, all in Brooklyn Museum of Art.

# Bibliography

Abrahams, Roger, ed. *African Folk Tales*. New York: Pantheon, 1983.
———. "Jump Rope Rhymes of South Philadelphia." *Key Stone Folklore Quarterly* 1, no. 8 (1963): 3–15.
Abrahams, Roger, and John F. Szwed, eds. *After Africa: Extracts of Travel Accounts and Journals of the Seventeenth, Eighteenth and Nineteenth Centuries Concerning the Slaves, Their Manners, and Customs in the British West Indies*. New Haven: Yale University Press, 1983.
———, eds. *Discovering Afro-America*. Leiden: Brill, 1975.
Adams, Hunter Havelin. "African Observers of the Universe: The Sirus Question." In *Blacks in Science: Ancient and Modern*, edited by Ivan Van Sertima. New Brunswick NJ: Transaction, 1983.
Albertson, Chris. *Bessie*. New York: Stein, 1982.
Allen, Paula Gunn. *Grandmothers of the Light*. Boston: Beacon, 1991.
Allen, Richard. *A Collection of Spiritual Songs and Hymns*. Philadelphia, 1801.
Allen, William Francis, Charles Pickard Ware, and Lucy McKim Garrison, eds. *Slave Songs of the United States*. New York, 1867.
Anderson, Martha G., and Christine Mullen Kreamer, eds. *Wild Spirits Strong Medicine: African Art and the Wilderness*. New York: Center for African Art, 1989.
Andrews, William L. *To Tell a Free Story: The First Century of Afro-American Autobiography*. Urbana: University of Illinois Press, 1986.
Aptheker, Herbert. "Maroons within the Present Limits of the United States." In *Maroon Societies*, edited by Richard Price. New York: Doubleday, 1973.
Ba Benzélé of Central Africa. *Anthology of World Music: The Ba Benzele Pygmies*. Rounder, 1998, CD.
Bacquart, Jean-Baptiste. *The Tribal Arts of Africa*. New York: Thames, 1998.
Baker, Houston. "The Blues as Literature." Interview. NPR, February 24, 2009.
———. *Blues Ideology and Afro-American Literature: A Vernacular Theory*. Chicago: University of Chicago Press, 1984.

Bakhtin, M. M. *Speech Genres and Other Late Essays*. Austin: University of Texas Press, 1986.
Baldwin, James. *The Amen Corner*. New York: French, 1968.
———. *The Price of the Ticket: Collected Nonfiction 1948–1985*. New York: St. Martin, 1985.
Bambara, Toni Cade. *The Black Woman*. New York: New American, 1970.
———. *Gorilla My Love*. New York: Random House, 1972.
———. *The Salt Eaters*. New York: Random House, 1980.
———. *Those Bones Are Not My Child*. New York: Pantheon, 1999.
Baraka, Inamu Amiri. *Blues People*. New York: Morrow, 1963.
Barnes, Sandra, ed. *Africa's Ogun: Old World and New*. Bloomington: Indiana University Press, 1989.
Barton, William E. "Hymns of the Slave and the Freeman." *New England Magazine*, December 1898.
———. *Old Plantation Hymns: A Collection of Hitherto Unpublished Melodies of the Slave and Freeman with Historical and Descriptive Notes*. New York, 1899.
Bascom, William. "African Folktales in America: The Talking Skull Refuses to Talk." *Research in African Literatures* 8 (1977): 226–91.
———. *Ifa Divination: Communication between Gods and Men in West Africa*. Bloomington: Indiana University Press, 1969.
———. *Sixteen Cowries: Yoruba Divination from Africa to the New World*. Bloomington: Indiana University Press, 1993.
Basho. *On Love and Barley*. Translated by Lucien Stryk. New York: Penguin, 1985.
Bastide, Roger. *African Civilizations in the New World*. Translated by Peter Green. New York: Harper, 1971.
Bauer, Marion, and Ethel Peyser. *Music through the Ages*. New York: Putman, 1932.
Bayliss, John, ed. *Black Slave Narratives*. New York: Macmillan, 1970.
Beckwith, Carol, and Angela Fisher. *African Ark: People and Ancient Culture of Ethiopia and the Horn of Africa*. New York: Abrams, 1990.
———. *African Ceremonies*. 2 vols. New York: Abrams, 1999.
Beier, Ulli, ed. *The Origins of Life and Death*. London: Heinemann, 1966.
Bena Lulua of Angola and Zaire. *Sanza and Guitar Music of the Bena Lulua of Angola and Zaire*. Lyrichord, 1977, CD.
Bennett, Lerone. *Before the Mayflower*. New York: Penguin, 1969.
Bennett, Louise. *Anancy and Miss Lou*. Kingston: Sangster, 1979.
———. *Anancy Stories and Dialect Verse*. Kingston: Pioneer, 1957.
———. *Jamaica Labrish*. Kingston: Sangster, 1966.
———. *Laugh with Louise*. Kingston: City Print, 1961.
———. *Lord Di Ridim Sweet*. Sangster, 1999, CD.
———. *Yes Me Dear*. Sonic, 1982, CD.

Berlin, Ira, and Ronald Hoffman, eds. *Slavery and Freedom in the Age of the American Revolution*. Urbana: University of Illinois Press, 1983.

Bernal, Martin. *Black Athena: The Afro-Asiatic Roots of Classical Civilization*. New Brunswick NJ: Rutgers University Press, 1987.

Biebuyck, Daniel, and Kahombo Manteene. *The Mwindo Epic*. Berkeley: University of California Press, 1973.

Biesele, M. "Women Like Meat." In *The Folklore and Foraging Ideology of the Kalahari Ju/hoan*. Johannesburg: University of Witwatersrand Press, 1993.

*Black Banjo Songsters of North Carolina*. Smithsonian, 1998, CD.

Blassingame, John, ed. *Slave Testimony: Two Centuries of Letters Speeches, Interviews and Autobiographies*. Baton Rouge: Louisiana State University, 1977.

Bleek, Wilhelm. *Reynard the Fox in Southern Africa or Hottentot Fables and Tales*. London, 1864.

———. *Specimens of Bushman Folklore*. London: Allen, 1911.

Blight, David. *Slave No More*. New York: Harcourt, 2007.

Bontemps, Arna, ed. *Great Slave Narratives*. Boston: Beacon, 1969.

Boone, Sylvia Ardun. *Radiance from the Waters: Ideals of Feminine Beauty in Mende Art*. New Haven: Yale University Press, 1986.

Botkin, B. A. *Lay My Burden Down: A Folk History of Slavery*. Chicago: University of Chicago Press, 1969.

Boyer, Paul, and Stephen Nissenbaum, eds. *The Salem Witchcraft Papers: Verbatim Transcripts of the Legal Documents of the Salem Witchcraft Outbreak of 1692*. New York: Da Capo, 1977.

Bradford, Sarah. *Harriet Tubman: The Moses of Her People*. New York, 1886.

Brady, Margaret. "Gonna Shimmy till the Sun Goes Down." *Folklore Annual of the University Folklore Association*, no. 6 (1974).

———. "This Little Lady." In *Black Girls at Play: Folkloric Perspectives on Child Development*. Texas: Southwest Educational Lab, 1975.

Brathwaite, Edward. *The Development of Creole Society in Jamaica*. Oxford: Clarendon, 1971.

Brawley, Benjamin, ed. *Early Negro American Writers*. Chapel Hill: University of North Carolina Press, 1935.

Braxton, Joanne M. "A Poet's Retreat: The Diaries of Charlotte Forten Grimke (1837–1914)." In *Wild Women in the Whirlwind*, edited by Joanne Braxton and Andree McLaughlin, 70–88. New Brunswick NJ: Rutgers University Press, 1990.

Brentjes, Burchard. *African Rock Art*. New York: Clarkson, 1965.

Brooklyn Museum. *Africa in Antiquity: The Arts of Nubia and the Sudan*. New York: Brooklyn Museum, 1978.

Brown, William Wells. *Clotel; or, The President's Daughter*. 1853. Boston: St. Martins, 2000.

———. *My Southern Home*. Boston, 1880.

Budge, E. A. Wallis. *The Book of the Dead*. 1926. New York: Citadel, 1960.

———. *The Gods of the Egyptians*. 1904. New York: Dover, 1969.

Burr, George L., ed. *Narrative of the Witchcraft Cases, 1648–1706*. New York: C. Scribner's Sons, 1914.

Busby, Margaret. *Daughters of Africa*. New York: Pantheon, 1992.

Byrd, Alexander X. "Ebo, Country, Nation, and Gustavus Vassa's *Interesting Narrative*." *William and Mary Quarterly*, 3rd ser., 63, no. 1 (January 2006): 123–48.

Cabrera, Lydia. *El monte: notas sobre las religiones, la magica, las supersticiones y el folklore de los negros crillos y el pueblo de Cuba*. Miami: Coleccion del Chichereku, 1986.

Campbell, Joseph. *The Masks of God*. New York: Viking, 1964.

Carby, Hazel. *Afro-American Women Novelists*. New York: Oxford University Press, 1987.

———. *Reconstructing Womanhood*. New York: Oxford University Press, 1987.

Carretta, Vincent. *Equiano the African: A Biography of a Self-Made Man*. Athens: University of Georgia Press, 2005.

Cesaire, Aime. *Lost Body*. New York: Braziller, 1986.

Chamoiseau, Patrick. *Solibo the Magnificent*. New York: Pantheon, 1997.

Chappell, Louis. *John Henry: A Folklore Study*. Jena, Germany: Biedermann, 1933.

Charters, Samuel. *The Roots of the Blues*. New York: Putnam, 1980.

Chase-Riboud, Barbara. *Echo of Lions*. New York: Morrow, 1989.

———. *The President's Daughter*. New York: Crown, 1994.

———. *Sally Hemings*. New York: Crown, 1979.

Chestnut, Charles. *Paul Marchand F. M. C.* Jackson: University Press of Mississippi, 1998.

Chomsky, Noam. *Language and the Mind*. New York: Harcourt, 1968.

Christaller, J. G. *Twi mmebusem mpensa-Ahansi mmoaana: A Collection of Three Thousand and Six Hundred Tshi Proverbs among the Negroes of the Gold Coast Speaking Asante and Fante*. London, 1879.

Christian, Barbara. *Black Feminist Criticism*. New York: Pergamon, 1985.

Clarke, John Henry. *African People in World History*. Philadelphia: Black Classics, 1991.

Clarke, Margaret Courtney. *Ndebele*. New York: Rizzoli, 1986.

Clarke, Veve A., and Sara E. Johnson, eds. *Kaiso: Writings by and about Katherine Dunham*. Madison: University of Wisconsin Press, 2005.

Cliff, Jimmy. "Many Rivers to Cross." *The Harder They Come*. Mango, 1972, CD.

Cody, Cheryll Ann. "Naming Kinship and Estate Dispersal on a South Carolina Plantation 1786–1833." *William and Mary Quarterly* 39 (1982): 457–62.

Cohn, Lawrence. *Nothing but the Blues: The Music and the Musicians*. New York: Abbeville, 1993.

Collins, Julia. *The Curse of Caste; or, The Slave Bride*. 1865. Edited by William Andrews. New York: Oxford University Press, 2006.

Conde, Maryse. *I, Tituba, Black Witch of Salem*. 1986. Charlottesville: University of Virginia Press, 1992.
Cone, James. *The Spirituals and the Blues: An Interpretation*. New York: Seabury, 1972.
Cooper, Anna Julia. *A Voice from the South*. Xenia OH: Aldine, 1892.
Coulson, David, and Alec Campbell. *African Rock Art: Paintings and Engravings on Stone*. New York: Abrams, 2001.
Courlander, Harold, ed. *Afro American Folklore*. New York: Crown, 1976.
———, ed. *The Cow-Tail Switch and Other West African Stories*. New York: Holt, 1987.
———, ed. *The Crest and the Hide and Other African Stories*. New York: Putnam, 1982.
———, ed. *The Drum and the Hoe*. 1960. Berkeley: University of California Press, 1985.
———, ed. *Haiti Singing*. New York: Cooper Square, 1939.
———, ed. *Negro Folk Music USA*. New York: Columbia University Press, 1963.
———, ed. *Olode the Hunter and Other Tales from Nigeria*. New York: Harcourt, 1968.
———, ed. *A Treasury of African Folklore*. New York: Crown, 1975.
Craft, Ellen. *Running a Thousand Miles to Freedom; or, The Escape of William and Ellen Craft from Slavery*. 1860. London, 1863.
Crafts, Hannah. *The Bondwoman's Narrative*. Edited by Henry Louis Gates. New York: Warner, 2002.
Curtin, Phillip D., ed. *Africa Remembered: Narratives by West Africans from the Era of the Slave Trade*. Madison: University of Wisconsin Press, 1967.
———. *The Atlantic Slave Trade*. Madison: University of Wisconsin Press, 1969.
Da Gama, Vasco. *The Journal of the First Voyage of Vasco da Gama*. Translated by G. Ravenstein. London, 1898.
Dalphinis, Morgan. *Caribbean and African Languages*. London: Karia, 1985.
Davidson, Basil. *The African Past*. Boston: Little, Brown, 1964.
———. *Black Mother*. Boston: Little, Brown, 1961.
Davis, Angela Y. "The Blues as Literature." Interview. NPR, February 24, 2009.
———. *Blues Legacies and Black Feminism*. New York: Vintage, 1999.
———. *Women, Culture, and Society*. New York: Vintage, 1990.
———. *Women, Race, and Class*. New York: Random House, 1981.
De Mille, Agnes. *The Book of the Dance*. New York: Golden, 1963.
Demos, John. *Entertaining Satan*. New York: Oxford University Press, 1982.
Deren, Maya. *Divine Horsemen: The Living Gods of Haiti*. 1953. New York: McPherson, 1983.
Diegues, Carlos, dir. *Quilombo*. New York: New Yorker Films, 1984.
Diop, Cheikh Anta. *The African Origins of Civilization: Myth or Reality*. New York: Hill, 1974.
———. *Black Africa*. New York: Hill, 1978.
Dixon, Melvin. *Ride Out the Wilderness: Geography and Identity in Afro-American Literature*. Urbana: University of Illinois Press, 1987.

Doob, Leonard W., ed. *Ants Will Not Eat Your Fingers*. New York: Walker, 1966.

Douglass, Frederick. *Narrative of the Life of Frederick Douglass an American Slave*. Boston, 1845.

Dowson, Thomas. *Rock Engravings of Southern Africa*. Johannesburg: University of Witwaterstrand Press, 1992.

Drake, Samuel G. *Witchcraft Delusion in New England*. Roxbury MA, 1866.

Drewal, Margaret Thompson. *Yoruba Ritual: Performers, Play, Agency*. Bloomington: Indiana University Press, 1992.

Driberg, J. H. *People of the Small Arrow*. New York: Payne, 1930.

Dubois, Sylvia. *A Biography of a Woman Who Whipped Her Mistress and Gained Her Freedom*. New York, 1883.

Du Bois, William Edward Burgart. *Black Reconstruction in America 1860–1880*. 1935. New York: Atheneum, 1992.

———. *The Philadelphia Negro*. 1899. New York: Kraus Thomson, 1973.

———. *The Souls of Black Folk*. In *The Norton Anthology of African American Literature*, edited by Henry Louis Gates, 613–739. New York: Norton, 1997.

Dunham, Katherine. *Island Possessed*. New York: Doubleday, 1969.

———. *Journey to Accompong*. New York: Holt, 1946.

———. *Kassamance: A Fantasy*. New York: Odarkai, 1974.

———. "The Negro Dance." In *Kaiso: Writings by and about Katherine Dunham*, edited by Veve A. Clarke and Sara E. Johnson, 217–26. Madison: University of Wisconsin Press, 2005.

———. "Notes on the Dance." In *Kaiso: Writings by and about Katherine Dunham*, edited by Veve A. Clarke and Sara E. Johnson, 388–97. Madison: University of Wisconsin Press, 2005.

Dunlap, Sara Jackson. "Letters of Phillis and Susana Wheatley." *Journal of Negro History* 57 (April 1972): 211–15.

Elder, J. D., Alan Lomax, and Bessie Lomax Hawes. *Brown Girl in the Ring: An Anthology of Song Games from the Eastern Caribbean*. New York: Pantheon, 1997.

Eldridge, Eleanor. *Memories of Eleanor Eldridge*. Providence RI, 1883.

Ellis, Normandi. *Awakening Osiris*. Grand Rapids MI: Phanes, 1988.

Ellison, Ralph. *The Collected Essays*. New York: Modern Library, 1995.

Epstein, Dena. *Sinful Tunes and Spirituals*. Urbana: University of Illinois Press, 1977.

Equiano, Olaudah. *The Interesting Narrative of the Life of Olaudah Equiano or Gustavus Vassa the African Written by Himself*. In *The Classic Slave Narratives*, edited by Henry Louis Gates, 1–182. New York: Penguin, 1987.

Erdoes, Richard, and Alfonzo Ortiz. *American Indian Myths and Legends*. New York: Pantheon, 1984.

Feelings, Tom. *The Middle Passage*. New York: Dial, 1995.

Fenner, Thomas P. *Cabin and Plantation Songs*. New York: Putnam, 1901.
Fisher, Angela. *Africa Adorned*. New York: Abrams, 1990.
Fisher, Miles Mark. *Negro Slave Songs in the United States*. New York: Citadel Press, 1953.
Fisk University. *Unwritten History of Slavery: God Struck Me Dead: Religious Conversion Experiences and Autobiography*. Nashville: Fisk University Social Science Department, 1945.
Foner, Eric. *A Short History of Reconstruction*. New York: Harper, 1990.
Foster, Francis Smith, ed. *A Brighter Coming Day: A Frances Ellen Watkins Harper Reader*. New York: Feminist Press, 1990.
Fox-Genovese, Elizabeth. *Within the Plantation Household*. Chapel Hill: University of North Carolina, 1988.
Franklin, John Hope. *From Slavery to Freedom: A History of African Americans*. 1947. New York: Knopf, 1967.
Frazier, Franklin E. *The Negro Family*. Chicago: University of Chicago Press, 1966.
———. *The Negro in the United States*. New York: Macmillian, 1967.
Frazier, James George. *Leaves from the Golden Bough*. New York: Macmillan, 1924.
Frederick, Charles. "Singing Freedom into Being: The Spirituals." MA thesis, Empire State College, 2003.
Galeano, Eduardo. *Memory of Fire: Century of the Wind*. New York: Pantheon, 1988.
———. *Memory of Fire: Faces and Masks*. New York: Pantheon, 1987.
———. *Memory of Fire: Genesis*. New York: Pantheon, 1985.
Gates, Henry Lewis, ed. *The Classic Slave Narratives*. New York: Penguin, 1987.
———, ed. *Collected Black Women's Narratives*. Schomberg Library of Nineteenth-Century Black Women Writers. New York: Oxford University Press, 1988.
———, ed. *The Collected Works of Phillis Wheatley*. Schomberg Library of Nineteenth-Century Black Women Writers. New York: Oxford University Press, 1988.
———, ed. *Norton Anthology of African American Literature*. New York: Norton, 1996.
———, ed. *Race Writing and Difference*. Chicago: University of Chicago Press, 1986.
———. *Signifying Monkey: A Theory of Afro-American Literary Criticism*. New York: Oxford University Press, 1988.
———, ed. *Six Women's Slave Narratives*. Schomberg Library of Nineteenth-Century Black Women Writers. New York: Oxford University Press, 1988.
———, ed. *Spiritual Narratives*. Schomberg Library of Nineteenth-Century Black Women Writers. New York: Oxford University Press, 1988.
———. *Wonders of the African World*. New York: Knopf, 1999.
Gautz, Jeffery. *The Mabinogion*. New York: Penguin, 1976.
Geertz, Clifford. *The Interpretation of Culture*. 1973. New York: Basic, 2000.
Giddings, Paula. *Where and When I Enter: The Impact of Black Women on Race and Sex in America*. New York: Bantam, 1984.

Gilroy, Paul. *The Black Atlantic: Modernity and Double Consciousness*. Cambridge: Harvard University Press, 1993.
Gonzalez-Wippler, Migene. *Rituals and Spells of Santeria*. New York: Original, 1984.
———. *The Santeria Experience*. Englewood Cliffs NJ: Prentice-Hall, 1982.
———. *Tales of the Orisha*. New York: Original, 1985.
Graves, Robert. *The Greek Myths*. New York: Penguin, 1955.
———. *The White Goddess*. 1948. New York: Farrar, Straus, and Giroux, 1975.
Green, Mildred. *Black Women Composers*. New York: Farrar, Straus, and Giroux, 1983.
Greenberg, Joseph. *Language, Culture and Communication*. Stanford CA: Stanford University Press, 1971.
———. *Language in the Americas*. Stanford CA: Stanford University Press, 1987.
———. *The Languages of Africa*. Bloomington: Indiana University Press, 1966.
Greene, Lorenzo. *Negro in Colonial New England*. New York: Columbia University Press, 1962.
———. *The Negro Wage Earner*. 1930. New York: Russell, 1969.
Grimke, Charlotte Forten. *The Journals of Charlotte Forten Grimke*. New York: Oxford University Press, 1988.
Gutman, Herbert. *The Black Family in Slavery and Freedom*. New York: Random House, 1976.
Hanson, Chadwick. *Witchcraft in Salem*. New York: Braziler, 1969.
Harding, Vincent. *There Is a River: The Black Struggle for Freedom in America*. New York: Harcourt, 1981.
Harper, Francis. *Iola Leroy*. 1892. Boston: Beacon, 1987.
Harrison, Daphne Duval. *Black Pearls: Blues Queens of the 1920s*. New Brunswick NJ: Rutgers University Press, 1988.
Harrison, Paul Carter. *Totem Voices*. New York: Grove, 1989.
Hashaw, Tim. *The Birth of Black America: The First African Americans and the Pursuit of Freedom at Jamestown*. New York: Carroll and Graff, 2007.
Heaney, Seamus. *Beowulf: A New Verse Translation*. New York: Farrar, Straus, and Giroux, 2000.
Herodotus. *The History of Herodotus*. Translated by David Green. Chicago: University of Chicago Press, 1987.
Herskovits, Melville. *Dahomey: An Ancient West African Kingdom*. 2 vols. Evanston IL: Northwestern University Press, 1967.
———. *The Myth of the Negro Past*. Boston: Beacon, 1941.
Herskovits, Melville, and Francis Herskovits. *Surinam Folklore*. New York: Columbia University Press, 1936.
Higginson, Thomas Wentworth. "Negro Spirituals." *Atlantic Monthly* 19 (1867): 685–94.

Hill, Errol, ed. *The Theater of Black Americans: Roots and Rituals*. Vol. 1. Englewood Cliffs NJ: Prentice-Hall, 1980.

Hill, Errol, and James Hatch. *African American Theater*. Cambridge: Oxford University Press, 2004.

Holloway, Joseph. *The African Heritage of American English*. Bloomington: Indiana University Press, 1983.

———, ed. *Africanisms in African American Culture*. Bloomington: Indiana University Press, 1990.

Homer. *The Iliad*. Translated by Robert Fagles. New York: Viking, 1990.

———. *The Odyssey*. Translated by Robert Fagles. New York: Viking, 1996.

Huggins, Nathan Irvin. *Black Odyssey*. New York: Random House, 1977.

Hughes, Langston. *The Collected Poems*. New York: Knopf, 1994.

Hughes, Langston, and Arna Bontemps, eds. *Book of Negro Folklore*. New York: Dodd, 1958.

Hughes, Ted, trans. *Tales from Ovid*. New York: Farrar, Straus, and Giroux, 1997.

Hull, Richard W. Munyakare. *African Civilization before the Bantuuree*. New York: Wiley, 1972.

Hurston, Zora Neale. *Barracoon: The Story of the Last Black Cargo*. New York: Amistad, 2018.

———. *Mules and Men*. Bloomington: Indiana University Press, 1935.

———. *The Sanctified Church*. Berkeley CA: Turtle Island, 1981.

———. *Tell My Horse*. 1938. Berkeley CA: Turtle Island, 1983.

———. *Their Eyes Were Watching God*. 1937. Urbana: University of Illinois Press, 1978.

Innes, Mary, trans. *The Metamorphoses of Ovid*. New York: Penguin, 1955.

Jackson, Bruce, ed. *Wake Up Dead Man: Afro American Work Songs from Texas Prisons*. Cambridge MA: Harvard University Press, 1962.

Jackson, Gale. *Bridge Suite*. New York: Storm Imprints, 1998.

———. "If He Asks You Was I Running You Tell Him I Was Flying If He Asks You Was I Laughing You Tell Him I Was Crying: Reading John Henry as American History 1870." In *Racing and (E)racing Language*, edited by Ellen Goldner and Safiya Henderson Holmes, 57–76. Syracuse: Syracuse University Press, 2001.

———. "The Way We Do: A Preliminary Investigation of the African Roots of African American Performance." In *African American Literary Criticism, 1773–2000*, edited by Hazel Arnett Ervin, 312–27. New York: Twayne, 2000.

Jacobs, Harriet. *Incidents in the Life of a Slave Girl*. 1861. Edited by Jean Fagen Yellin. Cambridge MA: Harvard University Press, 1987.

Jahn, Janheinz. *Neo-African Literature: A History of Black Writing*. New York: Grove, 1969.

James, C. L. R. *A History of Negro Revolt*. New York: Haskell, 1969.

Janzen, John, and Wyatt MacGaffey, eds. *Anthology of Kongo Religion: Primary Texts from Lower Zaire*. Lawrence: University of Kansas, 1974.

Jeffries, Rosalind. "The Image of Woman in African Cave Art." In *Black Women in Antiquity*, edited by Ivan Van Sertima, 98–123. New Brunswick NJ: Transaction, 1992.

Jochannan, Yusef Ben. *The Black Man of the Nile*. Philadelphia: Black Classics, 1989.

Johnson, Guy. *John Henry: Tracking Down a Negro Legend*. Chapel Hill: University of North Carolina Press, 1929.

Johnson, James Weldon, and J. Rosamond Johnson, eds. *American Negro Spirituals*. 1928. New York: Da Capo, 1985.

Jones, Bessie, and Bess Lomax Hawes. *Step It Down: Games, Plays, Songs and Stories from the Afro-American Heritage*. New York: Harper 1972.

Jones, Jaqueline. *Labor of Love, Labor of Sorrow: Black Women Work and Family from Slavery to the Present*. New York: Random House, 1985.

Jordan, Winthrop. *White Over Black: American Attitudes towards the Negro 1550–1812*. Chapel Hill: North Carolina University Press, 1968.

Joyner, Charles. *Down by the Riverside: A South Carolina Slave Community*. Urbana: University of Illinois Press, 1984.

Kaplan, Sidney. *The Black Presence in the Era of the American Revolution*. Amherst: University of Massachusetts Press, 1989.

Karasch, Mary C. *Slave Life in Rio de Janeiro 1808–1850*. Princeton: Princeton University Press, 1987.

Karlsen, Carol. *The Devil in the Shape of a Woman*. New York: Norton, 1987.

Katz, Bernard. *The Social Implications of Early Negro Music in the United States*. New York: Arno, 1969.

Katz, William Loren, ed. *Five Slave Narratives*. New York: Arno, 1968.

Keckley, Elizabeth. *Behind the Scenes*. New York, 1868.

Kilson, Marion Dusser De Barenne. "The Ga Naming Rite." *Anthropos* 63–64 (1968).

King, Jeff. *Where the Two Came to Their Father: A Navaho War Ceremonial*. 1943. Princeton: Princeton University Press, 1991.

Kolchin, Peter. *American Slavery 1619–1877*. New York: Hill, 1993.

Kreamer, Christina Mullen, ed. *African Cosmos Stellar Arts*. Washington DC: National Museum of African Art, 2012.

Krehbiel, Henry Edward. *Afro American Folk Songs*. New York: Ungar, 1962.

Landeck, Beatrice. *Echoes of Africa in Folk Songs of the Americas*. New York: McKay, 1961.

Laye, Camara. *The Guardian of the Word*. New York: Vintage, 1980.

Leacock, Ruth. *Spirits of the Deep*. New York: Doubleday, 1975.

Lee, D. N., and H. C. Woodhouse. *Art on the Rocks of Southern Africa*. Capetown: Purnell, 1970.

Lerner, Gerda. *Black Women in White America: A Documentary History*. New York: Random House, 1972.

Lester, Julius. *To Be a Slave*. New York: Dell, 1968.

Levine, Lawrence. *Black Culture Black Consciousness*. New York: Oxford University Press, 1977.

Lewis, David Levering. *W. E. B. Du Bois: Biography of a Race*. New York: Holt, 1993.

Lieb, Sandra. *Mother of the Blues*. Amherst: University of Massachusetts Press, 1981.

Litwack, Leon. *Been in the Storm So Long: The Aftermath of Slavery*. New York: Knopf, 1979.

———. *North of Slavery: The Negro in the Free States 1790–1860*. Chicago: University of Chicago Press, 1961.

Loewenberg, Bert, and Ruth Bogin, eds. *Black Women in Nineteenth-Century American Life*. University Park: Pennsylvania State University Press, 1976.

Lomax, Alan. *Folk Songs of North America*. New York: Doubleday, 1960.

———. *Folk Song Style and Culture*. Washington DC: American Association for the Advancement of Science, 1968.

———, ed. *Prison Songs: Historical Recordings from Parchman Farm 1947–48*. Rounder, 1997, CD.

Lomax, Alan, and John Lomax. *Folk Song USA*. New York: Meredith, 1947.

Lorca, Gabriel Garcia. *In Search of Duende*. 1955. New York: New Directions, 1998.

Lovell, John. *Black Song: The Forge and the Flame: The Story of How the Afro-American Spiritual Was Hammered Out*. New York: Macmillian, 1972.

Lucas, J. O. *Religion of the Yoruba*. Lagos, 1948.

MacGaffey, Wyatt. *Art and Healing of the BaKongo Commented by Themselves: Minkisi from the Laman Collection*. Stockholm: Folken Museum, 1991.

———. "The Eyes of Understanding: Kongo Minkisi." In *Astonishment and Power*. Washington DC: National Museum of African Art, 1993.

———. *Religion and Society in Central Africa: The Ba Kongo of Lower Zaire*. Chicago: University of Chicago Press, 1986.

Major, Clarence. *Juba to Jive*. New York: Penguin, 1970.

Makeba, Miriam. *Africa*. Novus, 1991, CD.

Marley, Bob, and the Wailers. *Trenchtown Days: Birth of a Legend*. Sony, 2001, CD.

Martinez-Ruiz, Barbaro. *Kongo Graphic Writing and Other Narratives of the Sign*. Philadelphia: Temple University Press, 2013.

Mbiti, John. *African Religion and Philosophy*. New York: Praeger, 1969.

Mbuti of Central Africa. *Mbuti Pygmies of the Ituri Rainforest*. Smithsonian, 1992, CD.

McClusky, Pamela. *Art from Africa: Long Steps Never Broke a Back*. Seattle: Seattle Art Museum, 2002.

McKim, James Miller. "Negro Songs." In *The Social Implications of Early Negro Music in the United States*, edited by Bernard Katz, 1–2. New York: Arno, 1969.

McKinney-Johnson, Eloise. "Egypt's Isis." In *Black Women in Antiquity*, edited by Ivan Van Sertima, 64–71. New Brunswick NJ: Transaction, 1992.

McLaurin, Melton. *Celia, a Slave*. Athens: University of Georgia Press, 1991.
Miller, Arthur. *The Crucible*. New York: Penguin, 2003.
Mintz, Sidney, and Richard Price. *An Anthropological Approach to the Afro-American Past: A Caribbean Perspective*. Occasional Papers in Social Change, no. 2. Philadelphia: Institute for the Study of Human Issues, 1976.
Moore, Lillian. "Moreau de Saint-Mery and 'Danse.'" *Dance Index* 5 (1946).
Morgan, Edward. *American Slavery American Freedom: The Ordeal of Colonial Virginia*. New York: Norton, 1975.
Morrison, Toni. *Beloved*. New York: Knopf, 1987.
———. *What Moves at the Margins: Selected Non-Fiction*. Jackson: University Press of Mississippi, 2008.
Ndoma, Ugina. "Kongo and Personal Names Today." *Names* 25 (1977): 88–98.
Neff, Robert, and Anthony Connor. *Blues*. Boston: Godine, 1975.
Nettleford, Rex M. *Caribbean Cultural Identity: The Case of Jamaica*. Kingston: Institute of Jamaica, 1978.
———. *Dance Jamaica: Cultural Definition and Artistic Discovery*. New York: Grove, 1986.
———. *Dance Jamaica: Renewal and Continuity*. Kingston: Randle, 2009.
———. *Inward Stretch Outward Reach*. New York: Caribbean Diaspora, 1995.
Ngũgĩ wa Thiong'o. *Something Torn and New: An African Renaissance*. New York: Basic Civitas, 2009.
Niane, D. T. *Sundiata: An Epic of Old Mali*. London: Longmans, 1965.
Nketia, Kwabena. "Akan Poetry." In *A Treasury of African Folklore*, edited by Harold Courlander, 92–95. New York: Crown, 1975.
Northup, Solomon. *Twelve Years a Slave, Narrative of Solomon Northup, a Citizen of New York, Kidnapped in Washington City in 1841, and Rescued in 1853, from a Cotton Plantation Near the Red River in Louisiana*. 1853. Baton Rouge: Louisiana State University Press, 1968.
Norton, Mary Beth. "The Afro-American Family in the Age of Revolution." In *Slavery and Freedom in the Age of the American Revolution*, edited by Ira Berlin and Ronald Hoffman. Urbana: University of Illinois Press, 1983.
Nunley, John W., and Judith Bettlheim, eds. *Caribbean Festival Arts*. Seattle: University of Washington Press, 1988.
Odetta. "A Life within Music." *American Legacy* 19 (Summer 2008).
Odum, Harold. *Negro Workday Songs*. Chapel Hill: University of North Carolina Press, 1926.
Okpewho, Isidore. *The Epic in Africa*. New York: Columbia University Press, 1979.
Oliver, Paul. *Savannah Syncopators: African Retentions in the Blues*. New York: Stein, 1970.
Omedele, Oluremi. "Traditional and Contemporary African Drama: A Historical Perspective." Diss., University of California, 1989.

O'Neale, Sandra. "A Slave's Subtle War: Phillis Wheatley's Use of Biblic Myth and Symbol." *Early American Literature* 21 (Fall 1986): 144–65.

Ositola, Kolawole. "On Ritual Performance: A Practitioners View." *Drama Review* 32, no. 2 (1988): 31–41.

Ottley, Roi, and William Weatherby. *The Negro in New York: An Informal Social History, 1626–1940*. New York: Praeger, 1969.

Paiewonsky, Isidor. *Eyewitness Accounts of Slavery in the Danish West Indies*. St. Thomas: printed by the author, 1987.

Painter, Nell Irvin. *Sojourner Truth: A Life a Symbol*. New York: Norton, 1996.

Palcy, Euzhan, dir. *Sugar Cane Alley*. New York: New Yorker Films, 1983.

Palmer, C. A. *Passageways: An Interpretive History of Black America to 1865*. New York: Harcourt, 1993.

Park, Mungo. *Travels in the Interior Districts of Africa, Performed under the Direction and Patronage of the African Association in the Years of 1795, 1796, and 1797 by Mungo Park Surgeon*. New York, 1800.

Parrish, Lydia. *Slave Songs of the Georgia Sea Islands*. Hatboro PA: Folklore Society, 1942.

Patterson, Lindsay, ed. *International Library of Negro Life and History: The Negro in Music and Art*. New York: Publishers Company, 1967.

Patterson, Orlando. *Slavery and Social Death*. Cambridge MA: Harvard University Press, 1982.

———. *The Sociology of Slavery*. 1967. Rutherford NJ: Fairleigh Dickinson University, 1969.

Pennington, James W. C. *The Fugitive Blacksmith*. In *Great Slave Narratives*, edited by Arna Bontemps, 193–268. Boston: Beacon, 1969.

Petry, Anne. *Tituba of Salem Village*. New York: Random House, 1968.

Phillips, Ruth B. *Representing Woman: Sande Masquerades of the Mende of Sierra Leone*. Los Angeles: University of California Regents, 1995.

Piersen, William. *Black Yankees*. Amherst: University of Massachusetts Press, 1988.

Plutarch. *Moralia*. Vol. 5. Cambridge MA: Harvard University Press, 1936.

Power, Camilla, and Ian Watts. "The Woman with the Zebra's Penis: Gender Mutability and Performance." *Journal of the Royal Anthropological Institute* 3 (September 1997).

Price, Richard, ed. *Maroon Societies: Rebel Slave Communities in the Americas*. Baltimore: Johns Hopkins University Press, 1973.

Prince, Mary. *The History of Mary Prince, a West Indian Slave Related by Herself*. In *Six Women's Slave Narratives*, edited by Henry Louis Gates. New York: Oxford University Press, 1988.

Quarles, Benjamin. *Black Mosaic: Essays in Afro-American History and Historiography*. Amherst: University of Massachusetts Press, 1988.

———. *The Negro in the Civil War*. 1953. New York: Da Capo, 1989.

———. *The Negro in the Making of America*. New York: Macmillan, 1964.

Radin, Paul, and James Sweeney. *African Folktales and Sculpture.* New York: Pantheon, 1952.

Ramanujan, A. K., ed. *Folktales from India.* New York: Pantheon, 1991.

Rawick, George P., ed. *The American Slave: A Composite Autobiography: Oral Histories of Slavery Complied by the Works Progress Administration.* 19 vols. 1941. Westport CT: Greenwood, 1972.

———, ed. *The American Slave: A Composite Autobiography.* Supplement Series 1, 12 vols. 1941. Westport CT: Greenwood, 1977.

Reagon, Bernice Johnson. *If You Don't Go, Don't Hinder Me.* Lincoln: University of Nebraska Press, 2001.

Richmond, M. A. *Bid the Vassal Soar: Interpretive Essays on the Life and Poetry of Phillis Wheatley and George Moses Horton.* Washington DC: Howard University Press, 1974.

Riefenstahl, Leni. *Vanishing Africa.* New York: Harmony, 1982.

Rilke, Rainer Maria. "I, 25." In *The Selected Poetry,* edited and translated by Stephen Mitchell, 239. New York: Vintage, 1982.

Robeson, Paul. *Here I Stand.* 1958. Boston: Beacon, 1971.

———. *The Odyssey of Paul Robeson.* Omega Classics, 1992, CD.

Robinson, William G. *Black New England Letters.* Boston: Boston Public Library, 1977.

———. *Phillis Wheatley in the Black American Beginnings.* Detroit: Broadside, 1975.

Rodger, George. *Village of the Nubas.* 1955. Translated by Liz Heron. London: Phaidon, 1999.

Rodney, Walter. *How Europe Underdeveloped Africa.* London: L'Ouverture, 1973.

Rose, Willie Lee. *Rehearsal for Reconstruction: The Port Royal Experiment.* New York: Oxford University Press, 1964.

———. *Slavery and Freedom.* New York: Oxford University Press, 1971.

Rudner, Jalmar, and Ione Rudner. *The Hunter and His Art.* Capetown: Struik, 1970.

Ruhlen, Merritt. *On the Origin of Languages: Studies in Linguistic Taxonomy.* Stanford CA: Stanford University Press, 1994.

———. *The Origin of Language: Tracing the Evolution of the Mother Tongue.* New York: Wiley, 1994.

Saadawi, Nawal. *The Circling Song.* London: Zed, 1989.

Sackheim, Eric. *The Blues Line.* New York: Da Capo, 2003.

Scarborough, Dorothy. *On the Trail of Negro Folk Songs.* Cambridge MA: Harvard University Press, 1925.

Schneider, Gilbert D. "Daniel Decatur Emmett's Stump Sermons: Genuine Afro-American Culture, Language and Rhetoric in Negro Minstrel Shows." *Journal of Popular Culture* 19, no. 9 (Spring 1988).

Seale, Lee, and Marianna Seale. "Easter Rock: A Louisiana Negro Ceremony." *Journal of American Folklore* 55 (1942).

Sembene, Ousmane, dir. *Moolade.* New York: New Yorker Films, 2004.

Shockley, Ann Allen, ed. *Afro-American Women Writers: 1746–1933: An Anthology and Critical Guide*. New York: New American, 1988.

Shostak, Majorie. *Nissa: The Life and Words of a !Kung Woman*. Cambridge MA: Harvard University Press, 1981.

Silverman, Jerry. *Folk Blues*. New York: Oak, 1958.

Simone, Nina. *Don't Let Me Be Misunderstood*. Polygram, 1988, CD.

Sistrunk, Albertha. "Phillis Wheatley: An Eighteenth-Century Black American Poet Revisited." *College Language Association Journal* 23, no. 4 (June 1980): 391–98.

Smith, Barbara. "Toward a Black Feminist Criticism." In *All the Women Are White, All the Blacks Are Men, but Some of Us Are Brave*, edited by Gloria T. Hull, Patricia Bell Scott, and Barbara Smith. New York: Feminist Press, 1982.

Smith, Bessie. *The Essential Bessie Smith*. Columbia, 1997, CD.

Sobel, Mechal. *Trabelin' On: The Slave Journey to an Afro Baptist Faith*. Princeton: Princeton University Press, 1988.

———. *The World They Made Together: Black and White Values in Eighteenth-Century Virginia*. Princeton: Princeton University Press, 1987.

Sofola, Adeyemi. *African Culture and the African Personality*. Lagos: African Resource, 1973.

Southern, Eileen. *The Music of Black Americans*. New York: Norton, 1971.

———, ed. *Readings in Black American Music*. New York: Norton, 1971.

Spillers, Hortense. *Conjuring*. Bloomington: Indiana University Press, 1985.

Starkey, Marion L. *The Devil in Massachusetts*. New York: Knopf, 1949.

Starling, Marion. *The Slave Narrative*. Washington DC: Howard University Press, 1988.

Stedman, J. G. *Narrative of a Five Years Expedition against the Revolted Negroes of Surinam in Guiana on the Wild Coast of South America from the Years 1772–1777*. 2 vols. 1796. Amherst: University of Massachusetts Press, 1972.

Sterling, Dorothy. *We Are Your Sisters: Black Women in the Nineteenth Century*. New York: Norton, 1984.

Still, William. *The Underground Railroad*. 1872. New York: Arno, 1968.

Stuckey, Sterling. *Slave Culture*. New York: Oxford University Press, 1987.

Taylor, Suzie King. *Reminiscences of My Life in Camp with the 33rd United States Colored Troops Late First South Carolina Volunteers*. Boston, 1902.

Thomas, Elizabeth Marshall. *The Old Way: A Story of the First People*. New York: Farrar, Straus, and Giroux, 2006.

Thompson, Robert Farris. *Aesthetic of the Cool: Afro-Atlantic Art and Music*. Pittsburgh: Periscope, 2011.

———. *African Art in Motion*. Berkeley: University of California, 1979.

———. *Face of the Gods: Art and Alters of Africa and the African Americas*. New York: Museum for African Art, 1993.

———. *Flash of the Spirit*. New York: Random House, 1983.

Trent-Jones, Altona. *Play Songs of the Deep South*. Washington DC: Associated, 1944.
Truth, Sojourner. *The Narrative of Sojourner Truth*. 1878. New York: Arno, 1968.
Turner, Darwin. *Africanisms in the Gullah Dialect*. Chicago: University of Chicago Press, 1949.
Van Sertima, Ivan. *Blacks in Science: Ancient and Modern*. New Brunswick NJ: Transaction, 1983.
———, ed. *Black Women in Antiquity*. New Brunswick NJ: Transaction, 1992.
———, ed. *Golden Age of the Moor*. New Brunswick NJ: Transaction, 1992.
Vilson, Georges. *Kandelab: 101 Notated Haitian Folk and Vodou Songs*. Vol. 1. Kandelab Foundation, 2013, CD.
Virgil. *The Aeneid*. Translated by Robert Fagles. New York: Viking, 2007.
Walker, Alice. "In Search of Our Mother's Gardens." In *In Search of Our Mothers Gardens*, 231–43. New York: Harcourt, 1983.
Walker, Barbara. *The Woman's Encyclopedia of Myths and Secrets*. New York: Harper, 1983.
Warner-Lewis, Maureen. *Central Africa in the Caribbean*. Kingston: University of the West Indies Press, 2003.
Washington, Mary Helen. *Invented Lives*. New York: Anchor, 1987.
Weischhoff, Heniz. "The Social Significance of Names among the Ibo of Nigeria." *American Anthropologist* 43 (1941).
Wheatley, Phillis. *Memoir and Poems of Phillis Wheatley*. Boston: Mnemosyne Publisher, 1969.
———. *Poems on Various Subjects*. In *The Collected Works of Phillis Wheatley*, edited by Henry Louis Gates. New York: Oxford University Press, 1988.
Willet, Frank. *Ife in the History of West Africa*. New York: McGraw, 1967.
———. *The Sculpture of Western Nigeria*. Ibadan: Ministry of Information, 1966.
Williams, David Lewis. *Believing and Seeing: Symbolic Meaning in Southern San Rock Paintings*. London: Academic, 1981.
———. *A Cosmos in Stone: Interpreting Religion and Society Through Rock Art*. Oxford: Altamira, 2002.
———. *The Mind in the Cave*. London: Thames, 2002.
———. *The Rock Art of Southern Africa*. Cambridge: University of Cambridge Press, 1983.
———. *San Spirituality: Roots Expressions and Social Consciousness*. Oxford: Altimira, 2004.
———. *Stories That Float from Afar: Ancestral Stories of the San of Southern Africa*. College Station: Texas A&M University Press, 2000.
Williams, David Lewis, and David Pearce. *Inside the Neolithic Mind: Consciousness, Cosmos and Realm of the Gods*. London: Thames, 2005.
Williams, David Lewis, and Jean Clottes. *Shamans of Prehistory*. New York: Abrams, 1998.

Williams, Issac. *Aunt Sally; or, The Cross, the Way of Freedom: A Narrative of the Slave Life and Purchase of the Mother of Reverend Isaac Williams of Detroit Michigan.* 1858. Miami: Mnemosyne, 1969.

Wilson, Harriet E. *Our Nig; or, Sketches from the Life of a Free Black.* 1859. New York: Vintage, 1983.

Wolf, Virginia. *A Room of One's Own.* 1929. New York: Harcourt, 1957.

Wood, Peter H. *Black Majority: Negroes in Colonial South Carolina from 1670 through the Stono Rebellion.* New York: Knopf, 1974.

———. "It Was a Negro Taught Them: A New Look at African Labor in Early South Carolina." In *Discovering African America*, edited by Roger D. Abrahams and John F. Szwed, 26–45. Leiden: Brill, 1975.

Work, John. *American Negro Songs and Spirituals.* New York: Bonanza, 1940.

Yetman, Norman, comp. *Life under the Particular Institution: Selections from the Slave Narrative Collection.* New York: Holt, 1970.

Zwick, Edward, dir. *Glory.* Culver City CA: Tristar/Sony, 1989.

# Index

*Page numbers in italics refer to illustrations.*

Abaku, 35, 38. *See also* Cuba
abolition, 60–61, 83, 107, 123–24
Africa: Neolithic migrations in, 28–29, 39; Pan-African cultural practices and continuities in diaspora performance of, 9, 12–19, 21, 24, 27–30, 39, 50, 51, 66, 77–78, 83, 84, 86, 107, 117, 127, 134, 139–40, 148–49, 153; slave trade in, 12, 20–21, 40–41, 51, 178. *See also specific countries and regions*
African Methodist Episcopal Church, 23, 96
Africatown, 19, 20
Afro-Christian performance practices, 29, 30, 81, 95
Agwe (Dahomean deity), 25
Ailey, Alvin: *Revelations*, 18, 25–26
Akan: storytelling traditions of, 37, 178. *See also* Asante (Ashanti)
Alice (of colonial Pennsylvania), 83
Allen, Richard, 23, 96
Allen, William Francis: *Slave Songs*, 32, 123, 152, 155–56
Amharic liturgy, 28
Anansi (Anancy Spider trickster/hero), 11–12, 174
ancient Egypt: cosmology, mythos, and ritual performance in, 75–77, 95, 111–12, 175; and Nubian artifacts, xx, 1–2, 5, 174–77; roots of theater in, 107, 111

Andrews, William L.: *To Tell a Free Story*, 30
Angola, 36, 40, 63; Tu-Chokwe cosmograms in, 35
Angola, Isabella de, 55, 178
Anozier, Shelia (Chela), *46*, 66, *73*
Asante (Ashanti), 4, 11–12, 19, 22–23, 103, 105, 114, 134, 174
Ast, 2, 5, 75, 177, 183. *See also* Isis and Osiris
Azaka (Haitian deity), 66

Ba Benzélé (Central Africa): cultural practice and influence of, 4, 83–84
"Backwater Blues" (B. Smith), 171, 179
Baker, Houston, 59
Bakongo: cultural traditions and influence of, in African diaspora performance, 34–37, 56, 77, 94, 112, 128, 153, 174, 178, 179. *See also* Kongo
Baluba (Luba Zaire/Democratic Republic of Congo), 28, 111, 178
Bambara (Mali): cultural traditions and influence of, in African diaspora performance, 52, 72, 85, 140, 174, 178, 179. *See also* Mali
Bambara, Toni Cade, 6
Bangwa (Cameroon), 111
baptism, 24–26, 39, 101

Barbados: African and neo-African performance in, 21, 56–57; slavery in, 55–56. *See also* Caribbean
Bascom, William: *Ifa Divnation*, 20, 21, 22, 33–34; *Sixteen Coweries*, 22
Belinda (of colonial Massachusetts), 80–81
Benin: cultural performance and African diaspora influence in, 27–28, 40, 63
Bennett, Louise, 8, 12, 62–63, 90
Biesele, M., 106–7
"Bile the Cabbage Down," 136, 138, 140, 142
Bleek, Wilhelm: *Specimens of Bushman Folklore*, 47–48, 103
blues, 1, 4, 6, 10, 15–16, 18, 19, 30, 32, 43–44, 78, 84, 99, 101, 133–71, 174, 178, 179, 182, 183
"The Blue Tailed Fly," 164
"The Boll Weevil," 163–64
Boston: early African presence in, 55, 84
Botkin, B. A.: *Lay My Burden Down*, 145
"Bound to Go," 119
Braithwaite, Kwame, 12
Brazil: African presence and neo-African performance in, 12, 21, 22, 35, 38, 62, 95, 131–32; sacred songs in, 131–32
Brooklyn Museum, xx, 174–77
Brown, Henry "Box," 124
Brown, Sterling, 169, 171
Brown, William Wells: *Clotel*, 124, 125; *My Southern Home*, 167
"Brown Girl in the Ring," 108–9
Byard, Carole, *102*
"Bye Bye Baby Bunting," 82, 86, 90, 91, 93–94

Cabrera, Lydia: *El monte*, 8, 56
call-and-response (antiphony), 14, 15, 19, 28, 32, 35, 36, 37–39, 43, 49, 51, 52, 54, 64, 70, 71, 77, 78, 110, 116, 129, 134, 139, 153, 170, 178, 180
Cambindas (Macumbas), 131

Cameroon: cultural practices in, 17, 111
Campbell, Joseph, 85
Candomblé, 38. *See also* Brazil
Candy (of Salem), 56, 72
Cape Verde, 21
Carby, Hazel, 6, 161
Caribbean: African and African diaspora performance practices in, 1, 8, 11, 15, 16, 21, 50, 57, 68, 80, 90, 109, 111, 155; slavery in, 55, 123, 138, 155
carnival, 15, 115
Central Africa: indigenous music of, 83–84, 148–49. *See also* Ba Benzélé (Central Africa); Mbuti
Cesaire, Aimee, 8; *Lost Body*, 24
chain gangs, 162–63
Chamoiseau, Patrick: *Solibo*, 38
Cherokee, 11
Chinese character for "art," 181
Choctaw, 81
Christian, Barbara, 6, 29
"A City Called Heaven," 42
civil rights, 14, 26, 149, 162
Civil War, 31, 118, 143–44, 152, 154, 160, 165, 171. *See also* Truth, Sojourner (Isabella Bomfree); Tubman, Harriet
Clarke, John Henry, 175
"The Click Song" (Makeba), 83
Cliff, Jimmy: "Many Rivers to Cross," 26
Collins, Julia: *The Curse of Caste*, 97, 126
Colombia, 21
Cone, James, 114, 171
Congo. *See* Democratic Republic of Congo
Congo Square, 69
Cooper, Anna Julia, 7
cosmograms and sacred ground signs, 34–35, 77
cosmology, 1–2, 5, 27, 28, 33–38, 47, 48, 84, 95, 100, 104, 107
"Cotton Eyed Joe," 151, 153, 166, 168
Curry, James, 123

Craft, Ellen and William: *Running a Thousand Miles to Freedom*, 9, 124, 126
Craft, Hannah: *The Bondswoman's Narrative*, 9, 126
Cuba: African and neo-African performance in, 21, 42, 43, 56, 64, 113; sacred songs in, 7, 131; work songs in, 43. *See also* Caribbean

Da Gama, Vasco, 51
Damballah (Dahomean deity), 25
Da Mosto, Cada, 51
Davidson, Basil: *The African Past*, 12, 29; *The African Slave Trade*, 29
Davis, Angela, 6; *Blues Legacies*, 169, 170, 171; *Women, Race, and Class*, 44, 137
"Day-O" ("The Banana Boat Song"), 62–63
"Deep River," vi, 26
Democratic Republic of Congo: reference to "congo" in early diaspora songs of, 44, 63; Tabwa cosmological performance in, 107
Deren, Maya: *Divine Horsemen*, 112
Didinga (Sudan): children's play of, 49–50, 105
"Didn't My Lord Deliver Daniel," 43
Dine: mythology of, 11
Dixon, Melvin: *Ride Out the Wilderness*, 24
Dogon (Mali): cosmological practice of, 28, 95, 176–77, 179; proverb of, 8; *Togu No* and visual narrative of, 176–77
domestic work, 81, 140, 146, 161, 169
Douglass, Frederick: *Narrative of the Life of Frederick Douglass*, 42, 88, 96, 100, 123, 124, 175
Drewal, Margaret Thompson: *Yoruba Ritual*, 22
Du Bois, Sylvia, 80
Du Bois, W. E. B.: *Black Reconstruction*, 162–63, 175; *The Souls of Black Folk*, 23, 24, 72–79, 82, 96, 152, 155, 162

Dunham, Katherine, 8, 16, 65; essays of, on Afro-Caribbean dance, 112, 113; *Journey to Accompong*, 116

"East Coast Blues," 166
Egypt. *See* ancient Egypt
Elder, J. D., 16
Ellison, Ralph, 18
Equiano, Olaudah (Gustavas Vasa): *The Interesting Narrative*, vii, 9, 23, 40–43, 63, 119, 178
Ethiopia: Amharic liturgy in, 28; Hadza cosmological performance in, 106
Ewe: cultural practice and influence of, in African diaspora, 33, 65

*fanga*, 111, 121
"Fanga Alafiya," 121
Fanti (Fante, Ghana): cultural practice of, 53, 55
field hollers, 139, 148, 169
First Michigan Regiment of Colored Soldiers, 143
Fisher, Mark Miles, 93, 97, 98
Fisher, William, 98
Florence, Nellie: "Jacksonville Blues," 170
folk ballads, 92, 143, 151, 164, 175, 178
Fon (Dahomey): cultural practice and influence of, in African diaspora performance, 12, 25, 27, 33–34, 112, 178, 179
Foner, Eric: *A Short History of Reconstruction*, 31
Frederick, Charles: *Singing Freedom into Being*, 38
Freedman's Bureau, U.S., 156
Freeman, Elizabeth ("Mumbet"), 80

Galeano, Eduardo, 8; *Memory of Fire*, 8, 60
Gambia: cultural practice and influence of, in African diaspora performance, 85, 138. *See also* Senegambia

Garifuna (of St. Vincent): cosmograms and ground signs of, 35
Garner, Margaret, 61
Gates, Henry Louis: *Signifying Monkey*, 7, 23, 42
Geertz, Clifford, 175
Georgia: narratives of experience in, 124, 149, 169. *See also* Gullah; South Carolina and Georgia Sea Islands
Georgia Sea Islands. *See* South Carolina and Georgia Sea Islands
Gonzalez-Wippler, Migene, 22
"Go Round the Border Suzy," 119–20
Great Migration, 158, 162, 167
Greece and Rome, 4, 40, 47–48, 75–76, 94, 95, 98
Green, Mildred: *Black Women Composers*, 83
Greenberg, Joseph: *Language Culture and Communication*, 29
griot traditions, 4, 15, 27, 28, 30, 84, 85, 94, 101, 108
Gronomiosaw, James Albert Okawsaw, 23
Guinea: cultural practice and presence in African diaspora performance in, 44, 51, 63, 173
Gullah, 25, 35–36, 116

haiku, 78, 115
Haiti: African and neo-African performance practice in, x, 18, 25, 35–38, 62, 66, 112, 113; sacred performance and revolution in, 62; Zabeth in, 60
Hall, Pat, 111
Hall, Stuart, 8
"Ham Bone," 18, 19, 33, 66, 115, 129, 130. *See also* Juba
Handy, W. C., 168–69
Harper, Francis Ellen Watkins, 150–51, 161
Hashaw, Tim: *The Birth of Black America*, 138
Hathor (Egyptian deity), 2

Hazda (Ethiopia): rites-of-passage performance in, 106–7
"Head and Shoulders," 13–19, 109–14, 116
Hemings, Sally, 125–26
Herskovits, Melville: *Surinam Folklore*, 66
Higginson, Thomas Wentworth, 118
Hill, Errol, 8
"Hold Your Light," 118
Holiday, Billie: "Strange Fruit," 169
Hughes, Langston, 26
Hurston, Zora Neale, 6, 8; *Mules and Men*, 112; *Tell My Horse*, 112; *Their Eyes Were Watching God*, vii
"Hush, Hush, Somebody's Calling My Name," 40

Ibo/Igbo (Ebo): cultural practice and African diaspora presence of, 41, 63, 64, 178, 179
Ifa. *See* Yoruba
Ijaw (Nigeria): cosmology and folklore of, 133–35, 178, 183
"I Know Moon Light," 117–18
"I Know Moon Rise," 118
Isis and Osiris, 2, 39, 75–76, 77, 95, 98, 107, 134, 150, 171, 175, 183
Ivory Coast: stamper of, 177

"Jacksonville Blues" (Florence), 170
Jacksonville FL: and the Great Migration in song, 159, 170
Jacobs, Harriet: *Incidents in the Life of a Slave Girl*, 6, 9, 100, 122
Jamaica and the Jamaican diaspora: African and neo-African performance in, 1, 8, 11–12, 14, 18, 21, 44–45, 58–64, 90, 116; lullabies of, 90
James, C. L. R., 8
jazz, 4, 18–19, 28, 149
Jochannon, Yusef Ben, 175
"Joe Turner," 162–63

John Henry, 151, 162, 175
Jones, Bessie: *Step It Down*, 37, 65
Jones, Jaqueline: *Labor of Love, Labor of Sorrow*, 137
Jordan, June, 6
Joyner, Charles: *Down by the Riverside*, 115–16, 138
Juba: performance and lyrics of, 9, 47–73, 94, 120, 128–31, 135, 147, 149, 179, 181. *See also* "Ham Bone"; Lane, William ("Master Juba")
Ju/ hoan (!Kung), 106–7

//Kabbo, 5, 47–48, 104, 106
Kaplan, Stanley, 81
Kassola, Oluale (Cudjoe Lewis), 20
Katanga, 177
"Keep Inching Along," 160–61
Khoisan. *See* San (Khoisan); /Xam
King, Martin Luther, 24
Kom (Cameroon), 17
Kongo: and Ki-Kongo language, 19, 37, 64; performance traditions and influence of, in African diaspora, x, 19, 34–35, 56, 59, 63–65, 94, 112, 128. *See also* Bakongo; Lemba Society (Kongo); MacGaffey, Wyatt
Koyate, Mamadou, 27
Kreamer, Christina: *African Cosmos*, 107
!Kung (Zhun/twasi). *See* Ju/ hoan (!Kung)

Lane, William ("Master Juba"), 68
Legba, Esu Elegba (Yoruba deity), 2
Lemba Society (Kongo): verse of, 34
Lewis, David Levering: *W.E.B. Du Bois*, 76
Liberia: cultural practice and influence in diaspora performance in, 27, 50–51; *Nodli* of, 198. *See also* Sande Society
"Little Liza Jane," 120–21, 123, 125
Lomax, Alan, 84, 109, 135, 152, 160, 164
Lorca, Federico Garcia, 8

Lovell, John: *Black Song*, 26
Lozi (Zambia): cosmological performance practices of, 107
Luba. *See* Baluba (Luba Zaire/Democratic Republic of Congo)
lullabies, 7, 10, 30, 75–102, 183
"Lynchburg Town," 160–61, 165

Maafa, 20–21, 109. *See also* Middle Passage (transatlantic slave trade)
MacGaffey, Wyatt: "Eyes of Understanding," 112
Maderia, 21
Makeba, Miriam: "The Click Song," 83
Mali: epic ballad of, 94; performance traditions and influence of, in African diaspora performance, 4, 27, 28, 83, 85, 94, 95, 108, 176; and Sundiata empire, 94. *See also* Bambara (Mali); Dogon (Mali); Mande; Mandinga; Mende
Malunga, 138
Mande: cultural practice and influence of, in African diaspora, 21, 104, 178. *See also* Mende
Mandinga, 28
"Many Rivers to Cross" (Cliff), 26
"maroon" societies (*quilombos, mocambos, palenques, cumbes, ladeiras, mambises*), 62, 94, 116
Marshall, Paule, 1
Martinique: African and neo-African performance in, 37–38
"Ma Teodora," 43–44, 64
Matoposa: cosmological performance of, 106–7
Mbuti: music and influence of, 4, 83–84. *See also* Central Africa
Mbwetete, 95
McClusky, Pamela: *Art from Africa*, 25
McKim, James, 32

McKim, Lucy: *Slave Songs*, 32, 123, 152, 155–56
Mende: cultural traditions and influence of, in African diaspora, 25, 27, 36, 108, 116, 160, 178. *See also* Mande
Mexico: Mande round houses in, 21, 104
Middle Passage (transatlantic slave trade), vii, 20–22, 26–27, 55, 81, 89, 171, 177
*minkisi*, 56, 94, 112
"Miss Mary Jane," 165
"Miss Mary Mack," 130–31
Moreton, J. B., 62
Morrison, Toni, 6, 98; *Beloved*, 61

Nettleford, Rex, 8, 15, 18; *The Crossing*, 18
New York City: street games in, 13–19, 108–15, 128–29, 130–31
Ngugi, wa Thiong'o: *Something Torn but New*, 4, 26, 95, 98, 134, 184
nkisi. See *minkisi*
"Nobody Knows the Trouble I See," 155–58, 166
Nok civilization, 22
"No More Auction Block," 30–32, 144, 147, 149
Northrup, Solomon: *Twelve Years a Slave*, 67, 128
Nubia (Sudan), xx, 1, 4, 105, 107–8, 174, 175
Nunley, John, 8, 15
Nyanga: language song of, vi, 173, 179–82

Ogun (Yoruba deity), 94
oral histories: indigenous storytelling and cosmologies in, 11; institution of slavery in, 31–32, 42, 59, 61–62, 85–86, 88, 115–16, 123–24, 143, 145, 149, 155, 161
Orisha, vii, 12, 16, 18, 131
Oromo, 4
Ortiz, Fernando, 8
Osanyin (Yoruba deity), 94
Oshoosi (Yoruba deity), 94

Oshun (Yoruba deity), 25
Ositola, Kolawole, 22, 33

Painter, Nell, 59
Palcy, Euzhan: *Sugar Cane Alley*, 37
Pan-African. *See* Africa
parietal (rock) art, 2, 5, 48, 107, 181
Park, Mungo, 52
Parrish, Lydia, 25, 36, 55, 116, 118, 150, 159, 160
Patterson, Orlando, 8
pedagogy: in performance, 8, 9, 16, 18, 24, 49, 53, 77, 83, 111, 114, 116, 134, 140, 153, 171, 177–80
Pende (western Zaire): cosmograms and ground signs of, 35
Pennington, James: *The Fugitive Blacksmith*, 123
Peru, 21
"Plumb the Line," 36
Plutarch: *Isis and Osiris*, 75, 95
"Poor Rosy," 151–57, 168, 178
Port Royal SC, 32, 152–57, 162, 166
"Possum-la," 135–36
Powers, Camille, 106
Price, Richard: *Maroon Societies*, 62
Prince, Lucy Terry, 83
Prince, Mary: *Narrative of the Life of Mary Prince*, 87–88, 122–23
Pueblo: stories of, 11

Rada, 112
"Rainbow Round My Shoulder," 138–39
Rainey, Gertrude "Ma," 168–70; "Southern Blues," 168
Ramanujan, A. K.: *Folktales from India*, 174, 182–83
Rashida, 28
Reagon, Bernice Johnson: *If You Don't Go, Don't Hinder Me*, 26
Reconstruction, 31, 148, 149, 152–57

Rilke, Rainer Maria, x, 22
ring games and ring plays, ix, 13–19, 54, 115–32, 145, 152, 159, 181
ring shouts, 35, 38, 66, 115–20
"Rise Sally Rise," 125
rites of passage, 48, 50, 103–33, 181
Robeson, Paul, 8
Rodney, Walter, 175
"Run Little Liza," 120, 121, 123

Saawadi, Nawal: *The Circling Song*, ix
sacred songs, vi, vii, 5, 10, 38, 131; in rebellion and revolution, 61–62. *See also* ring shouts; spirituals (African American)
Salem witch trials, 56–57
Sally (of Virginia), 60–61
San (Khoisan), 4, 9, 19, 20, 21; cosmology, mythology, performance practices, and influence of, vii, 26, 38–40, 47–48, 50, 58–59, 95, 103–7, 134, 174, 178, 182, 183; as "root" genetic and linguistic population, 3–4, 25, 38–40, 48, 59, 83–84, 148. *See also* Ju/'hoan (!Kung); /Xam
Sande Society, 177; philosophical principles of, 25, 27; rites-of-passage performance of, 108. *See also* Mende
"Sangaree," 158–60
São Tomé, 21
Scott, Michael, 3
Sembene, Osmane: *Moolade*, 108
Senegal: and agricultural knowledge in colonial Americas, 138; cultural traditions and influence of, in African diaspora, 85, 138–39; and origins of peoples of African diaspora, 63, 85, 138. *See also* Senegambia; Wolof
Senegambia, 51, 76, 85. *See also* Gambia; Senegal
sharecropping and tenant farming, 159–61, 164
Shockey, Ann Allen, 6

"Shoo Fly," 144–45
Shostak, Marjorie: *Nisa*, 106
Sierra Leone, 27. *See also* Mende; Sande Society
slave narratives, 6, 30, 42, 61, 97. *See also* abolition; oral histories; Works Progress Administration (WPA)
Smith, Bessie: "Backwater Blues," 171, 179; "Young Woman's Blues," 171
Smith, George "Geo," *172*
Smith, Ivy: "Third Alley Blues," 170
"Sometimes I Feel Like a Motherless Child," 99–101, 147
Son House (Eddie James), 32
South Carolina: African diaspora presence and experience in, 25, 32, 36–37, 41, 87, 91, 93, 99, 115–16, 118–19, 121, 138–39, 147, 152, 155, 160, 166. *See also* Gullah; South Carolina and Georgia Sea Islands
South Carolina and Georgia Sea Islands: African continuities in, 24, 36, 116, 121, 137, 139, 150, 155; and Reconstruction history, 155–57. *See also* Gullah
Southern, Eileen: *The Music of Black Americans*, 15, 18, 19, 50–51, 66; *Readings in Black American Music*, 70–71
"Southern Blues" (Rainey), 168
Spillers, Hortense, 6
spirituals (African American), vii, 4, 6, 10, 23–28, 30, 37–38, 76–79, 82, 96–101, 114, 129, 155–58, 166, 168–71; and blues, 114, 171; and lullabies, 75–102. *See also* sacred songs
"Steal Away," 97, 129
Stedman, John Gabriel, 59–60
Stewart, Maria, 161
"Strange Fruit" (Holiday), 169
St. Simons Island: African and neo-African performance in, 25, 118, 142. *See also* South Carolina and Georgia Sea Islands
Stuckey, Sterling: *Slave Culture*, 53, 116

Index

St. Vincent, 35
Sudan: performance practices in, 28, 49–50, 72, 75, 105–7, 112, 181. *See also* ancient Egypt; Nubia (Sudan)
Surinam: African and neo-African practices in, 59–60, 66, 98
"Swing Low Sweet Chariot," 79, 82, 96–101

Tabwa (Democratic Republic of Congo): cosmological performance practices of, 107
Tamil: folklore of, 182
Telugu: folklore and sacred ritual of, 182–84
Temme (Teme): cultural practice and African diaspora influence of, 178
"That Suits Me," 115–17
"Third Alley Blues" (I. Smith), 170
Thomas, Elizabeth Marshall: *The First People*, 4, 53
Thompson, Robert Farris, 15–17; *African Art in Motion*, 50–53, 65–66, 67, 109–11; *Face of the Gods*, 38–39; *Flash of the Spirit*, 2, 4, 34–35, 56–57, 104
Tituba (of Salem) 56, 72, 81
Tiv (Nigeria), 109
Towerson, William, 51
Trent-Jones, Altona: *Play Songs of the Deep South*, 90, 121, 128
Trinidad, 35
"Troubled in Mind," 158
"Trouble in Mind," 158
Truth, Sojourner (Isabella Bomfree), 9, 65, 82, 88, 95, 99, 143–44, 181
Tubman, Harriet, 26, 97, 161
Tu-Chokwe (northern Angola), 35. *See also* Angola
Turnage, Wallace, 124
Turner, Darwin, 8; *Africanisms in the Gullah Dialect*, 25, 36
Turner, Nat, 62, 97

Umbanda, 38. *See also* Brazil; sacred songs
Underground Railroad, 97–98
uprisings, revolts, and ritual performance, 60–63, 97. *See also* Haiti; "maroon" societies; sacred songs

vendor song, 167
Vilson, Georges: *Kandelab*, 132
Virginia, 41; African presence and practice in, 66, 67, 97, 123, 137, 138, 145, 147, 178
Vodun (Vodou), 25, 35, 38, 112

"Wade in the Water," 24–26, 37–38
Walker, Alice, 6, 7
Ware, Charles Picard: *Slave Songs of the United States*, 32, 123, 152, 155–56
Warner Lewis, Maureen, 16, 128
Washington, John, 124
Washington, Mary Helen, 6
Watusi (Tutsi), 4
Wells, Ida B., 161, 163
"We Mold the Pots," 49, 105
"We Shall Sleep but Not Forever," 99
West Africa: peoples, cultural practices, and convergences of, in African diaspora, 3, 11, 14, 18, 19, 21, 28, 35–36, 38, 58, 59, 64, 77, 84, 111, 115
Wheatley, Phillis, 9–10, 84–85
Williams, David Lewis: *A Cosmos in Stone*, 48
Williams, Eric, 8
Williams, George Washington, 139
"Willowbee," 128–29
Wilson, Harriet, 9; *Our Nig*, 146
Wolof: and Du Bois family lullaby, 76–78; griot traditions of, 27–28, 85. *See also* Gambia; Senegal
Wood, Peter: *Black Majority*, 138
work songs, 6, 10, 30–32, 43–44, 52, 62, 73, 93, 133–82; corn-husking song, 91; corn-

pounding song, 173–82; and lullabies, 152–68
Works Progress Administration (WPA), 6, 10, 152; Alec Bostick (Morgan County GA), 100; Annie Little (Springfield MO), 88; anonymous informant, 145; C. B. McCray (Jasper TX), 90; Chaney Mack (Memphis TN), 79–83, 94, 96, 101; Ellen Betts (Louisiana), 145; Ellen Godfrey (Georgetown County SC), 87; Fairy Elkins, 144; Francis Black (Grand Bluff MS), 144; George Fleming (Spartanburg SC), 147; Harriet Jones (South Carolina/Texas), 146; James August Holmes (Harrison County MS), 99; James Singleton (Simpson County MS), 123; Jennie Proctor (Alabama), 122, 141; Joanna Draper (Mississippi), 122, 146; Joanna Thompson (Lafayette County MS), 92; John Finney (Jackson County AL), 91; John Moore (Louisiana), 148; Julia Woodbury (Marion County SC), 99; Katherine Epps (Uniontown AL), 119; Laney Athens Van Hook (Georgia), 92; Lawrence Evans (Franklin County MS), 120; Lizzie Hughes (Nacogdoches TX), 120; Lorenzo Ezell (Sparta County SC), 91; Louisa Brown (Murrells Inlet SC), 87; Lucy Galloway (Harrison County MS), 166; Martha Richardson (Columbia SC), 93; Mary Kincheon Edwards (Baton Rouge LA), 148; Mary Kindred (Juniper TX), 92; Mary Wright (Kentucky), 127; Narcissus Young (Nashville TN), 90; Pauline Grice (Atlanta GA), 149; Ruby Pickens (Livingston AL), 99; Wayman Williams (Mississippi), 149

Worrell, Marilyn, 16

/Xam: cosmology and cultural performance of, 47–50, 56, 95, 104–8, 134, 179. *See also* San (Khoisan)
Xhosa: lullabies and pedagogy in, 83

Yaangalala, 15, 128
Yellin, Jean Fagan, 6
Yemaya (Yoruba deity) vii, 25, 131
yodeling, 39, 83–84, 139, 148
Yoruba: deities, 12, 25, 94, 131; founding histories and historic migrations, 21–22, 29; *Ifa* divination, 20–23, 33–34; ritual performance traditions and continuities in African diaspora, 4, 9, 12, 15, 17–19, 21–23, 25, 27–29, 33–34, 37, 56, 59–60, 77, 85, 94, 111–13, 121, 174, 178–79; welcoming dance and song, 121
"You May Bury Me in the East," 23–24, 76–77, 98
"Young Woman's Blues" (B. Smith), 171

Zaire, 35
Zambia: corn-pounding song in, 6, 173, 178–82; Lozi cosmological performance practices in, 107; Ndembu cosmograms and ground signs in, 35
*zepaules*, 113
Zimbabwe: cosmology and performance in, 98, 106–7
Zulu: lullabies of, 83

Index     225

www.ingramcontent.com/pod-product-compliance
Lightning Source LLC
Chambersburg PA
CBHW022008220426
43663CB00007B/1005